KILLER PRIEST

KILLER PRIEST

The Crimes, Trials, and Execution of Father Hans Schmidt

Mark Gado

Crime, Media, and Popular Culture
Frankie Y. Bailey and Steven Chermak, Series Editors

Westport, Connecticut
London

Library of Congress Cataloging-in-Publication Data

Gado, Mark, 1948–
    Killer priest : the crimes, trial, and execution of Father Hans Schmidt /
Mark Gado.
        p.   cm.—(Crime, media, and popular culture, ISSN 1549–196X)
    Includes bibliographical references and index.
    ISBN 0–275–98553–9 (alk. paper)
    1. Schmidt, Hans, d. 1916.   2. Schmidt, Hans, d. 1916—Trials,
litigation, etc.   3. Murder—New York (State)—New York—History—Case
studies.   4. Trials (Murder)—New York (State)—New York—History—Case
studies.   5. Catholic criminals—New York (State)—New York.   6. Murder in
mass media.   I. Title.   II. Series.
    HV6534.N5G34   2006
    364.152'3097471—dc22   2005034799

British Library Cataloguing in Publication Data is available.

Library of Congress Catalog Card Number: 2005034799
ISBN: 0–275–98553–9
ISSN: 1549–196X

First published in 2006

Praeger Publishers, 88 Post Road West, Westport, CT 06881
An imprint of Greenwood Publishing Group, Inc.
www.praeger.com

Printed in the United States of America

The paper used in this book complies with the
Permanent Paper Standard issued by the National
Information Standards Organization (Z39.48–1984).

10 9 8 7 6 5 4 3 2 1

"For all sorts of cruelty, piety is the mask."
William James, American psychologist and philosopher
(1842–1910)

For Jill and our sons, Mark and Chris

Contents

Series Foreword

This volume is part of an exciting interdisciplinary series on Crime, Media, and Popular Culture from Praeger Publishers. Because of the pervasiveness of media in our lives and the salience of crime and criminal justice issues, we feel it is especially important to provide a home for scholars who are engaged in innovative and thoughtful research on important crime and mass media issues.

This series will focus on process issues (such as the social construction of crime and moral panics), presentation issues (such as the images of victims, offenders, and criminal justice figures in news and popular culture), and effects (such as the influence of the media on criminal behavior and criminal justice administration).

With regard to this latter issue—effects of media/popular culture—as this foreword was being written the *Los Angeles Times* and other media outlets reported that two young half-brothers (ages 20 and 15) in Riverside, California, had confessed to strangling their mother and disposing of her body in a ravine. The story was attracting particular attention because the brothers told police they had gotten the idea of cutting off her head and hands to prevent identification from an episode of the award-winning HBO series, *The Sopranos*. As the *Los Angeles Times* noted, this again brought into the spotlight the debate about the influence of violent media such as *The Sopranos,* about New Jersey mobsters, on susceptible consumers.

In this series, scholars engaged in research on issues that examine the complex nature of our relationship with media. Peter Berger and Thomas Luckman coined the phrase the "social construction of reality" to describe the process by which we acquire knowledge about our environment. They and others have argued that reality is a mediated experience. We acquire what Emile Durkheim described as "social facts" through a several-pronged process of personal experience, interaction with others, academic education, and, yes, the mass media. With regard to crime and the criminal justice system, many people acquire much of their information from the news and from entertainment media. The issue raised by the report above and other anecdotal stories of "copycat" crime is how what we consume—read, watch, see, play, hear—affects us.

What we do know is that we experience this mediated reality as individuals. We are not all affected in the same way by our interactions with mass media. Each of us engages in interactions with mass media/popular culture that are shaped by factors such as our social environment, interests, needs, and opportunities for exposure. We do not come to the experience of mass media/popular culture as blank slates waiting to be written upon or voids waiting to be filled. It is the pervasiveness of mass media/popular culture and the varied backgrounds (including differences in age, gender, race/ethnicity, religion, etc.) that we bring to our interactions with media that make this a particularly intriguing area of research.

Moreover, it is the role of mass media in creating the much discussed "global village" of the twenty-first century that is also fertile ground for research. We exist not only in our communities, our cities, and states, but in a world that spreads beyond national boundaries. Technology has made us a part of an on-going global discourse about issues not only of criminal justice but of social justice. Technology places us to events around the world "as they happen." It was technology that allowed Americans around the world to witness the collapse of the World Trade Center's Twin Towers on September 11, 2001. In the aftermath of this "crime against humanity," we have been witnesses to and participants in an on-going discussion about the nature of terrorism and the appropriate response to such violence.

In this first volume in our new series, we have brought together scholars from a wide range of disciplines to examine the role of mass media in the social construction of reality in the wake of an event such as September 11 that affected all us in profound ways. This volume is only the first in a series that we expect to be both timely and significant.

Frankie Y. Bailey and Steven Chermak
Series Editors

Acknowledgments

The author made efforts to enlist the aid of the Catholic Church in the writing of this book. Their internal records concerning the assignments, travels, and duties of Father Schmidt would have been helpful to clarify some issues in the narrative. For whatever reason, the church did not cooperate in this project. But it would be incorrect to say they refused. They simply did not respond.

There are many people I would like to thank for their help in this undertaking. Alan Colsey, former chief of police of South Nyack/Grandview and now MBA director at St. Thomas Aquinas College in New York, supplied editorial assistance. Lydia Pletz of Cold Spring, New York, provided all the German translations in the text. Roberta Arminio of the Ossining Historical Society in Ossining, New York, the perennial source for numerous books and articles on the history of Sing Sing prison, was always available to answer questions. Captain Mort Childress (retired) of the Louisville Police Department provided vital research into the Alma Kellner murder case in Kentucky, as well as all the information concerning the Louisville Police Department. Lt. Mitchell Librett, Ph.D., of the New Rochelle Police Department in New York, provided essential research assistance. Additional support was received from the Municipal Archives of New York City, the helpful staff of the New York State Archives and the State Library in Albany, the Vassar College Library in Poughkeepsie, the Office of Personnel in the New York City Police Department, and the New York City Police Museum. Professor Frankie Bailey of the University at Albany and Professor Steve Chermak of Indiana State University sponsored this project to Praeger Publishing and contributed editorial comments to the manuscript as well. I would also like to thank my editor at Praeger, Suzanne Staszak-Silva, whose professional advice helped me through this long process. My wife, Jill, provided assistance throughout and, as my most enthusiastic supporter, a never-ending source of encouragement.

Introduction

The duality of man's existence, so masterfully portrayed in Robert Louis Stevenson's classic novel, *The Strange Case of Dr. Jekyll and Mr. Hyde* (1886), is a recurrent theme in Western literature. Teodor Jozef Konrad Korzeniowski, better known as Joseph Conrad, explored the alleged evil nature of man in *Heart of Darkness* (1902), one of the twentieth century's most enduring and enigmatic novels. While Stevenson declares that "man is not truly one, but truly two," Conrad surrenders man's soul over to evil with little resistance and illustrates what could happen when he confronts his dark inner self. In *Man Against Himself* (1938), Dr. Karl Menninger interpreted the situation in slightly different terms. "Love and hate, production and consumption, creation and destruction, the constant war of opposing tendencies would appear to be the dynamic heart of the world," is how he describes that conflict.

Edward Hyde was Dr. Jekyll, in a sense, without the allegorical mask. Once he drank the experimental potion, Dr. Jekyll "transformed" into Mr. Hyde, the emotional opposite of what he was in reality. Of course, there was no authentic conversion since Mr. Hyde *was* Dr. Jekyll buried under the subconscious strata. This alter ego, symbolized by the repulsive Mr. Hyde, is described as animalistic, hairy and ugly, a primitive creature whose appetites are out of control and dangerous. Stevenson used the word "troglodyte," a cave dweller. Those primal traits, which allegedly exist in every human being, can only be brought under control by society's laws and restraints. Without them, according to Stevenson, man is a beast. Eventually, Dr. Jekyll did not require the potion to turn into Mr. Hyde; the transformation occurred involuntarily. In time, the evil side of his psyche overcomes the good. And even more ominous, Dr. Jekyll disappears forever, leaving only his evil counterpart behind.

Conrad, on the other hand, may have seen evil as central to man's nature and, ostensibly, at the core of his soul. This pessimistic view, epitomized by the rapid descent of Colonel Kurtz in *Heart of Darkness*, leaves little room for optimism. But it is important to remember that Kurtz, in the beginning of the story, was an honorable man. He arrived in Africa with noble intentions, guided by the belief that civilization could offer a better way of life to the natives. His deterioration began when he became immersed in the ivory trade and was corrupted by undefined cruelties that he witnessed and, later, participated in. Having come face to face with evil, Kurtz was consumed and eventually destroyed by it.

This disturbing theme was explored once again in William Golding's *Lord of the Flies* (1954), in which the violent clash between good and evil takes place in isolation, far away from the calming effects of civilization and society. Golding, whose experiences in World War II undoubtedly affected his thoughts on the power of evil, employed a simple plot to illustrate his hypothesis. A group of innocent children left alone on a deserted island, without adult supervision, eventually descend into savagery and barbarism. The author's lesson may be that evil lives inside the soul of mankind and absent any restraint, he will revert back to the primordial savage. Again, the fragile balance of man's existence gave way to temptation, struggle, and, ultimately, final defeat.

The crimes of Father Hans Schmidt were many. The murder of Anna Aumuller, of which he was convicted in 1914, was so gruesome and satanic that it is sometimes difficult to believe he was, in fact, a Catholic priest. The daily revelations of his sexual perversions and debauchery, aptly reported in the New York press, shocked the public and reverberated all the way to the steps of the Vatican. Schmidt was a classic psychopathic personality, egotistic, self-absorbed, and oblivious to the feelings of others, much in the tradition of killers such as Nathan Leopold, Richard Loeb, or Ted Bundy.[1]

The story of *Killer Priest* is true. Details were gathered from a wide variety of sources, which included a voluminous library of newspaper reports from the New York papers the *Sun*, the *Evening Telegram*, the *New York Times*, the *New York Press*, and the *New York Herald*, as well as the *Courier-Journal* and

Times of Louisville, Kentucky. Much was learned from the court testimony of dozens of participants in the Schmidt trial, which held New York City spellbound during the winter months of 1913 and 1914. Sworn depositions from family members also provided valuable insight into the defendant's childhood development. His sister, Elizabeth Schmidt-Schadler, was particularly observant of her younger brother's pathological obsession with blood at a very early age. She was also aware of his sexual attraction to her when he was a boy, a trait that may have had a pivotal influence on his fixation for St. Elizabeth, the patron saint of Hungary. And finally, hundreds of pages of several sworn statements taken from Father Hans Schmidt provided a unique opportunity to hear the voice of the defendant himself, who seemingly never tired of discussing his life of crime and debauchery. Through this abundance of material, the author was able to faithfully reconstruct the events of September 1913 to a very high degree of certainty. However, despite all of this documentation, questions still linger over the activities of Father Hans Schmidt. Was he also responsible for the murder of little Alma Kellner in 1909? Were there other murders as well?

Without the existence of a handwritten confession, it will never be proven if Father Schmidt was the Louisville murderer. Though the man convicted of that killing, Joseph Wendling, served twenty-six years in a Kentucky prison, he claimed innocence until the day he died. Curiously, when Schmidt was questioned about Alma Kellner after he was arrested in New York, he replied, "I never heard of her!" That would have been impossible since her disappearance was front-page news in Louisville for months and she was a student at the Catholic school when he visited in August 1909. The Louisville diocese assisted in the police investigation as well, so it could not be feasible that he never heard her name. Some startling coincidences also exist between the two killings, such as Alma Kellner's body that was found yards away from the altar where Father Schmidt once prayed. One can only imagine the reluctance of Louisville officials to reopen the case after they had expended so much time, effort, and money to convict another man for that murder. That said, there simply is not enough evidence to convict Father Schmidt of the killing of Alma Kellner. His guilt or innocence in that murder will be left to the reader to decide.

Of course, it is impossible to know exactly what was said in conversations that took place, for example, in the privacy of someone's home or in an isolated cell-block. For that, some literary license had to be taken in order to maintain reader interest and story continuity. But the author is confident that in each and every instance, the words used in the narrative are supported by the evidence and dictated by common sense. For example, it is safe to assume that after his arrest, when Father Schmidt had conversed with his lawyer, they undoubtedly discussed the details of his case. When detectives canvass a neighborhood, whether in 1913 or in 2005, they are sure to ask questions of the people they find at home. It is in these types of situations that some additions and speculations were made. But in no occasion were the essential facts of the case altered or disturbed in any way.

In reality, Father Schmidt had two trials. The first took place in December of 1913, just three months after his arrest. That trial resulted in a hung jury or "jury disagreed," as it was described in the official record. The vote was 10–2 for a guilty verdict. The second trial began in January 1914, which is described at length in this book. Since the same witnesses testified in both proceedings, and defense and prosecution teams were identical, only the second trial is addressed here. Obviously, it would be repetitive to describe both trials, which were carbon copies of each other. Luckily, an official record still exists for the January trial, which was reviewed by the New York State Court of Appeals. That review also includes two separate depositions given by Father Schmidt on February 15 and March 13, 1914. Though not completely truthful, those depositions, as well as a final statement taken in October 1914 at Sing Sing, provide hundreds of pages of the defendant's words describing his thoughts and actions on the events of September 1913.

The trial record was also the source material for reconstructing the early life of Hans Schmidt in Germany. Testimony by his sister, Elizabeth, his brother, Karl, and his father, Heinrich Schmidt, furnished important clues to the nature of his childhood experiences and the origins of his psychological development. Clergy who served with Father Schmidt in the Mainz seminary, as well as those at the Church of St. Boniface and St. Joseph's Church in New York City, described his rather curious attitude toward Catholic dogma. Though he considered himself a blessed child, Hans Schmidt was disrespectful and dismissive of church tradition. Virtually every person with whom he served had strong reservations about Schmidt's fitness and viability as a Catholic priest. That may help explain why his ordination at the seminary at Mainz took place in private in the bishop's quarters. There was no ceremony and no guests. By then, Schmidt had already been arrested (on forgery charges) and his reputation as a sexual philanderer with both men and women was well known in local inns and taverns.

The astute reader will notice that there are discrepancies in statements made by some participants in the story. Often, they are at odds with each other and sometimes, they tell different versions of the same event. Sometimes, these statements were honest mistakes; other times, people deliberately tried to mislead investigators. It is important to remember that in murder cases, then and now, there are strong motives for people to blatantly lie, even in the face of evidence to the contrary. Their goal is usually to minimize their involvement and, therefore, their culpability.

1

The Chapel

NOVEMBER 1, 1802, WERTHEIM, GERMANY

Bitter November winds cut through empty trees and rattled the branches. Along the sprawling Tauber River, a wave of fallen leaves rolled down slippery banks and into frigid waters, covering its surface with a quilt of a thousand colors. Herds of deer scampered into the forests under ominous gray skies while rabbits crawled deeper into their holes. All across the valley, settlers dreaded the coming winter because it meant months of unbearable cold, isolation, and sometimes, an ignominious death. A restless flock huddled around a wood-burning stove inside the chapel as they listened to the morning mass and prayed on their calloused knees for a better life. Their bodies warmed by the fire and their souls comforted by God, they knelt in solemn silence while persistent winds pounded against thick wooden walls.

The tiny church was built by the townspeople over a period of one year. They chopped down tall pines with their axes, carved the stubborn logs into a workable form, and piled them on top of one another until the structure began to rise from its stone foundation—in the rain, in the snow, or in the wind, it did not matter. Month by month, they pushed on. They soon added the roof, floors, windows, and doors. Everyone contributed something to the church, even if it was just nailing the seats together or hanging lanterns in the vestibule. Children stuffed mud and dry straw between the logs to provide protection from the winter winds. The women kept fires burning and boiled huge vats of a rudimentary vegetable soup to keep the men well fed and contented. They worked with a fierce determination, a sense of singular purpose, and an ingenuity that was fundamental to the German people. The people of Wertheim never built anything that would not last. Even a basic item like a wooden bucket was put together with care and attention to the smallest detail. These people believed that if a person wanted to do something, it had to be done right. Their homes were built to last a hundred years, not twenty. Their wagons were sturdy and durable, they never fell apart. It was the German way: always perform duties conscientiously; never do anything poorly. A task well done is its own reward.

The Roman Catholic priest who said the mass that morning had arrived in the village two years before. He was ordained at the seminary in Mainz, where most young Germans went if they were serious about the priesthood. Wertheim was his first assignment since ordination, and already he longed to be somewhere else. Munich, Frankfurt, Stuttgart, or any of the larger cities would do. The smaller congregations in remote towns and villages simply did not appeal to him. Having been raised in the sprawling city of Hamburg, he considered farmers and their offspring less sophisticated than city people and certainly less educated. He also felt they did not maintain the same standards of cleanliness as those who lived in more populous regions.

Farmers spent long days working the fields, tilling the ground and harvesting the crops. It was an honorable living, of course, but they always seemed to be so grimy, the priest thought. On Sunday mornings, they would come to church still covered with farm dirt. It was embedded in their clothes, mingled with their hair, and pressed into their skin. A city person would never dream of showing up at church services in such a condition. But farm people were different. They seemed not to care how they looked or smelled.

Their faith was different, too. That is not to say it was not genuine. It was. But farmers had a more pragmatic view of the Catholic faith. They never expected big things from prayer. Maybe it was because they never asked for anything big. All a farmer wanted was a good crop, good weather, and ample rain. He did not think much beyond that. They were a simple lot and as a result, their prayers were simple. The young priest experienced that in the confessional as well. Their sins were, well, simple. They rarely stole anything, displayed little vice, and lived their frugal lives in a manner that did not leave much time for anything else except for work. If there was one word that could be used to describe the average landowner in Wertheim, it was diligent.

A man worked hard, tried to provide for his family, and instilled a sense of religion and realism in his children that he hoped would guide them through a difficult life. Women were usually supportive, obedient to their husbands, and dedicated to the common goal of raising a family. To the priest, it was a painfully boring existence. These musings were on his restless mind as he recited the prayers for the congregation. While some of the men stoked the fire in the stove, the priest moved to the center of the altar where he prepared for the consecration.

"Diesque nostros in tua pace disponas, atque abaeterna damnatione nos cripi," he recited almost mechanically, "et in electorum tuorum jubeas grege numerari. Per Christum Dominum nostrum. Amen."[1] He turned to the small crowd and lifted the chalice above his head, then gently positioned the golden vessel on the altar. In a few minutes, the ceremony would be over and he would be able to return to the comfort of his room. He grasped the chalice with both hands and spoke the Latin words.

"Quam oblationem tu Deus, in omnibus, quaesumus, benedictam, adscriptam, ratam, rationabilem, acceptabilemque facere digneris; ut nobis Corpus et Sanguis fiat dilectissimi Filii tui Domini nostri Jesu Christi."[2] He placed the cup back on the altar, slightly to his right. Then he turned his head to the left and read from the prayer book. As he did, his right elbow suddenly made contact with the chalice. The sacred vessel tipped over, spilling the red wine across the white linen. He immediately grabbed the chalice by the stem, but it had already emptied.

"Vater! [Father!]" cried one of the altar boys who assisted him. The priest secured the chalice, placing it to his left. He pushed the wet linen to the side and continued to say the mass. The cloth partially draped over the altar so that the red stain was visible to the flock. An elderly farmer in the front pew was the first to notice something. Others stared at the linen with puzzled expressions. Then, several people in the first row began to murmur softly to themselves.

"Himmlischer Vater! [Heavenly father!]" someone said.

"Ein Wunder! [A miracle!]" others gasped. The priest did not know what the commotion was about until he stepped back. "Sieh!" an old woman yelled from the wooden pews, "Jesu eigenes Gesicht! [Look, the face of Christ himself!]" The red wine produced a stain on the linen that had formed the rough shape of a human head. Its eyes became two white spots surrounded by circles of deep crimson. The cheeks were elongated narrow strips that flowed into what appeared to be a beard. The portion that appeared to be the face was framed by small streams of wine that had dripped into the resemblance of long hair. There was no mistake, the people whispered, it looked like the head of Christ.

"Ein heiliges Wunder! [A sacred miracle!]" someone said as the congregation seemed to gasp in one breath. People fell to their knees in ecstatic adoration. Their palms touched the ground as they bowed their heads. The priest stepped back to examine the linen, but could not see the image. To him, it looked like spilled wine.

"The blood of Christ has given us a sign!" one parishioner told the young priest. "Wait for us here, Father!" another man said. Some people fled from the chapel to summon their families. Everyone had to see what God had done for the long-suffering farmers of the Tauber River Valley. The villagers lit candles and placed dried flowers in front of the altar. Soon, the chapel was turned into a shrine. By nightfall, hundreds gathered around the tiny building to recite prayers and read the holy psalms of King David. They built huge fires to keep warm and made plans for a stone building to protect the sacred relic for future generations.

The young priest looked out at the massive throng in front of his chapel and tried to comprehend the transformation that had taken place over the past few hours. He could not understand it. He thought maybe he was at fault. Maybe he just was not as faithful as he should have been. In the seminary, he was taught not to question religious teachings because the brothers said that faith was about believing in something for which there was no proof. It was always a difficult concept for him.

He walked to the center aisle where the white linen was spread over the altar for all to see. People were on their knees in front of the cloth, praying in unison for salvation and mercy. They sang. They cried. They lifted their hands and hearts to the heavens. The young priest was overwhelmed by the fervor. He stared at the large blood-red stain and tried to see what the faithful saw.

But he could not.

2

The Sixth

Even as a boy, Hans Schmidt was self-absorbed, moody, and spoke very little, especially to his father. He had nine siblings, and each took notice of his unusual behavior, which ranged from being amusing one moment to terrifying the next. By the time he was eight years old, the boy would lock himself in his room, where he recited religious prayers with an ardor and in a language no one else could understand. His mother, Gertrude Miller Schmidt, a pessimistic woman raised on a farm and poorly educated, never objected, because she herself was a religious zealot who long ago abandoned her role as a mother and a wife. She simply prayed all day. "She was very religious, too much so," her husband once said. "She influenced him in that direction. I believe so."[1]

Hans Schmidt was born in 1881 in Aschaffenberg, a small town located thirty miles south of Frankfurt. His father, Heinrich Schmidt, was a well-known railroad official respected by everyone in the village. He made a decent living and, with the help of a generous vegetable garden and several farm animals, was able to provide ample food for a demanding family.

Heinrich and Gertrude Schmidt had ten children together, spread out over fourteen years. However, most of the responsibility for raising the formidable clan fell upon Gertrude, who, as it turned out, had little interest in family matters. Heinrich was away on railroad business most of the year and could not devote much time to the everyday chores of the Schmidt household. Gertrude became overwhelmed by the arduous task of motherhood, for which she was ill prepared, and could never adapt. She began to feel isolated and depressed. When she finally accepted the notion that she could no longer cope with the demands of her large family, she retreated into her own world, convinced that she had failed her husband, her children, and, ultimately, herself. For refuge, she sought the comfort of the Catholic Church. Each morning and evening, she attended mass, neglecting meal preparation and ignoring her children. In between services, she sat in her bedroom for hours and recited the rosary or read a prayer book. The children were left on their own, sometimes able to manage and other times not. The older ones tried to take care of their younger siblings but were not always successful.

At first, Gertrude took the children with her to church, but the steady stream of godly devotion was monotonous and difficult for a young child to understand. Only Hans seemed to accept it without question. He was the sixth born, neither the oldest nor the youngest, just one who was somewhere in the middle. He was known only as "the sixth." Occasionally, even his father forgot who he was, which may have been understandable because he was rarely at home; and when he saw the child, he sometimes called him by another name.

Gertrude Schmidt never made that mistake. She held him close. Of all her children, Hans seemed to be the favorite. When he was seven years old, the boy noticed a curious mark on the left side of his chest. It was a pink-colored splotch of skin just under his left nipple that extended sideways to the top of the rib area. It was about four centimeters by eight centimeters wide. When he asked his mother about it, Gertrude told him it was the mark of God. The birthmark, she said, was identical to the wound inflicted on Jesus by the Roman soldiers as He suffered on the cross at Calvary. Hans had been marked as a holy child. She took the boy to church every morning and sometimes again at night. Soon, they became a familiar sight in Aschaffenberg, traipsing off to mass, hand in hand, oblivious to the weather and careful to avoid the curious glances of neighbors who frequently wondered who was minding the children at the Schmidt home.

Hans took to piety as a rabbit takes to grass. He immersed himself in it. Gifted with a sharp intellect and a curiosity to match, he memorized lengthy passages of the Bible and could recite them at will, much to the bewilderment of his brothers and sisters. He said several rosaries each day and was careful to articulate the words perfectly on each recital, even when alone. By the time he was nine, he had erected an altar in his room, replete with candelabra, tabernacle, and pictures of the Stations of the Cross pasted to the walls. He had several cassocks, which his mother had sewn together for him.

At night, little Hans would practice saying the mass in Latin. "He went to church always," his father said, "always had prayer books with him and he always imitated sacred and priestly things, and his play was all about priests."[2] His mother often sat in his room with the child, and while he performed the holy mass, she made corrections and suggestions, and continually prompted Hans as to the proper stance of a Catholic priest. She made a white collar that was as stiff as wood, which fit neatly under the cassock. Hans became a picture-perfect little priest, and when he stood at his homemade altar, reciting the Latin words of mass with the chalice held high over his head, his mother fell to her knees in rapturous ecstasy, convinced that she was in the presence of a true holy child. Night after night, they repeated their sacred ritual in his room while the other children, mystified by the locked door and the shouts of adoration from within, huddled in the kitchen, giggling and making jokes among themselves about "Father Hans" and their crazy mother.

During these years, Hans developed a rather curious affliction. Wherever he was, whether in the fields, in the barn, at school, or at home, Hans frequently complained about not getting enough oxygen. The boy would suddenly stop whatever he was doing, loosen his collar, unbutton his shirt, and take several deep breaths as if he had just finished running a mile. His face bore a painful expression while his lungs strained to catch a breath. "What has God done with the air?" he would ask the heavens above. At times, he would climb to the highest elevation available, such as a tall tree or the loft in a barn. Once, he sat on the roof of the house, where he claimed it was easier to breathe. His father screamed at him until he came down and then beat the boy for his insolence.

Before he was ten years old, Hans experienced his first uneasy stirrings of sexual desire. Being raised in a rural area, the children were exposed to the random sexual activity of cows, horses, and other farm animals. Hans, like any other child, had a natural inquisitiveness about such things. A neighborhood boy named Fritz, who lived on the same street and was the same age, had similar curiosities. Together, they began to explore their bodies, and that year Hans had his first sexual encounter. "He did not know just how it happened," one doctor later told the court, "but they partly undressed and played with each other, and some attempts were made to penetrate by means of the rectum."[3] Deeply ashamed that he could not control his sinful desires, Hans became overwhelmed with guilt and felt the need for atonement. This constant struggle against temptation and his repetitive failure to redeem himself caused a deep psychological rift in the young boy.[4]

The more he sinned, the more he went to church. "When anybody in the house, or a neighbor went to church he always was glad to go along," his sister once said, "Always very devout. When he was a small child, the people said, 'That is a very devout, religious child,' and that he must be the priest. 'That is our little chaplain.'"[5] When he returned from church with the neighbors, Hans would rush into the house, flushed with excitement, and tell his mother what he had seen. During his first year in school, Hans began to hear voices. "Three weeks after his First Communion," his sister once said, "he visited me and I asked him, 'How did you like the day of your communion?' He said, 'This was the nicest day of my life. On the day before my communion I heard in the church the voice of God—"Du wilst mein Prieste weren! [You shall become a priest!]"—and shortly after that I went again to the church and I heard the same voice.'"[6]

When Heinrich arrived home from his business trips, the nightly prayer sessions between Hans and his mother had to be temporarily discontinued, due to the father's disapproval of his family's obsession with Catholicism. Heinrich was a Protestant, and though he tolerated Catholics as friends and acquaintances, he demanded that his wife be Protestant also, something she could never be and refused to become. For that reason, Hans had to be careful of his faith whenever his father was at home, lest his mother become the target of Heinrich's rage. Most times Hans would retreat to the safety of his room and wait until his father went away again. Hans avoided his siblings as well, but he continued his obsessive sexual interests. "He had a great admiration for the human body," said a doctor who once interviewed Hans, "and had practiced homosexuality continuously."[7]

During his childhood years, Hans failed to develop a meaningful relationship with any of his brothers. He became friendly only with one older sister, Elizabeth, whom he took to as a second mother. "From his talk I could always see that he always liked me the best," she once said.[8] Elizabeth was the only sibling to whom he would speak more than a few words. "He often retired to his own room in the house of our parents," a brother later said in court. "We weren't used to anything else from him. Already in the years of his youth, he did not appear to me as normal because he had too few pleasures. He also had no comrades of play, as other children have."[9] His behavior did not go unnoticed by his father, who saw that Hans was different from the others. He saw that the boy spurned friends and rejected his brothers, but Heinrich was away from home most of the time and could not focus his attention on such domestic issues.

About the same time that Hans became infatuated with religion, he developed a fascination with blood. On occasion, when his mother prepared dinner, she would slaughter chickens by cutting off their heads. Hans watched this activity very closely and became transfixed by the killing. Sometimes, he would take the heads of the chickens and play with them in his room or hide them for later use. His father once caught him with a bloody chicken head and scolded him for it. After that, Hans was careful to conceal the parts and play with them only when his father was not home.

According to later court testimony, Dr. Jeliffe said, "On one occasion he had taken the head of a rooster and put it while still bleeding on the end of his penis and had walked around strutting about with this decapitated head of this rooster on his penis until his father caught him and beat him."[10] Another time, Hans had a severe gash on his leg, and it bled profusely. His sister Elizabeth took him to her bed, where she dressed the wound. Hans became aroused at the sight of the blood, and the incident provoked a powerful sexual response in the young boy. Whenever he saw blood, he came to associate its appearance with sexual activity; but it was not until the geese were killed that Heinrich Schmidt realized his son was vastly different from most other children.

During the summer of 1891, Gertrude Schmidt brought three geese home from the market at Aschaffenberg. She purchased the birds at a good price and planned to breed them for food and also for their feathers, which were valued to stuff pillows and homemade quilts. The geese were kept in a small shed where the garden tools were stored. Heinrich and two of the older children had constructed a cage and placed the animals inside. Each day Gertrude would feed the geese and tend to their needs, looking forward to when she would be able to collect their feathers and assemble the bedding items. One August morning, she went out to feed the geese and found that two were missing. At first, she thought that the birds had slipped out of the cage somehow. But upon inspection, she found the walls were intact. Some-one had stolen the birds. When she questioned the children, all denied knowledge of the theft. That same afternoon, Heinrich, who happened to be home from a recent trip to Berlin, repaired part of the fence on the east end of the farm. As he packed up his tools on the wagon, he saw Hans coming out of the woods and called to him.

"Hans, bist Dud das? [Hans, is that you?]"

The boy seemed startled. He dropped something onto the ground and then hurried away without acknowledging his father. Heinrich finished loading his tools and then walked over to where he saw Hans a minute before. He searched through the grass to find what the boy had dropped. When he found it, he did not realize what it was at first. All he saw was a bloody lump of white feathers. When he touched it, he saw it was the head of a goose, neatly severed at the neck. Its eyes were open, staring into nothingness, while the blood, still fresh and wet, dripped from its gaping throat.

"Mein Gott! [My God!]" he murmured. A thick trail of blood led from the head of the bird toward the brook twenty yards away. Heinrich saw that the boy had quickly disappeared over the crest of the hill. He decided to follow the blood. When he arrived at the water's edge he saw the carcasses of two geese, lying side by side on a flat rock. The heads of both geese had been amputated. Heinrich went back to the house to find his son. He told Gertrude what he had found, but she did not become alarmed. She said that her Hans must have a reason for it and the birds were to be eaten anyway. When Heinrich went to Hans's room, the boy was gone. He noticed that Hans had changed his clothes because his pants were hanging on the back of the door. Heinrich saw blood on the pant legs, and when he picked up the clothing, more blood dripped from the inseams. He reached into the right front pocket and found the source. It was the missing head of the second goose. After that day, no one in the Schmidt family looked at Hans quite the same way again. He had no explanation for what he did and never displayed any remorse. He simply seemed to enjoy the texture of blood.

When his father questioned him about his mutilation of the farm animals, Hans responded, "Ich seh' gern blut! [I like to see blood!]"[11] But it did not end there. During their playtime, most of the other children could be found running through the fields with their friends, flying a kite or riding the newest bicycle. Not Hans. He wandered over to a nearby slaughterhouse where cows and pigs were prepared for local butchers. The boy would sit for long hours watching the relentless slaughter of the helpless animals. Mesmerized by the bloody spectacle, Hans frequently lost track of time and would miss lunch at home, and occasionally even dinner. At times, he stole a few apples from a neighbor's orchard so he could eat while he watched the killing.

The strange child, who sat as if hypnotized, eating fruit while the men cut the throats of squealing pigs, puzzled the workers at the slaughterhouse. Some of the butchers went to Heinrich to tell him of the little boy's visits. After his father discovered where his son was spending his time, he beat the boy. But it did not stop him. Soon, Hans took Fritz to the slaughterhouse, where they both became strangely aroused when they saw the killings take place. "He said that in going to the slaughterhouse he had a great deal of sexual excitement," said a doctor who interviewed Hans years later, "that the blood excited him and excited the friend with whom he went. They performed mutual acts of masturbation and that it continued at infrequent intervals up to the age of about fourteen."[12]

Hans continued his sexual relationship with Fritz for years. During that period, Hans also began to have sexual relations with his older brother, Karl. It was Karl who taught Hans about sexual intercourse between a man and a woman and frequently drew attention to their parents' activity in the bedroom. Since his father was away a great deal of the time, Hans slept with his mother in her bed. When the father arrived home, Hans was kicked out and sent back to sleep with the other children. On occasion, Hans could hear his mother in the bedroom moaning; but he did not believe it was from pleasure. "He had the idea that the father was cutting the mother and hurting her and he thought that when he heard a suppressed scream," one doctor later said.[13]

Throughout that year, chickens were killed mysteriously, rabbit limbs were found in the cellar, and squirrel carcasses, horribly mutilated, were discovered on the farm property. It could never be proven that Hans was responsible, though the entire family and most of the frightened neighbors knew who performed the bizarre rituals. Heinrich, a stern disciplinarian who believed that a family was bound to follow the father's orders, had a deep fear of inherited insanity. Like many people at that time, he was convinced that mental instability was a biological problem passed on from father to son. That fear was real because both sides of the Schmidt family suffered from a disturbing, enduring trend of madness and suicide that went back for generations.

Heinrich's grandfather, Nicola Schmidt, who lived in the city of Oberhessen, was institutionalized in a mental hospital for long periods due to severe alcoholism. In 1849, Gertrude's grandfather, Andrea Seppler, committed suicide by hanging. So grief-stricken was the family that her brother, Conrad Seppler, who lived in Angersbach, shot himself to death soon afterward. Before that, he went through a period of insanity that caused him to cut himself numerous times in the most horrible ways. Heinrich's beloved brother, Jacob Schmidt, was confined to a mental institution for the duration of his adult life and would die there.[14] And now, Heinrich was faced with the real possibility that one of his own sons, the reclusive boy with the name he could never remember, the sixth one, might join in this tragic parade of madness.

In 1895, when Hans was fourteen years old, the Schmidt family moved to Mainz, located thirty miles from Aschaffenberg. There, Gertrude convinced Heinrich that Hans needed professional guidance. She succeeded in enrolling him in a school where Latin was taught extensively and was considered the first step into a Catholic seminary. The boy dedicated his entire being to his studies. Wherever he went, his head was buried in books. "Without a book or a paper, one never met him," his brother once said of him.[15] He quickly learned to play the violin and studied the compositions of the classical German composers. But his behavior remained erratic. Townspeople saw the boy wandering the streets throughout the night. He would walk quickly and then come to an abrupt stop for no apparent reason, immersed in deep thought. After several minutes frozen in silence, Hans would continue on his way without a word. On several occasions, he was found sitting naked in a freezing bathtub, impervious to the cold, playing the violin.[16]

But he studied hard and always finished his course work at the top of his class. His brother Karl once described Hans as "an extraordinarily pious man, never smoked or took alcoholic drinks."[17] His understanding of the academic material was second to none, and though Hans had a tendency to debate in highly philosophical terms, most teachers agreed on one point: Hans Schmidt was a genius. At the age of nineteen, he was admitted into the St. Augustine Seminary at Mainz in preparation for the priesthood. It was his mother's dream come true. Gertrude Miller Schmidt, the farm girl from the hill country, would be mother to a priest.

But even as he entered St. Augustine's, Hans expressed concern that he was not meant for the priesthood. He confided in a priest, Father Peter Kraus, who was an instructor at the school. "He came to my sitting room and asked me to give him advice as to whether he should become a priest," Father Peter told the court years later. "He listened to me in a very earnest manner and made a very good impression on me. Then he went away. It appeared to me that he was strikingly absent-minded, very earnest and acted extravagantly. I later went to his room and there he lay in his bed with a cushion under his head and when I asked him what he was thinking, he said, 'Father, I am deciding whether I shall become a monk or an atheist.'"[18] He made his decision to continue after he heard a voice in the chapel by the statue of St. Augustine. It was the same voice he had heard years before when he made his First Communion. But this time, the voice spoke in Latin: "Se nones vocatus fac ut voceres! [If you have not the vocation, make yourself one!]" To Schmidt, the meaning was clear. "I thought I heard this voice from God," he said later. "I then took up my studies with more vigor!"[19]

For the next two years, Hans studied at the Mainz seminary. In much the same manner as when he was a child, he kept to himself and made few friends. To make money, he took to playing the violin in saloons in nearby towns. Dressed in a cassock and collar, Hans would play till all hours of the night and then attend classes the next morning. It was widely known that he had an obsessive desire to make money, but it was said that he never spent anything on himself. "It was noticeable that he always had a strong desire to make money but for himself, he used very little," his brother once said. "He always gladly gave to the poor and the needy. He himself was a teetotaler and did not spend anything for his clothes as well."[20]

Hans was hostile toward his colleagues and difficult to control, and his reputation was a tenuous one at the seminary. "He was much in conflict with the students and particularly with the house orders," said one doctor who interviewed Schmidt. "He frequently went out without asking leave, whenever he wanted to take a walk, or to buy things. He argued with the professors, so much so that his fellow students told him that if he did not change, he would not get along well."[21] But Schmidt could not be swayed. "I am in constant trouble about the house rules of the seminary," he later said. "I hated the so-called Haus-Ordnung with which I was confronted at every step. I liked to study while the others slept, and to sleep when the others studied. There was no end to the constant friction. I hated to ask permission for every little thing."[22] He complained that the professors "had no right to intimate that I was wrong. They all teased me and they called me crazy doctor. This happened whenever I argued matters of dogma or doctrine."[23]

Intense sexual conflict continued to plague him during the years Schmidt studied for the priesthood, and he was unable to resolve the subconscious guilt over his homosexuality. "I was frequently fighting my sexuality all the time I was at the seminary," he said during one interview. "At one time I would think that it was sinful and then I would say that God must allow it since he had given me the feelings, he had meant for me to enjoy them. I thought God would pardon me. Each one of us in this world was different and what God intended him to live up to, is the sole criterion. I know that my relations cannot be understood by others. I often confessed what I had done and made acts of contrition."[24]

In 1904, Schmidt continued with his ecclesiastical studies at the University of Munich. At night, he would leave the college grounds and play the violin in the city's worst taverns and saloons. During the day, in between classes, he gave away all the money he made the night before and then complained that he had none left with which to buy food. "Sometimes I felt very uncertain about myself during that period. There were very dark moments of despair for which I could not account myself and other times when I felt like an agent of God Almighty!"[25]

Hans told everyone that he was a doctor and insisted that people address him in that manner. "He printed his own doctor's diploma affixing the seal [t]hereto," said one official representative of the bishop. "He studied only one semester but tried to create an impression that he was there only for his studies. He had presented his doctor's dissertation and according to his statement before the ecclesiastical court it was a copy of something out of a periodical and was not original . . . he called himself Dr. Johannes Schmidt."[26]

In 1905, Hans was arrested in Munich, charged with forging graduation certificates for failing students. Because of his reputation for being so generous to the poor, many people could not believe that Hans Schmidt could do such a thing. However, German authorities were less forgiving and demanded that the young man be sent to jail. But his father hired a Munich attorney, Johann George Boxheimer, to defend him. Boxheimer prepared a deposition for the court that described the Schmidts' family history and their alarming tendency toward suicide. Boxheimer wrote, "in the family of the accused, many persons have been insane and not only near relatives from the father's side, but also from the mother's side."[27] He also pointed out to the court that Hans Schmidt had a reputation for mental instability at the seminary. "He was often missing at the official service to God and made himself busy in his room, very often with developing of photographic film. In the seminary for priests at Mainz the accused walked around sometimes for days as if in a dream and during this time it was impossible to get a sensible reply from him."[28] Upon learning that he might be facing a prison sentence, a curious thing happened to Hans Schmidt. He became crazier.

He was seen riding a bicycle through the city streets in broad daylight wearing nothing except his underwear. He spoke in broken sentences that often had nothing to do with the conversation at hand. "His behavior seemed very strange to me," said a cousin who saw the young man during this time. "He was unsteady and then again very quick moving. Then it seemed to me as if he was entirely preoccupied."[29] When he was allowed to preach during services, his lectures made no sense to anyone and had little to do with the church or the Catholic religion. His sermons were so disjointed and nonsensical that people believed Hans had become insane. As a result, his attorney concluded that an insanity plea for their client might be best. After a deluge of supporting depositions, which were easy to obtain in a city where everyone knew Hans as "the crazy doctor," the court agreed. It was decided that the young man should attend the cold-water sanitarium at Jordanbad in Wurtenburg.

Jordanbad was an institute where people went for rest and relaxation. Using the baths as a medical treatment, patients could immerse themselves daily in cold water, which was alleged to be therapeutic in value, both psychologically and physically. Schmidt entered Jordanbad and remained there almost a month. Records indicate that he took only one bath during that time.[30] Upon his release, he was sent to do penance at the Engelsburg monastery at Miltenberg. There, he fell into disfavor with the monks, who tired quickly of the headstrong young man who debated every order and refused to follow the simplest instructions. "If he had the duty to say prayers aloud, the most foolish matters came to light and he was not able to read the most simple prayers that were used every day. One day he ran around without pants, only wearing the cassock," said his lawyer in Munich.[31] After only a few weeks, Schmidt was sent back to Mainz.

In the spirit of forgiveness, the seminary tribunal agreed to let him return to class. It was one of the few periods in his young life when Hans was happy. Again, he plunged into the books, determined to complete his studies. He improved his knowledge of biblical verse and was able to converse and write fluently in Latin. He read Plato and Socrates, and could discuss the most intricate points of religious dogma, no matter how ancient. But still, Hans avoided companionship of friends and colleagues. "One could never persuade him to go into society," his brother once said of him.[32] Despite his combative attitude and lingering questions on his abilities as a clergyman, Hans Schmidt was ordained into the Catholic priesthood on December 24, 1906.

His ordination took place in the Mainz seminary in the dead of night and was performed by the bishop. Because of the controversial aspects of Schmidt's behavior, the ceremony took place in seclusion and was unknown to the other candidates. "The bishop ordained me alone," he said later. "I do not like to speak of it. The real ordination took place the night before. St. Elizabeth, she ordained me herself. I was praying at my bedside when she appeared to me and said, 'I ordain you to the priesthood.' She then disappeared. There was light during her appearance. I told no one. I thought it best to keep it to myself. They would make fun of me. They always made fun of me for these things. They always expect others to do as they do. God speaks to different people in different ways."[33]

He received his first assignment to a parish in the village of Burgel. But Father Hans did not take well to the parishioners. He did not seem interested in their welfare and was frequently absent from services. He stayed there for seven months, until July 1907, when he was transferred to Seelingstadt. A short time later, Schmidt was suddenly reassigned to a small chapel at Gonsenheim. "At both places they found fault with me about the way I preached," Schmidt said later. "I liked to talk about that which I wanted to. They were mostly uneducated farmers. They did not understand me."[34] Another chaplain, Jacob Sieben, served at Gonsenheim during the same period. "After the holy mass in the morning, he went immediately out of the church[,] which is not the custom of priests," Father Sieben once said.[35] But even after he became a priest, Schmidt experienced a bitter internal struggle with his sexual obsessions.

"Yes, there were some altar boys," he said. "I took walks with them, but did not dare to touch them. And in the confessional I felt it could not be wrong because I could not help it. I would confess to other priests who said I must try to overcome these faults."[36] Sometimes he was successful; other times he failed. By that time, he already had sexual relations with several women. These encounters left him unsatisfied and depressed. One psychiatrist who later examined Schmidt said, "He was very much disappointed but still it did not hinder him from continuing such relations."[37] On most occasions, he would leave the parish at Gonsenheim at night and seek out local prostitutes. He removed his collar and wore civilian clothes so as not to be recognized as a priest. Rumors of his late-night trips to the city's brothels made their way to the parish, but he was never discovered. On occasion, he would return to the church at dawn with barely enough time to change into his cassock and perform morning services.

His sermons, and the manner in which they were delivered, were widely ridiculed. "In August or September, he preached a very remarkable sermon entitled 'De Samaritano Misericorde,' in which he recited a poem, 'The Last Hours of Tiberius,'" Father Sieben later said. "I was present at the time of the service and must state that this sermon was absolutely eccentric. Particularly, the voice in which he delivered the sermon and the gestures which he used were all in the manner of an actor."[38] Father Kraus later declared, "it was entirely abnormal. It has been spoken of everywhere and laughed over."[39] In his deposition to the Munich court Johann Boxheimer wrote, "All listeners were shocked by this happening and believe[d] that they had a lunatic in the pulpit."[40] His other sermons were fiery speeches of damnation and condemnation and did not go over well in the community. He was caught stealing donations to the church but did not keep the money for himself. Instead, he personally gave out the funds to people he thought deserving. For that reason, the church was reluctant to punish him as a thief.

Other clergy thought Father Hans was unfit to be a priest and complained to the monsignor as well. One of the most common complaints concerned Schmidt's continuous violation of church teachings. "The greatest mistake he made was in the use of his fingers," one priest said during testimony. "According to the rubrics of saying mass, the priest, after the Host has been consecrated, must use only the thumb and index finger of each hand and no other parts of the hand must touch the Host until the Host is consumed at communion. That is a very strict law in the celebration of the mass. But Father Schmidt did not always use his fingers in that way, he used the second finger and the thumb."[41] The staff at the church was fully aware of this offense and reported it to their superior.

Father Schmidt also did not perform the mass in the traditional manner, a serious transgression of church dogma and one that should have been resolved by either a suspension or dismissal. "He would leave out part of the mass, part of the prayers and other parts of the mass," one priest complained. "After the communion when we must purify the chalice, he would consume more time than the ordinary priest in this way: that instead of going at the work steadily, he would raise and look around, up at the ceiling, up at the crucifix."[42] His failings in religious matters were well known. Most other priests had no respect for him, though parishioners were unaware that Father Schmidt was not performing the sacred mass according to church law.

In his relationships with the parish staff, he was an enigma. His strange comments at social gatherings both surprised and frightened other priests, who constantly complained to the monsignor about his behavior. "One incident is so fresh in my memory that it seems it just occurred," Father Jacob related to court, years later. "We were seated at the dinner table and Chaplain Schmidt told with such drastic realism of a burglary in a Munich bank that I gained the impression that he could only mean that he himself had been there!"[43] On another occasion, Father Schmidt openly discussed the Harry Thaw murder case and expressed empathy for the killer.[44] "He was very much interested in the case," said one priest, "and in a way, sympathized with Thaw, that the man was being persecuted, that he might have been right in what he did, killing this man White."[45]

It was also common knowledge to the staff at the church that Father Hans routinely stole food from the kitchen. This was considered puzzling since the priests could eat as much as they wanted and there were never any complaints about a lack of food. "I forgave much in him as he had come to Gonsenheim as a sick man," Father Sieben said. "After his departure I must say that it seemed to me it were best if he was no priest."[46] After several months of questionable behavior, Hans was asked to leave and find another assignment. However, the bishop would not reassign him, and he was unable to find a single church that was willing to take him in.

By the winter of 1908, Schmidt's career as a priest was in shambles. He had been arrested for forgery and publicly humiliated in court. He had a reputation as a thief who stole food and squandered church money. His sermons were famous for their lack of common sense, and many people fled services when he spoke from the pulpit. Everyone in the parish witnessed his odd behavior in the streets; he would wander about in a daze and stand as if paralyzed while people walked around him in amazement and fear. His late-night womanizing was whispered about in the community, and his perennial interest in young boys was well known. He had nowhere to turn.

And so, with financial help from his father, in addition to the money he had stolen from the meager collection plates at Gonsenheim and the funds he was able to extort from elderly parishioners by promises of salvation, Hans Schmidt decided to go to America. There he could begin a new life, unimpeded by the shadows of the past, free to pursue the sacred duties of his position and fulfill, at last, his promised destiny as a man of God.

In July 1909, the son of Heinrich Schmidt, the sixth one, boarded the steamship *Grosser Kurfurst* of the North German Lloyd Line at the docks in Frankfurt and set sail for New York City.

3

Alma

She disappeared. That was all there was to it. She left her home at 507 East Broadway in Louisville, Kentucky, at 9:45 A.M. on December 8, 1909, and was never seen alive again. Alma Kellner, eight years old, was on her way to attend mass at St. John's Church, located at Clay and Walnut streets, only six blocks from her home. After two hours had passed, her parents, Frederick and Elizabeth, became concerned. Since the mass was only one hour, Alma should have returned home no later than 11:15 A.M. By the afternoon, they were frantic and notified the police. By late evening, every available officer in the Louisville Police Department was out on the street looking for the pretty little girl who had vanished on her way to mass. But there was not a single lead as to what had happened to her.

When Alma awoke that morning, she first played with her baby brother, Frederick Jr., age four, for a while. That day was the Feast of the Assumption of the Virgin Mary and a solemn mass was planned at St. John's for the occasion. She then prepared for church, which she attended frequently with her classmates. Alma wore a brown plaid dress with cream velvet trim and collar. Over the dress, she put a dark brown coat and a red hat. Alma was looking forward to the ceremony. When she finished dressing, she kissed her mother and her baby brother goodbye and walked out the front door of the house. As she walked down Broadway toward the church, Alma turned to wave goodbye. Two neighbors, Mrs. Elizabeth Rush and Mrs. Martha Peace, saw Alma and exchanged greetings with her as she passed them on the street. Mrs. Kellner watched her daughter skip along until she was out of sight.

By noon that day, Alma had not returned home. Mrs. Kellner voiced her concerns to her husband, who told her not to worry. Since school was not in session, maybe she stopped off to play with friends. By two o'clock, Mrs. Kellner was very worried and went out to look for her daughter. When she could not locate her, Mrs. Kellner called Frederick, who then went to the police. Relatives and friends were called in, and they began to scour the neighborhood for little Alma. They went to St. John's Church, where they spoke to the pastor, Father Schuhmann. He said that the mass was celebrated at 9:00 A.M. instead of the usual 10:00 A.M., which further alarmed the Kellner family. It meant that by the time Alma arrived at the church, mass would have been either over, or very close to being over. She should have left immediately and returned home. Father Schuhmann also said that he did not recall seeing the little girl during mass at all.

Alma attended St. Mary's Academy at 1162 East Broadway. The school was part of St. John's Church, where most of the staff knew her well. Sister Mary Columbia, the mother superior of the school, immediately assembled her staff and made inquires about Alma. She also sent out aides to the homes of the children in the parish who were friendly with the little girl. Police arrived and searched the school building and the surrounding area. Playgrounds and parks in downtown Louisville were canvassed for anyone who might have made contact with Alma. The rectory was searched on the theory that she may have wandered into the dormitory and fallen asleep. By evening, all the city's hospitals had been contacted and asked if they had treated a female child in the last eighteen hours. Store owners along Broadway were questioned as police tried to retrace Alma's route to the church.

"Mrs. Kellner broke down when it began to grow dark and her child did not return," the Louisville *Courier-Journal* reported, "but Mr. Kellner bore up under the strain and left no stone unturned to find his child. Thinking that she may have gone to another church to attend mass, every Catholic pastor in town was asked to help in the search. These priests also sought to find some clue, but like the others in the searching party, their efforts were futile."[1] Slowly, the possibility of abduction began to crystallize in the minds of the family. Though kidnappings were rare in Louisville, it was a theory that police entertained almost from the beginning. Alma's grandfather, J. F. Kellner, was once the president of Central Consumers Company, a successful business in downtown Louisville. He was a wealthy man who died in 1908. His son, Frederick, had inherited his estate, and it was no secret that the Kellners were well off. Police speculated that Alma had been taken and held for ransom. Though kidnapping was still a new crime, it was not unknown. Every parent knew the legendary story of Charley Ross, America's most famous abducted child.

It was called the "crime of the century." Four-year-old Charley Ross disappeared from the front yard of his home in Germantown, Pennsylvania, on the afternoon of July 1, 1874. He was the youngest son in a family of seven children. The community was bewildered. They could not imagine why anyone would want to steal a four-year-old child. Several days later, a note arrived at the Ross household demanding money for his safe return. "You wil hav two pay us befor you git him," the poorly spelled note demanded.[2] A ransom kidnapping had never occurred in America before this. The police were dumbfounded. Thousands of volunteers assisted police in their search for the kidnappers. The suspects later demanded $20,000, or they would kill little Charley Ross. Though the family eventually agreed to pay the money, the transaction was never completed. Negotiations dragged on for months, while Charley Ross became a household name across the country. Newspapers reported every minute aspect of the case in huge headlines, along with spirited calls for the quick execution of the suspects. "What happened to Charley Ross?" was the most often asked question of the time. "The abduction of Charley set the pattern for subsequent abductions . . . and also opened up a cultural territory in the public exploitation of children, fed by the imaginings of the horrible abuse suffered by other people's children and the emotional dread of losing our own."[3]

In December 1874, New York City police apparently killed two of the kidnappers in a Brooklyn shoot-out.[4] As he lay fatally wounded inside the tenement building in Bay Ridge, one of the suspects told the cops, "It's no use lying now, I helped to steal Charley Ross, Mosher knows all about it!"[5] William Mosher was the second suspect killed in the same gunfight. A third man was eventually convicted of charges relating to the Ross case, but little Charley's body was never found.[6] His story became part of American folklore and, even in 1909, was well known throughout the country, thanks to periodic "sightings" of the still-missing Charley Ross.

Captain Francois Portman, of Louisville Police Department's Second District, was put in charge of the Kellner case. He quickly dispatched his investigators to all parts of town. "The alarm was spread throughout the entire city," the *Courier-Journal* said. "The detective force was put on the trail at once and every patrolman in Louisville was instructed not only to investigate every child seen on the streets, but also to arrest all persons who might be suspicious in their actions."[7] Throughout the night, the effort to find Alma Kellner intensified. Louisville was turned upside down and the more the police searched, the more desperate they became. "Alleys were scoured, old stables and tenements were searched by the police, but with the same result, the child could not be found. In fact, nothing known to the mind of the trained detective was left undone."[8]

B. C. Younts, who owned a pharmacy just two blocks from the Kellner home, told investigators he saw Alma that morning. He said he watched her walk by his storefront at about 9:50 A.M., though he could not be positive about the time. Police located W. R. Augustus, the local mail carrier, whose route extended down Broadway and along Clay Street. He told investigators that he saw the little girl earlier that day at about 10:00 A.M., walking on Hancock, near Clay Street, which was the correct way to the church. Augustus had the same mail route for many years. He knew the Kellner girl, so there was no reason to doubt his story. Sergeant Jerry Quill of the Louisville Police Department went to St. John's Church and located the janitor, who told him that he was at the rectory all that day and did not see Alma Kellner.

"Those detectives and friends who worked all night to find even the slightest trace of the child seem completely baffled at the mysterious disappearance," said the *Courier-Journal*. Relatives congregated at the Kellner home on East Broadway, which also became the command post for Captain Portman and his growing staff. Every few minutes, friends and concerned neighbors appeared at the Kellners' doorstep with food, water, or coffee for the police. They would enter the large living room where Mrs. Kellner reclined on the sofa, wracked by grief and worry. Her dutiful husband rubbed her forehead with a wet towel and tried to comfort her. One reporter described the scene as "a pathetic one, for not only were the mother and father in tears but those who came to comfort remained to weep as well. On the floor of the living room were a rocking horse and other playthings to delight the childish heart, with which the little girl had amused her baby brother before she started for church."[9]

Over the next few weeks, a routine developed. Police received dozens of tips, which originated from informants, jail inmates, reporters, other police departments, and the general public as well. Investigators tirelessly pursued these leads and then reported the results to the Kellner family. Always, the information led nowhere. On December 17, word came to Chief of Detectives John P. Carney that police in Indiana might have located Alma. Early that day, Davies County Police raided a gypsy camp in the woods near Washington, Indiana. A little girl who greatly resembled Alma was found in the custody of two gypsies. Frederick Kellner was immediately notified and he agreed to go to Washington to see the girl who was being held by the police. "The trip to Washington in the hope that the mystery which has baffled the police for nearly two weeks and which gained world-wide notoriety, was begun early Sunday morning," reported the *Courier-Journal*. "In company with three newspaper men, Mr. Kellner boarded a Baltimore and Ohio train at 8:10 o'clock this Sunday morning."[10]

Later that day, Mr. Kellner was taken off the train and placed on a private bus to take him to the Davies County Jail. By then, local residents had learned that the father of the missing girl was coming to their town. Hundreds of curiosity-seekers gathered at the train station and in the vicinity of the jail. "Many of the throng started in hot pursuit of the bus and chased it all the way to the jail," the *Courier-Journal* reported. "On the route, many more joined in the run and when Mr. Kellner alighted at the jail, he was forced to pass through a line of nearly a thousand excited, breathless people."[11] He greeted the jailer, and was taken up to the room where the little girl was being held for his identification.

The minute he laid eyes on her, Kellner knew she was not his missing daughter. "This is not Alma," he said. "But before he could say more," the *Courier-Journal* reported, "tears were streaming down his cheek and he gave way to grief as he has never done before since the disappearance of his child. . . . The scene was a most pathetic one and everyone gathered in the room was deeply affected."[12]

At first, the child was too frightened to speak. But in a few moments, she gave her name as Hazel Ramay Pitts and said that she had been with her mother and father as long as she could remember. "We travel about in the summer," she said. "This year we are out late but were on our way home. I have lived with pa and ma all my life and I didn't know what these big peoples was going to do with me. I was awful scared last night that was a goin' to take me from pa and ma but when they treated me so nice here I wasn't afraid no more. Yes, sir, I had roast turkey and cranberry sauce and a lot of other good things to eat today and I knowed that didn't look like much like they was a goin' to hurt me."[13]

Though Kellner was deeply disappointed, he held out hope for Alma's return. "I am still convinced that Alma was kidnapped and is being held for ransom," he told reporters. "I believe that when this matter quiets down, those who are holding her will state their terms and we will be able to arrange for her return. Although this is my belief, I cannot be certain that it is correct and the awful fact remains that we may never see her face again."[14] He bid his farewell to the Washington Police and caught the next train back to Kentucky. "The return trip was a sad one, though Mr. Kellner bore up bravely under the terrible strain," wrote one reporter for the local press.[15]

In the meantime, Frank Fehr, an uncle of Alma and a family spokesman, brought home the bad news to Mrs. Kellner. "Joy was transformed into gloom with harsh suddenness yesterday afternoon when Frank Fehr notified members of the family that the little girl at Washington, Indiana, was not the missing child," said the *Courier-Journal*.[16] Later that day, Frederick Kellner arrived home and faced his grieving wife once again. "There, there, mother, it's all right," Mr. Kellner said to his suffering wife. "She'll turn up. Don't worry. Mostly, she just went to play with her friends."

But he did not believe it himself. Alma was a conscientious child, very self-aware and obedient. In school, she was regarded as an intelligent and disciplined student. "She was not only a diligent and gifted child in her school work," said one published account, "but is known as a child of the most amiable and loving disposition. Sister Columbia and the other sisters who knew her, loved her dearly and they are almost as deeply affected by her disappearance as are her parents."[17] No, she would never go anywhere without her parents' permission. Alma was a good girl. Something had happened to her. Something terrible. Something evil.

4

Into the Cellar

The winter skies over the city of Louisville seemed even more depressing to the Kellner family. The months dragged on with no word of the missing Alma. No note was received from any kidnappers, and the police were totally puzzled by the little girl's disappearance. However, Captain Carney had his own ideas of what had happened, which he shared only with his colleagues in the police department. Not an outgoing man, but a tenacious investigator, Carney continued to work the case even as it faded from the headlines of the local press. "There were many who thought that she had been kidnapped," he told a reporter from the Louisville *Courier-Journal*, "but Chief of Police Watson Lindsey and I would not let the matter rest that easily. It never left the minds of the Chief and myself that a degenerate had done away with the child."[1] By February 1910, police suspected that Alma had not survived her abduction. Somewhere between her home and the church, a distance of less than one mile, she had met her fate, whatever it was. The suspect had managed to take her off the streets, or from the church, without anyone noticing. To the police, this fact indicated that the victim knew the person or at least had seen him before.

Captain Carney reviewed the interview list compiled on the day of her disappearance. The last person to see Alma walking along Broadway was the owner of a pharmacy located at Clay and Hancock Street. He said that he saw the girl go by at about 9:50 A.M., though he could not be sure of the exact time. At St. John's, no one remembered seeing Alma at the service, though several people reported seeing a little girl who could have been her. The nuns at the academy where she attended school spoke highly of Alma Kellner and her attachment to the church. "This was characteristic of the darling little girl," Sister Mary Genevieve said later. "She would often steal away from the other children and go to the chapel to spend a moment in prayer. Alma was no goody-good girl by any means but her devotion to the child Jesus was amazing."[2] The custodian at St. John's, Joseph Wendling, reported that he was at the church that morning to start the boilers and he did not see her in the pews. Carney assumed that Alma was taken either immediately before she reached St. John's or immediately after the service at the church itself. If she was murdered, her body could be in that same area. "I detailed the entire force to search for the body," Carney told the press. "Every sewer, outhouse, and basement in the radius of several miles of the child's house was searched. Any place that was large enough to conceal the body was examined."[3]

By the spring of 1910, the story of the missing girl from Louisville had moved off the front pages. The Kellners were numb with grief and were forced to face the possibility that Alma might never be found. No new information was forthcoming and police had no new leads to follow. The investigation was at a standstill. Other parents in the community feared that there could be a kidnapper or a child killer on the loose, and paid close attention to the activities of their children. No student walked to school at St. John's that semester without an adult guardian. Frank Fehr shared his thoughts with a newspaper reporter. "I entertained the theory all along that the child had met with foul play," he said, "but in desperation I clung to the kidnapping theory in order to buoy up the hopes of the family. When no one came forward and offered to negotiate with us to return the child for ransom, I felt sure she would not be found alive."[4]

On May 26, 1910, Father Schuhmann, the pastor of St. John's, was informed by the school custodian that the basement of the school building was filled with water. A pipe had broken and was leaking into the space beneath the ground floor. When the priest went to examine the situation, he found that the water was nearly four feet deep. A local plumbing firm, Haller & Zehnder, was summoned to the scene. Before they could do any repairs, the water had to be pumped out. One of the workers, Richard Baxter Sweet, descended into the dark waters using a lantern for light. He found the broken pipe immediately in a far corner of the basement. After making a temporary patch, he hooked up a pump and began to empty out the cellar. The plumbers worked on the project for several days, replacing the rusted pipes and draining the substantial amount of water.

On the morning of May 30, Sweet descended again into the cellar, where the water level now was only one foot. There was a distinctive, foul odor unlike the previous days, when the water level was much higher. He hung his lantern from a nail in the crossbeam above. Using a shovel, Sweet began to clear out the debris that had gathered in the furthest corner of the cellar. On his very first effort, the metal shovel struck something just under the water.

"Damn!" Sweet moved the lamp closer to get a better look. When the light hit the water, Sweet saw a tiny shoe and a foot sticking out from a pile of rubbish. "Oh Lord!" he whispered. He dropped the shovel and hurried up the ladder and through the trapdoor to where his boss, Jacob Haller, was waiting for him.

"Mr. Haller! Mr. Haller! I think there's a body down there!"

The police arrived ten minutes later. When the news spread that a body was found, excited crowds began to assemble outside St. John's and soon surrounded the school. "Excitement ran high as the word passed from mouth to mouth that the body of Alma Kellner had been found," said the *Courier-Journal*. "Hundreds came running from every direction and it was with greatest difficulty that order could be maintained." Students attending class at the school ran to the windows to see what was happening. Fear began to permeate the classrooms when it became known that their classmate had been murdered. "Father Schuhmann, as soon as he was told of the discovery, dismissed the pupils of St. John's School and they departed for their homes many of them with tear-stained faces."[5]

Captain Carney responded to the church along with his team of detectives. Following closely behind was Chief Lindsey, Louisville Mayor William O. Head, and Coroner Ellis Duncan. When more lanterns were brought to the trapdoor that led to the basement, investigators descended down the ladder. They located the mangled body of a child in the southeast corner of the basement, just as Richard Sweet had described. When they were able to clear the debris that covered the remains, police discovered that the body was wrapped in a carpet. They removed the bundle from its resting place and floated it over to the base of the ladder. With the help of Captain Carney and other detectives, they lifted the body out of the water and onto the dry floor above. The stench was overpowering.

Police slowly unraveled the rotting carpet. For the first time, they were able to see the corpse, and it was not a pretty sight. "As soon as Coroner Duncan touched the carpet, flesh fell from the bone," one reporter said. "With a stream of water, he cleaned the mass and laid aside every fragment of evidence." The remains were more skeletal than anything else. The right foot was missing from below the knee and both hands were gone. There was very little flesh apparent and what was present was highly decomposed, if not destroyed by water saturation. The skull was severely fractured and several pieces of the cranium had been broken off. "Coroner Duncan discovered that some of the bones were charred," said the *Courier-Journal*, "which gives rise to the belief that the murderer attempted to burn the body after the fiendish crime had been committed. The burning of the body probably would account for the absence of any trace of the child's clothing."[6] The remains were removed from the scene and taken to a nearby funeral home.

Almost immediately, Captain Carney and his detectives began to formulate theories on how the body of the girl came to be in the cellar. Father Schuhmann said he did not know the place even existed until the previous week, when he was alerted about the broken pipe. But it did not seem likely that someone from the outside could have come into the church, abducted the girl, murdered her, and dumped the body without anyone taking notice, especially since there was usually someone working in the church at all hours of the day, and most of the night. Captain Carney ordered a detailed search of the premises.

Within a few minutes, one detective located a portion of carpet that was identical with the carpet that was wrapped around the body. It was found in a closet that was used exclusively by the church janitor. In the same spot, police found a man's shirt that appeared to have bloodstains on the front panel. It was becoming more than likely that Alma had, in fact, reached the church on December 8 and was abducted in the chapel or immediately after leaving.

"The fiend, whoever he was, must have found her there, alone and unprotected," Chief Lindsey later said, "and the passion that burned in him overthrew his reason. He in some way got her to the cellar where the awful deed was committed. The fact that some of the bones were charred supports this theory for the furnace is the only place where the child's body could have been burned. It is a known fact that the body was hacked or chopped up in an effort to destroy it. As several members are missing, this theory is entirely possible and it is probably while engaged in this gruesome task the fiend was interrupted and decided to resort to the quicker means of burying the body and allowing some strong chemical, like quick lime, to do the work."[7]

But police were confident that the person who murdered Alma had to be familiar with the layout of St. John's Church. There was simply no way for a stranger to come to the grounds, enter the church, and kill a student undetected. "It is probable," said Lindsey, "that only one man knew of this dark hole and this is our clue, which we believe will solve the mystery of the child's murder and place in the clutches of the law the man who was guilty of it."[8] Police made inquiries about the school janitor, Joseph Wendling, who was originally questioned by detectives in December, when Alma first disappeared. Father Schuhmann reported that Wendling had suddenly walked off the job in January and had not been seen since, but his wife, Madelena "Lena" Wendling, still lived on the school grounds in the janitor's apartment.

When investigators questioned her, she denied knowing anything about the little girl's death. She told the police her husband Joe had a history of leaving his workplace without any reason whatsoever. He left no note and offered no explanation. According to a local press report, she said, "he deserted several of his former employers in Louisville before he secured the place at the parochial school and when he took his leave without saying why, she suspected nothing wrong."[9] Police searched her apartment and found several articles of clothing, including a shirt that appeared to have bloodstains. They also found a ring and a decorative pin, which, police suspected, could have belonged to Alma. When they showed the shirt to Mrs. Wendling, she identified it as belonging to her husband. But she could not adequately explain how she came into possession of the jewelry. "The woman could throw no light on the ring or pin. Although the articles were found in the trunk in her room," the Louisville *Courier-Journal* reported. "She cried out that a little boy found the articles and gave them to her."[10]

Father Schuhmann told Carney that Wendling and his wife first came to him in November 1909 looking for a job. He said the man had come to St. John's through a mutual friend, who told Father Schuhmann that Joe Wendling was a competent worker. He hired Wendling as the school janitor and his wife as a housemaid to help in the rectory. The keys to all the buildings on the church property were in the janitor's possession and he had access to the entire grounds. Father Schuhmann said he remembered seeing Joe on the day of Alma's disappearance, but it was after services, sometime in the afternoon. He did not recall anything suspicious about Joe's activities during that time or at any time thereafter.

On the night of December 8, 1909, the day Alma disappeared, a meeting of the Young Ladies Sodality of St. John's Church was held on the first floor of the school building. The room in which this meeting was held was located directly above the cellar where the girl's body was found. Police felt sure that if Alma was murdered during that meeting, the attendees would have heard a commotion. Police became more convinced that the victim was killed somewhere else on the church property and later taken to the cellar, or that the girl was already dead at the time of the ladies' meeting. Police did not find the body when they searched the school in December because they never looked in the cellar. Few people knew the space existed.

But Madelena defended her husband and said he had nothing to do with the little girl's murder. She knew Joe was not a reliable person, she told Captain Carney. "He said he was going into town and would be back later," she said to detectives when questioned. "When he was going, he wanted my money. I said no. He has his own head, comes and goes when he pleases. He never liked it here in America."

"Is he German?" asked Captain Carney.

"He is French. I am German, born in Alsace."

"Did he like children and little girls? Did he play with them?"

"Yes," Mrs. Wendling replied, "he liked boys as well. I never saw him play much with boys though. He sometimes had girls around him."

"On that morning in December when the girl disappeared, was your husband there that morning?"

"Yes, he was," she said, "but he was not worried. I remember."

Captain Carney was handed the stained shirt that was found in the janitor's room. He held it in front of Mrs. Wendling, who was trembling. "Did he say to you wash this shirt?"

"No, sir. I saw the shirt sometime after, but thought nothing of it. His clothes were always dirty. He was the janitor."

"When the detectives came around, was he nervous?"

"No, he was not worried. He was always nice, genial to me and talked a good deal. He rarely drank."

"Did it ever occur to you that he had something to do with the disappearance of that child?"

"No. Never. He was a good man to me."

"Did he say he was scared?"

"No, not at all."

"What does he look like, Mrs. Wendling?"

"He is about twenty-seven years old, about five feet eight inches or ten. I can't tell about weight, small black mustache, dark hair and dark eyes. He had no scars but had a blue-colored tattoo on his arm, and spoke with a French accent."

"Thank you, Mrs. Wendling," said Captain Carney, "We may want to talk to you later again." He gathered up his notes and the shirt and walked to the door. "Oh, by the way, was he ever arrested before?"

She paused for a moment and seemed to think about the question. She placed her hand on her chin as if to support her head. "Yes, I think but only once. For fooling with girls at Bryant and Stratton College."[11]

At that very moment while Carney spoke with Madelena Wendling, across the narrow courtyard, a tired and exasperated Father Schuhmann entered the chapel. He slipped inside the vestibule and closed the thick wooden door behind him. The serenity and stillness of the empty building became his armor against the world outside, especially that day. The center aisle was illuminated by the gentle glow of burning candles positioned on both walls. Two large hurricane lamps posted on the rear doorframe provided a soft, flickering light at the entry. The old priest dipped his right hand into the Holy Water basin and made the sign of the cross. As he began the short walk down the aisle, he saw someone kneeling in prayer at the railing by the tabernacle. Because the chapel was lit only by candlelight and lantern, it was difficult to see very clearly. As he moved closer, Father Schuhmann saw the young German priest who had arrived in Louisville only a few months before.

According to his papers, Hans Schmidt was ordained in 1906 at the highly regarded Mainz Seminary in Germany. Louisville was his first official assignment in the United States, though he had spent some time at a parish in Trenton, New Jersey. He was only twenty-nine years old, of medium build, with dark hair and a pleasant face. His demeanor seemed friendly, though a bit too intense; but that intensity was something that was not uncommon in those new to the priesthood. Father Schuhmann had been the host for many new priests from various seminaries around the world. He knew that youth frequently inspired a strong, unrelenting devotion, perhaps because of the many challenges that lay ahead. Schmidt had come to his parish with a strong letter of recommendation from a German diocese. The chaplain prayed with his head bowed and hands extended over the railing.

"Hans?" Father Schuhmann said softly. "Is that you in the dark there? I didn't expect to see you."

The young priest, whose hands cradled his forehead, did not seem to hear the monsignor. The old priest moved a little closer until he almost touched the railing.

"Hans?"

Father Schmidt seemed startled. He ran his hands through his smooth, black hair and straightened his cassock without standing.

"Schoenen Gruss, [Greetings] Father George," he whispered. "I didn't hear you come in."

"Das tut mir Leid [I'm sorry]."

"Oh, that's all right, you're not disturbing me."

"Hans, I thought you would be in the library with the rest of the staff at this hour. By the way, coffee will be served shortly. Please join us in the dining room, if you like."

Father Schmidt removed a handkerchief from his vest pocket and wiped his brow. "Of course, Father, I would be happy to. I was just praying, Father, praying for that little girl, Alma. Her family must be suffering greatly. It is up to us to provide them with spiritual support."

"Yes, it's awful, awful. I am worried, Hans. Nothing like this has ever happened before. I am concerned about what it will do to our church."

"Gott wird uns helfen. Er hat das immer getan. [God will see us through. He always has.]"

Father Schuhmann knelt in the first pew and prayed silently for a few moments. He needed to be in the rectory shortly to meet with the school staff and the other brothers. Making the sign of the cross, he rose to his feet and glanced over at the young priest.

"Hans, kommst Du mit? [Hans, coming with me?]" Father Schuhmann called.

"In a moment," the young priest answered. "I should pray for her killer as well."

Father Schuhmann nodded and clasped his hands in front of his chest. Schmidt was a true Christian, thought the old priest. God never turns his back on the sinner, only the sin. Father Schuhmann walked up the aisle, determined not to be late for the evening coffee. He dipped his fingers into the holy water once again and rubbed his forehead with the cool liquid. Down the aisle, he saw that Schmidt was still on his knees, engrossed in holy prayer.

"Yes, Hans," he said as he nodded his head in agreement. "We mustn't forget him either."

5

The Pursuit

For the next several weeks, Captain Carney and his team of investigators followed the nebulous trail of Joseph Wendling. Inquiries were sent to Washington, D.C., and wanted posters dispatched to all major cities in Kentucky, Missouri, Indiana, Tennessee, and Mississippi. Carney was convinced that Alma had been killed on the very day she disappeared because Wendling was a man of little means and had no secure location to keep the little girl. Therefore, it was unlikely that she could be held captive for a long period without anyone taking notice.

"I believed all along that my little daughter would come back to me alive and well," Fred Kellner told the press. "Something seemed to assure me that she had been stolen by designing persons anxious to extract money from us and this feeling kept my hopes high. I never expected to hear that she had met with such an awful fate for we would not believe anyone capable of such an outrage on an innocent child."[1]

Carney sent circulars outlining the details of the case to the American Consuls in France, Germany, and Italy. He sent 900 posters to every major police department in the United States. Carney was able to trace Wendling to New Orleans, where the fugitive stayed in flophouses along the waterfront and on Bourbon Street. It would not be a problem for Wendling to blend in because he was French. The city's French Quarter was a bewildering mixture of sailors, vagabonds, drifters, and hoodlums who were running from the law. Working with the New Orleans Police, Carney just missed capturing Wendling by a few hours; it was discovered that he had checked out of his boarding room just before the detectives arrived.

From Bourbon Street, Wendling went to Houston, where he got a job as a chef. Carney jumped on a train and arrived in the city only to find out that Wendling had left a few weeks before for Galveston. Carney lost track of his prey for several weeks afterward and spent most of his time showing wanted posters at the local saloons in the Galveston area. Carney received information that Wendling was in San Antonio. "I learned he had a job at a ranch twenty-two miles outside San Antonio," Carney told reporters. "He had worked there fourteen days and left under a sudden impulse and had gone back to downtown San Antonio."[2] But after a week of searching, Carney concluded that Wendling had left Texas for good.

In late June, detectives learned that Wendling had mailed a letter to a friend in San Antonio. When Carney secured the letter, he noticed the postmark was dated the week before in Rio Vista, California, a small town located forty miles south of Sacramento. Wendling wrote that he got a job on a brush gang, clearing roads of debris for ten dollars a week. It was a good lead and needed to be followed up immediately. Carney took a train out to California and, with several detectives from Sacramento, went to the work camp described in the letter. Again, Wendling was gone. But after checking the payroll records, Carney saw that Wendling had worked at the camp for several weeks. He told another employee that he was leaving the job because of a woman and would not be coming back. With the help of local detectives, Carney was able to identify this woman as Corrine Munea, who lived in Hume, Montana. The following day, Captain Carney was on the road again.

He arrived in Hume on July 15, after a week's travel. "I was delayed by washouts and slides," he told reporters later. "I rode forty-nine miles on the tail end of a freight train." Nevertheless, Mrs. Munea was eventually located and interviewed. She said that she did not know a man named Joseph Wendling but when she visited her mother in June, she did meet a Frenchman in Houston, Texas. When Carney showed her the wanted poster from Louisville, she immediately identified him as the stranger in Houston. He had introduced himself as Henry Jacquemin and spoke with a heavy French accent. He said he was a cotton trader out of New Orleans. But as far as she knew, Jacquemin was still in California. Furthermore, Mrs. Munea said, a postcard from him arrived that very day. The card was postmarked from Vallejo, California, and, better still, included an address: 633 Virginia Street.

"I was shown the postal card in Hume, Montana, on the night of Saturday, July 15," he told the press later. "Immediately, I started to San Francisco." But this time, Captain Carney decided to contact the police before he arrived. He wired San Francisco Police and gave them the latest information, including the Vallejo address. He requested that they go to that location and look for the suspect. "I was held up two days by a washout," Carney said. While his train waited out the heavy rains, San Francisco Police found Wendling. He was sleeping in his room when detectives burst in and arrested him. When he heard the news, Carney was elated.

"Am I glad the chase is over?" Carney told the press. "If you had traveled as far as I have you would be too. I have traveled 11,000 miles on this search."[3] The prisoner was taken to the local jail, where he was charged as a fugitive from justice and held without bail. Captain Carney arrived two days later, and for the first time the two men came face to face with each other. Though tired from his haphazard journey across the country and back, Carney was eager to learn what Wendling would say for himself.

"This fellow is a bright one," he said later. "He speaks French and German fluently and is a good mechanic and all around man. But he is a degenerate. When the body of the girl was found in the basement of the church, Wendling's wife admitted that she washed her husband's bloodstained clothing. I don't care to say what other evidence we have."[4] But Wendling strongly denied killing the girl. San Francisco Detective Thomas Burke and his partner, Detective Michael Ryan, were the two officers who found the fugitive in the Third Street flophouse. "We asked him if he committed the murder," detective Burke said in an interview with reporters. "He said, 'I know something about it and will tell when I get back.' He is the coldest-blooded man I ever came into contact with." But Wendling said that he never even knew he was a suspect in the girl's murder until the day before he was arrested. He was walking down a street in San Francisco with a friend and saw his own photograph in the newspaper.

When Carney first spoke with Wendling, he asked him how he could have killed a little girl who posed no threat to him. "I no kill the little girl so I get free as soon as I go back home," he told frustrated detectives. "I'd rather stay in California 'cause I make more money here." Carney wanted Wendling to agree to come back to Kentucky voluntarily to avoid the necessary paperwork that was sure to follow if he decided to fight extradition. Surprisingly, Wendling agreed to return to Louisville as soon as possible. Carney indicated that he would begin his return trip home as soon as he got some rest and a bath. "To the police," said the *New York Times*, "Wendling, after his capture, talks as coolly as if he had never been charged with any crime. He was absolutely unmoved under questioning but protested his innocence of the

Kellner murder declaring he knew nothing of it until he read of the finding of the body. He told Captain Carney that he would not resist extradition and the latter said he would start for home with his prisoner as soon as he was rested from his long chase."[5]

In the meantime, telegrams of congratulations poured into the Louisville police headquarters. Mayor Head said to Captain Carney, "On behalf of the people of Louisville, I congratulate you on your notable achievement which places you in the front rank of great American detectives. I had faith at all times in your ability. Extend to San Francisco detectives and to all officials my thanks and best wishes." News of Captain Carney's pursuit of the killer was reported in the nation's press, which followed his dramatic chase across the continent. Wendling began to realize that he had become famous. His photograph was in all the papers and he took pleasure in reading about himself. He asked to see the *San Francisco Examiner* every day. But he was adamant about one thing. He did not kill Alma Kellner.

Even so, Captain Carney was not taking any chances with his prisoner. "I am not at liberty to give my reasons," he said, "but I am convinced that he is plotting to attempt to break away en route to Kentucky. He'll never live to tell the tale. I told him frankly that I would shoot him like a dog if he made the least side step." Reporters were allowed to interview the prisoner, who spoke from his jail cell. When he was asked if he would have an attorney represent him on the murder charge, he responded with a shrug and a smile. "Why should I? I am innocent and can prove it. Innocent men do not need attorneys." On the morning of August 2, Captain Carney boarded a train in downtown San Francisco and left California with his prisoner.

Two days later they arrived in Denver, where Wendling was lodged in the city jail overnight. Again, local reporters descended upon the police station demanding to speak with the celebrity prisoner. "The volatile Frenchman is in a continued gale of merriment," said one press report. "He laughed when he learned that the officers were closing in on him after a chase of 11,000 miles, laughed when the heavy hand of the law fell on his shoulder, grinned with merriment when his captor threatened to shoot at the first attempt at escape, and through the bars of a solitary cell in the Denver city jail told his story punctuated with bursts of laughter."[6] But Wendling did not take the charges seriously because he claimed innocence and was confident he would be released as soon as he got back to Louisville.

The next day, the train arrived in St. Louis, where the two men again settled in for the night. In the meantime, Wendling's wife had hired an attorney, J. R. Clements, who appealed to the courts to stop the illegal transport of his client across the country without any extradition papers. Clements made several requests to obtain the itinerary from the Louisville

Police Department but met with no success. He then contacted the St. Louis City Court and filed a writ of habeas corpus asking for more time to file additional motions. But Captain Carney would not cooperate. He kept his travel plans a secret and refused to answer messages left at his hotel. "I am forced to act like a fugitive myself in order to escape this effort to hinder justice," he said to reporters. When Clements's motion arrived in court late on the day of August 10, city court Judge George Hitchcock put off a decision until the following day.

By morning, Captain Carney, Wendling, J. R. Clements, prosecutors from the St. Louis District Attorney's Office, and a legal team from the Kentucky Governor's office assembled in the city court to decide if the prisoner had to be released from custody. When Carney took the stand, he pointed out that Wendling had already been indicted for murder by a Kentucky court and was considered a fugitive from justice. He also produced papers that proved he was acting as a duly appointed agent of the governor of the state of Kentucky. The defendant's attorney, J. R. Clements, pointed out that such papers, including the indictment, had no standing in the state of Missouri and that if his client was to be taken back to Kentucky, Carney had to apply for extradition. "The boldness of these men to come into this court with such a pretense at a defense of their actions is more surprising than their previous conduct," Clements told the court. "We dare them to produce a single document, warrant, indictment, or process of law giving them any custody over this poor unfortunate man whom they are trying to accuse of a crime of which he is innocent."[7]

No sooner had Clements uttered these words, than when the lawyers from Kentucky dropped a package of documents on the table in front of the judge. "Gentlemen, nothing gives me greater pleasure than to offer this proof," said George Rowe, one of the Kentucky attorneys. In the bundle were certified copies of the bench warrant for Wendling, the Grand Jury indictment, and requisition papers for his return to Louisville. "I submit these papers to the court as proof of the legality of this prisoner's transfer," added Rowe.

At this point, J. R. Clements addressed the court and said that his client was intimidated into coming back to Kentucky before the papers were produced in St. Louis. He said no such papers existed when the prisoner was transported from California. But Judge Hitchcock was not convinced.

"The only point at question here is the validity of the papers produced by the prosecution," he said. "The point of whether it was legal for the defendant to be taken from California is a question for that state's courts. My recommendation to you, Mr. Clements, is to take that issue up in California. This writ is refused and the prisoner is remanded to Captain Carney, the duly authorized agent of the state of Kentucky."[8]

Carney walked over to Wendling, who was slumped in his chair. "Come along, Joe," he said. The men left the courtroom and went directly to the downtown train terminal. They boarded the 2:45 P.M. train of the Louisville, Henderson, St. Louis Railroad and settled in. Within the hour, the train rumbled down the tracks headed for Louisville. All along the route, curious crowds gathered at the scheduled stops. In Evansville, Indiana, a near riot broke out when it was thought that the prisoner had escaped. Over 1,000 angry citizens surrounded Carney and his prisoner as the police captain carefully explained that they were just stretching their legs. The men reached Louisville at 4:00 A.M., and Wendling was brought to the county jail. "He had no sooner been ushered into the Chief's room than he took a position in one of the large windows and busied himself whistling and waving his hand to the crowd which had gathered in the street below. His smile was much in evidence."[9] Carney left for home to get some well-earned rest.

"The first meeting between Joseph Wendling, the accused murderer of Alma Kellner, and his wife, Mrs. Lena Wendling, since the famous prisoner was lodged in the Jefferson County Jail took place shortly before noon yesterday and according to those present, it was most affectionate."[10] Mrs. Wendling told the press that she would support her husband and that he was innocent of the crime of which he was charged.

In the meantime, claims for part of the reward offered for Wendling's capture poured into the mayor's office. Everyone from the Houston Police to homeless people in San Francisco said they were entitled to some of the reward. In the forefront of those who were clamoring for the cash was none other than the new chief of the Louisville Police Department, George Ellis, who wanted the largest share. "I am in a position to furnish unassailable proof that Joseph Wendling would never have been captured without my aid," the chief told reporters the next day. "My claim for half the reward is a just one and if it is not recognized I shall file a suit in the United States Court."[11] Captain Carney demanded, and later received, $1,000 of the reward money. Chief Ellis settled for the same amount when it was pointed out that an attorney's fee would exceed the amount of the reward.

On the morning of November 28, 1910, the murder trial of Joseph Wendling began. The defendant was brought into the Jefferson County Court where Judge James Gregory called the proceedings to order. Wearing a gray suit, white shirt, and a dark green tie, Joe took his seat between his two attorneys. His hair was long and he appeared to be freshly shaven. He seemed to be unconcerned and in a jovial mood. "He wore the same cynical smile that has characterized him since his arrest," said the *Louisville Times*, "although close scrutiny revealed a tenseness about the corners of his mouth and a shiftiness about his eyes."[12] Jury selection required all of two days, and by the afternoon of November 30, Prosecuting Attorney Joseph Huffaker called his first witness, the father of Alma Kellner, to the stand.

Frederick Kellner's testimony was brief. He described for the court what his daughter was wearing on the morning of December 8, 1909, the last time he saw her alive. Prosecutors then put on the stand several witnesses who saw Alma walk to church that morning. Two of these witnesses claimed to have observed her in the pews of St. John's after the mass ended. One of them, Rosa Stauble, told the court that she attended mass the same morning and saw the girl sitting at the rear of the church. She also said that she saw two other women sitting together in the pew next to her. Mrs. Stauble said she remained in the church for a minute after mass ended to say a prayer. At that time, she saw Joe Wendling moving candles to the altar. The witness told the court that the janitor seemed to watch the girl during the time he was in the church. "If she was on the right side, he watched the right side and when she went to the left side, he watched the left side. He was in the church when I left . . . and the girl was at the railing."[13]

Next called to the stand was Mrs. Ann Graehle. She said that she was also at the church that morning and saw a girl there but could not say if it was Alma because she did not know her. Mrs. Graehle told the court that while she sat in the pew, she saw a man come into the church and take a seat in the rear row. When J. R. Clements asked the witness if she knew the man, Mrs. Graehle said that she did not recognize him but that he was dressed all in black and wore a black overcoat. She thought he came into the church from the sacristy door where the priests usually enter and exit, but could not be sure. When asked about Wendling, she recalled that she did see the janitor at about the same time but that he stayed only for a minute and left the church by the rear door. Mrs. Graehle said she walked outside herself a few minutes later but never saw the man who was dressed in black leave the church. After Mrs. Graehle's testimony, the court recessed for the day. The scheduled witness for the next morning was Joe Wendling.

"While externally calm and unperturbed, an undercurrent of uneasiness, an indication that the seriousness of his predicament is realized, is apparent in the demeanor of Joseph Wendling," said the *Courier-Journal*. "On the witness stand he appears collected and at ease, but a clenching of the hands, a shifting of the feet and a crossing and a re-crossing of his legs tell the tale of iron nerves strained to the breaking point as the grueling cross examination proceeds."[14] Wendling told the court he never saw Alma Kellner that morning and did not know her. He said that he was the only person responsible for the church grounds and had the keys to the buildings with him at all times. When he was shown some bloody clothes that police had found in his apartment, he identified the articles as belonging to him. But he added that he had not worn those clothes since he lived in France. Joe said he was once accidentally shot in the hand and the blood could have been from that injury.

During his testimony, Wendling held a handkerchief close to his face and wiped his brow periodically, giving the impression that he was nervous. "Wendling's smile is elusive and hard to describe," said one reporter. "It is not a facial contortion in any sense of the word. There is something weird and uncanny about it. The muscles of the mouth and cheek do not appear to move, yet he is distinctly smiling, a cynical, sneering, yet pathetic smile."[15] Again and again, Wendling denied he killed the little girl and explained away all the evidence offered by the prosecution.

After his testimony, it was decided that the jury should have a chance to examine the crime scene. At 3:00 P.M., Judge Gregory, the prosecutors, the defense attorneys, the twelve-man jury, and Joseph Wendling (guarded by the sheriff's deputies) left the courthouse and walked to St. John's Church, which was almost a mile away. Before they left the building, the Judge implored the spectators to remain at the courthouse. But it was to no avail. They had barely walked a block when a large crowd followed the parade. Within minutes, hundreds of people had joined in and they shouted for others to come along.[16] Soon, over a thousand people were behind the judge and the lawyers, yelling, teasing, and howling while the ragtag group continued their way through the narrow streets.

Once they arrived at St. John's, the jury viewed the furnace where the body was alleged to have been burned and the cellar where the victim was found. Some jurors tried to climb into the furnace to see if it was large enough for a little girl. After an hour at the church, the group began the trek back to the courthouse, pushing their way through the spectators, who by then had assembled along the sidewalks, lined the streets, and sat in their wagons as they watched the group march by.

On the morning of December 3, closing arguments were given to the court. Large crowds gathered in and about the building in anticipation of the final moments of the trial. "Large throngs hung on the outside, despite the fact that they could hear nothing and that they could not even see the inside of the courtroom," said one press account. "Others, more agile, clamored to the window ledges on the outside and hanging by their eyebrows peered through the windows."[17] The courtroom was overflowing and uncomfortable. Judge Gregory constantly reminded people to maintain silence as defense attorney Clements made his points to the jury.

Clements said that there was no conclusive evidence that his client even saw Alma Kellner on the day of the murder. The bloodstained clothing had been explained as defense witnesses substantiated that Wendling had been accidentally shot in the hand while he was a soldier in France. Clements told the court that Wendling left Louisville in January because of marital problems and was not running from the law. Furthermore, on the day of the murder, the identity of the man dressed in black who was in the church had never been established. He could have easily killed the little girl after the parishioners left. "I never saw a man get on the witness stand and acquit himself with more dignity than Wendling did," said Clements. "He answered every question truthfully."

But prosecuting attorney Huffaker countered the defense by pointing out that other witnesses had stated that the defendant was the only one in the church with the little girl. Huffaker said that the bloody clothing was damning because even Wendling's hat contained bloodstains. Furthermore, Wendling was one of the few people, besides the priests, who even knew of the existence of the cellar where the body was found. Since he was the janitor, Huffaker questioned, how could a stranger come into the church, take the victim, and kill her without Wendling noticing? The killer had to be someone associated with the church, he explained to the court. Huffaker walked over to the defense table and pointed to the defendant, who cowered in his seat, and said loudly, "We ask a conviction in this case because the evidence points to you and you alone as the man who committed this horrible deed."[18]

Judge Gregory then gave a lengthy charge to the jury, in which he explained the different degrees of murder and cautioned the jury to carefully consider each one in their deliberations, and reminded the panel of the presumption of innocence. "The law presumes the innocence of the accused," he said, "and it is the duty of the jury to reconcile all the facts and circumstances of the case with that presumption."[19] In less than two hours, the jury returned with a verdict. Wendling was found guilty of murder in the first degree. When he heard the foreman announce the decision, the defendant fainted to the courtroom floor.

On December 24, Wendling appeared in the same court for sentencing. Reporters and spectators crammed into the room shoulder to shoulder to hear the final word on the defendant. At 10:00 A.M., deputies brought the defendant into the court and sat him next to J. R. Clements. He was shabbily dressed and seemed to have lost weight. Gone were the crooked smile and the self-confident airs he displayed during the trial. He seemed confused as he glanced around the courtroom for a friendly face. Judge Gregory asked the defendant to stand and inquired if there was any reason why sentence should not be passed.

"Me no understand," came the reply.

Judge Gregory ignored the defendant's statement and sentenced Wendling to life imprisonment. "He listened to the reading of the opinion of Judge Gregory with the same half-smile and half-sneer that has characterized him since his arrest in San Francisco," said the *Louisville Times*.[20] Judge Gregory denied a motion by the defense for a new trial and thanked the jury for their dedication and patience. Later, J. R. Clements told reporters that he intended to appeal the decision and ask for a new trial in the Kentucky State Court of Appeals. In the meantime, Wendling was escorted out of the courtroom by a crew of stern-looking deputies. Some spectators jeered as the convicted murderer passed them on the way to the door.

At about the same time, a confident and introspective man, dressed all in black, read the newspaper while he sat at the train depot in downtown Louisville. He had followed the trial each day and had correctly guessed the outcome weeks before. As he dropped the paper to the floor, he picked up his suitcase and walked to the ticket counter where the wall clock indicated it was nearly 11:00 A.M. His train was scheduled to leave shortly. He reached into his pocket and removed a thick fold of cash, which he had stolen from St. John's collection plates the day before. The ticket clerk looked up.

"New York City," the man said with a German accent.

"Round trip, Father?" the clerk asked.

"One way only," the man replied.

He accepted his ticket and walked toward track six as indicated on the schedule board. He strolled through the darkened corridors, down the hallways and onto the barren platform, where he paused for a moment to look behind. The man thought he heard a noise in the distance, a slight tapping on the brick beneath his feet. It might have been someone. He narrowed his eyes and tried to see into the darkness at the other edge of the platform, where the light fragmented and the shadows played tricks on the imagination. The man took a few faltering steps forward to get a better look.

"Hallo?" he called out. "Hallo, ist jemand hier? [Hello, is anyone there?]"

But there was no one.

6

At Dawn

At 5:30 A.M. on Tuesday, September 2, 1913, seventeen-year-old Lucy Grace Cure left her Prospect Street home in Brooklyn and headed for the sea. She inherited a passion for fishing from her father, a longshoreman on the busy East River docks, where massive ocean cruisers discharged an avalanche of goods from Europe each day. She knew to fish either in the early morning hours, or at dusk when the chances for success were much higher than during midday. Not being a very good student at school, she did not care if she showed up late on the first day of class. At the dock near Constable Point, she tossed a fishing pole and a few crabbing traps into her father's rowboat. It was a sturdy, twelve-foot wooden skiff that her father bought when she was only three years old. For the past thirteen summers, she had spent many contented hours on the skiff in the waters off the Brooklyn shore.

The morning was a bit chilly. A slight but persistent breeze blew in, off the sea from the south as packs of gulls flew overhead, totally absorbed in their lifelong search for food. Their familiar noises echoed across the bay, a comforting sound to all who travel the sea. Behind her, the first tinges of sunlight appeared over the eastern edge of Long Island. Lucy boarded the boat and lifted the tie rope off the dock. She gave a mighty push off the dock with the oar, then placed both the oars in their locks and turned the boat toward the rising sun. She estimated about two hours of fishing before she would have to return to reach school.

"Fishes, here I come," she said.

Within minutes, Lucy fell into the familiar routine of rowing methodically out into the bay. She patiently guided the craft to an area off Constable Point where she had much success in the past catching blackfish, a bottom feeder that was one of her father's favorite dinners. Not much for fighting or sport, but they were good eating and fairly easy to catch. And with a little luck, she could get a passing striped bass or even a flounder that fed on much the same as blackfish. About a quarter mile off shore, she dropped anchor. It hit bottom at about thirty feet, she estimated. She knew she was in the right spot by checking her position with the chimney of the paint factory in south Brooklyn and coordinating it with another building behind it. If the two structures lined up, she knew she was in the proper lane.

Across the choppy waters, the lights of Manhattan pulsated with a sparkling rhythm that made the buildings seem alive. Lucy wondered if there was ever a city of such beauty and magnitude as New York. In the past decade, the city had grown at a furious pace, and it was not just the population that had expanded so dramatically. For the first time in its history, New York had grown vertically. Shantytowns, which were located everywhere on the fringes of the expanding city, were being razed and replaced with three- and four-story walk-up apartment buildings. These tenements would become the trademark dwelling of the immigrant era in Lower Manhattan.

Uptown, on Fifth Avenue and Ninety-first Street, a huge dilapidated shantytown was torn down at the turn of the century to make way for the Andrew Carnegie mansion. Skyscrapers, a word invented in the 1890s to describe any building more than a few stories tall, seemed to be everywhere. When the first steel-skeleton building was constructed at 50 Broadway in 1888, people actually ran away from the site in terror, because they thought the structure would topple at any minute. Bradford Gilbert, the architect who designed it, was later forced to move into the top floor just to encourage prospective tenants. "So wary were New Yorkers of a building whose walls were supported by the metal frame, rather than vice versa, that Gilbert had to reassure them by occupying the topmost offices himself."[1]

But by 1894, *Harper's Weekly* noted that people were no longer startled by skyscrapers. "We are getting to be more accustomed to the lofty structures, and so conventional ideas, born of what we are accustomed to look at, are gradually being modified."[2] Gilbert's "skyscraper" was all of thirteen stories. After Gilbert's success, Joseph Pulitzer commissioned a design for the new home of his newspaper, the *World*. He wanted it to be a personal monument and the tallest building in New York. It was fifteen stories tall.

Eventually, steel-girder construction was proven to be safe and economical. Building codes were reviewed and revised. The new method gained the approval of construction engineers and, later, the enthusiastic support of the general public. By 1900, the race to build the tallest building was on. Theoretically, steel-cage construction made it possible to build structures to unpredictable heights. There seemed to be no limits to the imagination of a new breed of architects. Opposite Trinity Church, on lower Broadway, a twenty-story tower was built, dwarfing everything around it. Every day hundreds of spectators gathered to watch the soaring progress of the steel monoliths. Other buildings of similar height quickly followed, each one adding one floor more than the competition. For only eighteen months, the title of "the tallest building in the world" belonged to the 612-foot Singer Building on Liberty Street.

Lower Manhattan was an area of enormous activity as thousands of steel workers, bricklayers, plumbers, painters, window framers, and day laborers clogged the streets each day on the way to their job sites. By 1910, the skyline of New York City had transformed itself into a modern-day fantasy, unimaginable only a decade before, a vast concrete wall of unprecedented height. Larger buildings brought more industry. Hundreds of businesses relocated to Lower Manhattan, which brought tens of thousands of people into the narrow, twisting streets of the financial district each day. Wall Street became an area of frantic activity fueled by the excitement of the stock exchange located at the corner of Broad Street. America's major banks and financial institutions set up their headquarters within walking distance of the exchange. Speculators bought up every inch of available land in the surrounding area, driving real-estate prices to the highest levels in history. At Broadway and Wall Street, land sold at an astounding price of $700 a square foot.

This caused developers to put up higher buildings in order to make a profit. A landlord could not make money on a small building because he had to charge rents so exorbitant that no tenant would lease space. He was forced to build higher. When steel-frame construction was perfected, buildings soared; and when passenger elevators were invented, the sky seemed to be the limit. Lower Manhattan became a city within a city. "Three centuries ago, it lay on the outskirts of an isolated trading post, today it is the financial center of America. It will remain, for generations, the commercial barometer of a vast teeming land whose terrific, restless energy it reflects."[3]

Though the financial district contained some of the most modern buildings in America, it was surrounded by the oldest neighborhoods in the city, and some of the poorest as well. The dramatic contrast between rich and poor in the metropolis of New York was never so pronounced as it was during the early twentieth century. On Varick Street, where Aaron Burr's old mansion once stood, broken-down, decayed houses lined the avenue, an incestuous breeding ground for crime and a persistent battlefield for some of the city's most violent street gangs.[4] West Houston Street had row after row of dilapidated, topsy-turvy buildings that seemed ready to keel over at the slightest breeze. Hudson, Canal, and Vandam streets offered the same dreary landscape of crumbling tenements and living conditions so foul that they inspired one contemporary author to ask, "What kind of children do you think will develop in such an atmosphere? If you wished to rear a criminal, do you think you could devise a better training place?"[5] Ironically, many of these wretched slums, including the 138 buildings on Hudson Street, were part of the vast real-estate holdings of the richest parish in America, Trinity Church, located on lower Broadway at the entrance to Wall Street.[6]

In the distance, Lucy could see the towering spire of Trinity Church off the Brooklyn shoreline. The ocean liner *Lusitania*, which was due to arrive at the West Forty-third Street docks that day, crawled across the horizon by the Jersey shore.[7] At times, several of these luxurious ships were parked in the bay, all in a row, patiently waiting for their turn to enter the New York harbor. To the starboard side of the *Lusitania*, the Statue of Liberty rose up out of the sea, its torch plainly visible against the morning sky. As spectacular as it was, the statue was dwarfed by the monolithic structures clustered in the tiny space of Lower Manhattan. Lucy tried to imagine what it would look like in fifty years, or a hundred. Would the buildings still be there? Would they be even taller? Where would all the people live? Where would they dock all the ships? She wondered all these things, and more, until she heard a solid thud against the side of the rowboat.

She leaned over to take a look, but saw nothing. She heard the thud again. It was on the starboard side and sounded like a small piece of driftwood striking the side of the hull. Though it was a fairly calm sea, gentle swells rocked the boat from side to side. She placed the oar in its holder and looked over into the murky waters. Just inches away from the side, she saw it. Blank, lifeless eyes stared out from a human head. It was floating faceup, trailing a two-foot long expanse of fine blond hair that lay on the surface of the darkened waters like a leaf. Individual strands fanned out from the skull and swayed softly with the rolling motion of the waves. The mouth was open, revealing a row of straight, clean teeth.

Neatly severed at the neck, the head bumped into the boat once again. Lucy sat absolutely still, her hands grasped the ridges of the boat tightly, not daring to let go. Two small moss bunkers nipped at the base of the neck, tearing minute pieces of flesh from the throat. The head rubbed alongside of the wooden skiff from stern to bow, trailing its mane of hair gracefully behind. Within seconds, it was gone, drifting back into the quiet darkness from whence it came.

Lucy screamed. Her voice shattered the delicate morning air and startled the gulls off the pilings on shore. Hundreds of birds launched into the sky simultaneously, pumping their wings up and down angrily, yapping and crowing in all sorts of sounds. The flock soared overhead as if it were a single entity and formed into a huge cloud that for a moment blocked out the morning sun and cast an ominous shadow over the tiny boat.

Lucy picked up the oars and began to row furiously to shore. She was not aware that she was still screaming. The gulls continued their flight out to the bay, glancing only for an instant at the young girl making her way to shore. Not too far from the skiff, the woman's head bobbed in and out of the water like an apple, twisting and turning at the whim of an indifferent sea. One curious bird broke from the flock and glided down to investigate the strange object. But to a seagull, it was just another meal.

7

Cliffside Park

Three days later, on Friday, September 5, New York City was experiencing the last remnants of a comfortable summer. The temperature was in the sixties, skies were unusually clear, and people enjoyed a gentle preview of the autumn season ahead. The sprawling beaches at Coney Island and Rockaway were still packed with bathers, while Long Island Sound was crammed with the usual fleet of inept weekend sailors. In the farmlands of Brooklyn, growers were preparing for the apple harvest and tending to the pumpkins, which would be the major sellers during the month of October. From City Island, huge schooners built in the island's family-owned shipyards were launched that week and made their trial run down the bay toward Newport, Rhode Island. The Astors, Morgans, and Vanderbilts all docked their magnificent steam-powered yachts at City Island, one of the world's finest sail-producing communities. All around Manhattan, thousands went to their favorite spots along the waterfront to fish, bathe, or catch the sun. The Jersey side was no different.

Mary Bann, age eleven, who lived in Cliffside Park, took her little brother, Albert, age nine, to the shores of the Hudson to play in the water and enjoy the sunny day. They splashed in the meager waves and tried to build castles from the sand on the beach. When she first saw the oddly shaped package floating in the shallow waters, she imagined it to be a bag of garbage or a rolled-up, discarded blanket. Being a curious child, Mary waded in ankle deep and pushed the item with a piece of driftwood. It had some weight. She snagged the edge of the bundle and pulled it closer. Just then, her class-mate and friend, Alice McKnight, who frequently came to the river with the others from the Weehawken neighborhood, called over to her.

"Mary! What do you have there?" Alice sat down on the edge of the shore, placing her bare feet in the water. "Cold!"

"I don't know! Whatever it is, it's kind of heavy!" Mary struggled to get the bundle up on the shore. It slipped away from her and threatened to drift out of her reach. "Give a hand!" Mary called.

"It's junk! It's always junk," Alice complained. "Why don't you leave it alone? Hey! Did you see that new boy in class today?" She smiled as she grabbed an end of the bundle and gave a pull. Albert also came over, grabbed the edge of the item, and tugged on it.

"Well, it's not so heavy!" The girls giggled as they dragged the sopping load onto the rocky shore of Cliffside Park. From where they stood, the girls could see the city skyline. In the middle of the Hudson River, sailboats drifted lazily over the water. There were so many, it seemed impossible that none of the vessels collided with each other. Directly across the waterway, the ocean liner *Vincente Torria*, a recent arrival from Genoa, was comfortably docked at the wharfs of West Forty-second Street. Alongside, the *Grosser Kurfuerst* of the North German Lloyd Line prepared for the next day's sailing to London. Resting in the next slip and dwarfing both ships was the fantastic *Lusitania*, awaiting a September 24 departure to Paris and Berlin.

The largest berth along the docks was occupied by White Star Line's luxurious *Olympic*, built as a challenge to Cunard's fleet, advertised as the "fastest steamers in the world." The *Olympic* was launched in October 1910 and quickly became the epitome of modern-day excellence in ocean travel. White Star, badly wounded by the *Titantic* disaster in 1912, depended on the *Olympic* to salvage its reputation and protect it from the ruin of bankruptcy. Next, and last in line, was the *Mauretania*, sister ship to the *Lusitania*, waiting to sail to Paris the very next morning. As spectacular as these ocean liners were, it was a routine sight for residents on the Jersey side. They barely gave the great ships a second glance.

With a little effort, the girls succeeded in pulling the strange package onto the grassy shelf of the shore where they rolled it into a safe position. A heavy blue sheet was wrapped around the item several times. A length of string, tied into a tangled knot, kept the package together.

"What do you think it is?" asked Mary.

"I don't know. Let's unwrap it. There's something inside, I think," said Alice.

The children managed to untie the line. Mary grabbed one edge of the bedding and pulled it smartly toward her. The bundle rolled away, making several rotations until something popped out. It fell onto the ground, its shapeless form making several rotations until it came to rest. At first, the children thought it was a broken statue or one of those new dummies that department stores used in their windows to model clothes. Only Mary understood that it was the upper part of a human torso, cut neatly in half just below the rib cage. There were no arms or head attached to it. At the bottom end of the chest, several crabs emerged from within and quickly scurried off the bloody sheet onto the ground.

"Oh!" Mary uttered as her brother looked on. It took a minute for the truth to dawn upon everyone. It was real. Then, together, the children went screaming into the woods. Behind them, the limbless, headless torso lay still in the grass.

"Rivermen and others who viewed the body were certain it had not been in the water long enough for the water to have destroyed the missing parts," reported the *New York Press* the next day. "The only alternative to the murder theory that could be suggested was that the body had come into contact with the propeller or paddle wheels of a steamer and thus had been dismembered." [1] But, since the parts were wrapped, this theory seemed ludicrous to investigators, and propellers do not amputate both arms and both legs in such a neat fashion. The victim appeared to be about twenty-five years old but beyond that, there was not much to be learned from the remains. "An examination of the trunk which was severed from the lower part of the body just below the ribs, convinced Dr. King of the coroner's office, the missing parts were amputated by someone with a fair knowledge of anatomy," one report said. "It was evident a long knife, possibly a butcher's knife was used." [2]

By the time the Hudson County Police arrived, a small crowd had already gathered around the soggy remains. Though they could not help but stare at the body, people lingered far enough away so that they could not smell the offensive odor. Mary Bann and Alice McKnight had receded into the crowd of dozens of onlookers who were milling around. Police pushed the mob back so they could begin their work.

Investigators carefully examined the corpse, which appeared foul, grayish-green, and not even human. The surface of the body was very smooth, almost ceramic-like, and seemed not to have any definitive shape. It was more like a gelatinous mass. Since there were no hands or feet, no jewelry was found. Although it was wrapped in what appeared to be a pillowcase and similar bedding sheets, there were no identification papers found anywhere. "Careful search was made along the Hudson shore, for several miles in both directions," said the *New York Press*, "but no tracks were seen and no trace was found of the missing members."[3] After several minutes of lively debate, while the remains lay at their feet, police agreed that it was once a female.

"God awful!" said Inspector Frank Viggiano, a cop for twelve years and a veteran of the Spanish-American War of 1898. He joined the police department when he returned from the jungles of Cuba, where he had seen exactly one day of real combat. Unlike a lot of his Italian colleagues, Viggiano was actually born in America, in New York City's notorious Five Points, in 1878. His parents fled the district when they realized it was more dangerous to live there, where fanatical gangs fought to the death in vicious street battles, than it was in the old country where a careless insult to a local Mafia warlord could result in a shotgun blast to the head. In 1890, the Viggiano's took their four kids, including Frank, and fled to the farmlands of Weehawken in eastern New Jersey. There, Frank was raised in the relative quiet and safety of rural Hudson County.

"Really awful," he said again. His partner, Mike Farrell, a sturdy, red-faced Irishman who had seen lots of floaters in his nineteen years of police work, shook his head from side to side.

"Frankie, she been chopped up damn good, no? Look at the way the arms were cut. Pretty nice job, I'd say." Farrell went down on his knees and leaned within inches of the body. "And look here. The bone was cut as smooth as a baby's ass. I wish I could cut my beef as well."

When he examined the remains, Viggiano saw that the limbs and the head had been neatly, maybe even surgically removed. There were no chopping injuries or burns indicating an explosion. The body was probably white, but had no visible means of identification. Police knew from experience that a coroner's postmortem in a case like this would provide them with little assistance. As dozens of people milled around the grassy field where the body was dragged from the waters, Mary and Albert Bann stood among the crowd watching the police go about their business. "What was it?" said Albert.

"Shhhh!" replied Mary. "Don't talk about it! It's not nice." She was trembling so badly that she had to put her hands under her armpits so that Albert could not see. She told herself it was from the cold. "Come on! Let's go home!" She turned and led Albert away. "As mommie would say, it's none of our business." They saw the police walking along the riverbanks a hundred yards away. The men were looking under the bushes, pushing away debris, and climbing over rocks. One of the officers stopped Mary and asked her name.

"Mary Bann," she said.

"And you found the bundle in the water?"

"Yes, it was me. I'm sorry!" she pleaded.

"Nothing to be sorry about, little girl," replied the officer. Mary saw the attendants lift the torso off the ground and carry it to the rear of their parked truck. She suddenly grabbed her brother's hand and pulled him away. Though only eleven years old, Mary had the presence of mind to guard the child from such ugliness.

The wrappings, which included a blood-stained sheet and a single pillowcase, lay on the ground not far from the shoreline. They were collected by the police, placed in a large sack, and brought to Hudson County Police Headquarters for a more thorough examination. The body was transported to the coroner's office. "County Physician King at once began an investigation," reported the *Press*. "Although identification seemed an almost hopeless task, he directed the body be scrutinized closely, in the hope that some birthmark or peculiarity might be found."[4]

"Whaddya think, Frankie?" asked Farrell, as he walked in the front door of the police headquarters. "Whaddya think? It was a pissed-off husband, no doubt. Why, I tell ya' many times, I be sitting with the little lady at home and thinkin' along the same lines." The big Irishman let out a huge laugh and slapped his partner on the back. Viggiano did not mind. He knew Farrell was a good investigator, even if he was a little too cynical at times.

"Where's the sheets?" he said to Farrell. "Our office?"

"That's where I told that new boy to bring 'em. 'Course, he don't look too smart, you know," said Farrell.

At the detective's office, the items were laid out on a table. There were no papers or other indications of the identity of the corpse. The blanket appeared to be the common variety that was easily available in any department store, such as Woolworth's or Sears. The sheet was plain and unmarked. When detectives turned the pillowcase inside out, they found a cloth tag attached to its lining that read "ROBINSON-BODERS COMPANY, NEWARK, NEW JERSEY." In the meantime, investigators began to canvass nearby police departments for missing-person reports. "Records of various counties on both sides of the river were scanned with the idea of finding some woman missing from home whose relatives could be asked to look at the body," reported the *Press*.[5]

Some detectives thought that the woman had been thrown off a dock or fell from a boat, and was later torn up by propeller activity. Teams were dispatched to local marinas to search for witnesses or other clues. Beginning a mile north and a mile south of Cliffside Park, investigators began to work their way toward the point where the body was discovered. Not surprisingly, on September 6, Hudson County Physician George King declared the woman had been a victim of foul play. "His report set to rest the idea that medical students had placed the torso in the water as a joke," said a story in a local newspaper. "After an autopsy, Dr. George King announced the young woman had been murdered."[6]

8

Weehawken

Two miles from Cliffside Park, the rocky shoreline of Weehawken extends southward along the Hudson into the community of Hoboken. The site is directly opposite West Thirty-eigth Street in Manhattan where the Lincoln Tunnel would be constructed in 1934. Even in 1913, the area was an industrial one, consisting mostly of warehouses and manufacturing plants. The Baxter Wrecking Company maintained a large building and work yard that abutted the river. The company shared a common slip with the Hudson and Delaware coal docks where huge barges unloaded raw coal for the area's heating needs. On Sunday, September 7, at 6:00 A.M., Joseph Hagmann, age twenty-three and his partner, Michael Parkman, age twenty-one, set out in a small, dilapidated skiff from the Baxter company docks. They were well-known "crabbers" who set traps at the bottom of the river for blue-claw crabs. It was a lazy man's way of fishing. A piece of bait, usually chicken, was wired inside a wooden cage with an open door. The trap was lowered by a line to the river bottom; after a time, it was hoisted back up, causing the door to slam shut. More often than not, several crabs would be trapped inside, for once a crab crawled into the cage, the design of the trap prevented it from crawling out.

By noon, Hagmann and Parkman caught dozens of blue-claws, a respectable haul for their morning's work. As they waited to pull up the traps, the men lay back in the boat, sipping homemade beer and smoking cigarettes. They idled away the morning in this manner until they heard someone from shore calling over.

"Ahoy! Ahoy there!" About a hundred yards distant, two Erie County railroad workers, Steven Sullivan, age thirty-eight, and Edward Hamilton, age forty-nine, were sitting on the riverbanks having lunch when they noticed something in the water near the crabbers.

"Ahoy! I say!" called Hamilton.

"Aye!" Hagmann answered. "You calling us?"

"What be in the water there?" Hamilton yelled back, pointing to the stern of Hagmann's boat.

"I think he's pointing to us," said Parkman. "What's he mean?" The tide had receded and the water line was much lower than when the men first set out in the morning. The depth of the water now was only a foot or two, even less in some places. When Parkman looked to the stern, he noticed a large bundle partially submerged in the water. It was wrapped in brown paper and tied with string similar to the kind used in a butcher's shop.

"Hey, Mike, what's that there?" He looked in the skiff for the short gaff. As Hagmann maneuvered the skiff a little closer, Parkman carefully gaffed the package with the hook and pulled it on board.

"Hey, this damn thing's heavy!" With effort, he managed to lift the heavy item on board and rested it on a crossbeam. Parkman cut the string off and a load of stones fell out onto the deck. One newspaper later reported that the bundle was stuffed with about ten pounds of rock. "The rock was Manhattan schist, a form of mica schist, which is granite rock peculiar to Manhattan Island and the Bronx. It abounds in the quarries along the Manhattan banks of the Hudson and is the shiny, sparkly rock one sees cropping up in Central and other parks. It is not found on the Jersey side."[1]

"What the hell?" Parkman cut the remaining string off the bundle. He ripped the paper off and more rocks fell onto the deck. Once the paper was removed, he found a white sheet rolled up over a large object. Hagmann held the item still while they removed the sheet.

"God!" he cried as the last of the linen came off. Both men took a step backward and almost fell off the boat. They were staring at the lower half of a woman's torso, minus the legs. It was a pale white color and of a very smooth consistency, and the amputation marks seemed precise. A tiny amount of blood stained both sides of the sheet. The internal organs were partially eviscerated, though a portion of the intestines hung out from the bottom section of the body.

"Oh my God!" said Hagmann as he set one leg over the side of the boat as if to get out into the water. "Cover it up, man, for God's sake, cover it up!" Parkman took the sheet and laid it back over the ghastly remains.

"I say, what do you have there?" yelled out Ed Hamilton from the shore. "What do you have there?"

Parkman began to pull up the remaining trap and prepared to take the boat in. He carefully wrapped the torso again with the sheet. Hagmann took the oars and placed them into the holders, careful not to look at the large bundle directly in front of him.

"You don't want to know," he answered the men on the shoreline. "Really!"

The crabbers began to row toward the docks. The police were notified, and while a curious crowd gathered around the remains that lay near the wooden pilings of Baxter's Wrecking Company, the men off-loaded their crabs and traps. As they completed their chores, four police officers finally arrived. "Captain A. O. Hossner of the Weehawken Police was soon on the spot and superintended the removal of the latest find to Volk's morgue," reported the *New York Press*. "Sergeant Michael Lyon of Weehawken's Police led a body of men in a search up and down the banks of the river near the basin in hope other parts of the body had washed ashore."[2]

The torso was taken to the county medical examiner's office, where tests were performed and attempts made to identify the body. The upper portion of the remains, found by Mary Bann on the previous Friday, was compared to the latest discovery and proved to be an obvious match. "When Dr. George King, County Physician of Hudson County, viewed the completed torso, he pronounced the amputation one of the neatest pieces of surgical work he had seen in a long time. So closely did the two parts fit together it seemed as if one blow had severed them. The legs had been cut and sawed from the trunk with great skill, the doctor said."[3] The New York *Sun* reported, "It had been cut away with a very long and very sharp knife used by one familiar with anatomy and with surgical knives. The lower part had been cut away just below the navel and just above the hip joint."[4]

But police were even more interested in the wrappings. The linen seemed to match the cloth wrapped on the upper portion of the torso found on September 5. Under the linen was a pillowcase of the same type and size as the previous find. It was of higher-than-average quality, approximately thirty-two inches long and twenty-one inches wide. The letter A had been embroidered on one of the ends of the pillowcase. The edges were also hand embroidered, which indicated a custom-made piece. This supported the theory that the killer might be someone who had more money to spend than the ordinary person. That fact, in addition to the neat surgical work on the torso, "led to the theory by detectives that this young woman was murdered by a physician. That opinion was strengthened by the discovery that the brown wrapping paper, in reality, was insecticide tar paper, such as one buys in drug stores."[5]

After the Weehawken discovery, the press began to refer to the incident as the "Hudson River mystery" and speculated on every aspect of the case. There was a widespread belief that the killer had to be a doctor because the cuts were so neatly performed, though it seemed just as likely the suspect could have been a butcher. "Knife wounds were all over the body," said one report, "and there were signs the victim was beaten before her slayer either hacked or sawed off her limbs and head."[6] But without further evidence, it was improbable that the woman would be identified. Even if fingerprints had been found, identification would still be difficult since that aspect of criminology was still in its infancy. "So successful was the attempt of the murderer to prevent identification of his victim that for a time, the police and county officials shook their heads doubting that the mystery would ever be solved," said the *New York Press*.[7]

In the meantime, investigators followed what leads they had. "Last night, the New York Police were inquiring of all hotels that come under the letter "A" in the directory, seeking to locate the hotel from which the pillow slip had been taken," said the *Sun*. "That work was, of course, only a shot in the dark. The "A" embroidered on the pillow slip might have been a family initial, the initial of the murdered girl or of the murderer. It was a pretty tenuous clue at best."[8]

A few days later, on the sunny afternoon of Wednesday, September 10, Irving Broander, age fifty-six, and his neighbor, Norman Carhart, age sixty-two, were enjoying a walk along the shoreline in Keansburg, New Jersey. They were members of the Morris Bathing Pavilion, where hundreds of Jerseyites frequently visited the beaches to enjoy the water or watch the activities of the New York harbor. There was hardly a day when the bay was not full of colorful ships, pleasure craft, barges, colossal ocean liners, and tiny sailboats. One never knew what to expect at the Morris Bathing Pavilion. On a clear day, the wonderful skyline of southern Manhattan could be seen from the shore. The beaches of Coney Island, only ten miles away, were plainly visible, and many sailors from the town of Keansburg made the boat trip on weekends. If one stood on the easternmost point at Sandy Hook, where a grand lighthouse stood guard over the bay like a silent soldier, the view of the New York harbor was truly magnificent.

"A fine day, Norm. What do you say?"

"Yeah, it is. If the weather holds, the family is gonna make that trip to Wildwood this Saturday. You're free to join us, Irv, no problem," replied Carhart. "I miss being down there, you know? It's a nice town. And the sea. It can get pretty tough at times. But the kids love it so."

"I was thinking about it," Broander said as he trudged through the sand along the beach. A slight breeze came off the water, making it feel a little colder than it really was. The tide was ebbing, leaving the shiny, green side of beach rocks exposed. A multitude of various forms of sea life, left behind by the tide and trapped in sand depressions, struggled to find their way back into the water. Crabs burrowed their way quickly into the wet sand while gulls circled overhead looking for easy prey. Thirty feet ahead, a shallow wall of ancient pilings obstructed the way. As the men climbed the wooden barrier, they helped each other across. When they reached the other side, they saw something embedded in the pilings. As they moved closer, they were able to get a better look.

"Damn!" said Broander, "is that what I think it is?" Ten feet away, lying on its side near the base of a two-foot-thick piling, was part of a human leg. It seemed to be cut off below the hip and just below the knee joint, but it was hard to tell.

"Yeah, Irv, I think it is."

The remains were taken to the Red Bank morgue within the hour, where an examination was conducted. Immediately after the find, authorities speculated that the leg was part of the same body found at Weehawken. It was nude and measured approximately fourteen inches long. Like the mutilated torso found by Mary Bann, the cuts were precise and neatly performed. Again, police imagined the amputation was done by a surgeon. "The work of cutting was clean and the bones had been sawed through as in the case of the bones of the dismembered body of the woman now at Volk's morgue in Hoboken," said the *Sun*.[9] The New York City Police Department was notified of the latest find because investigators still were not sure on which side of the Hudson the killing took place.

However, it seemed probable that all the body parts found to date were from the same victim. It was too much of a coincidence that various parts would suddenly turn up within such a short period of time and not be related. The *Sun* said, "In order to determine beyond doubt it belongs to the torso of the murder victim it will be sent to the Hoboken morgue and there fitted to the sawed off femur."[10] "The leg apparently came from a female victim," said the *New York Press*. "The white skin gave evidence of the sex of the owner of the amputated leg. The cut was clean as if made with a sharp knife."[11]

Dr. Edwin Fields, assistant coroner for the Hoboken morgue, conducted the initial examination. He decided that the limb had been in the water for only a few days and expressed hope that additional parts, including the head and hands, would soon surface. "Should one of the arms with the hand be found," he said to reporters, "identification will be made easy."[12] Dr. Fields also said the cut was "a clean amputation of the leg with a saw in the upper third of the trochanter[13] and another amputation through the leg and below the knee joint. The part measures fourteen inches in length and is seven inches wide at the thigh and five inches wide at the lower end."[14]

In the meantime, a bloodstained shirt washed up on the Hudson shore near Cliffside, New Jersey. The garment was of the same size as the torso and had large spots of blood on the front. The heaviest concentration of staining was in the neck area, along the collar. "It was of ordinary material and had no laundry or other marks upon it that might lead to the identification of its wearer," reported the *Sun*. "The chemise was stained with what looked like blood around the neck, in the center and along the lower edges."[15] The shirt was also partially charred, as if someone had tried to burn it up. Bergen police chief Leonard Marcy took possession of the article when a bather, who found it snagged in some bushes, gave it to him. He brought the shirt to Volk's morgue and turned it over to Dr. Fields.

But authorities knew that the more time passed, the less likely it would be that the missing head would be found. "In the case of the head, they are fearful that if it was cast into the water, it will never reappear," said another press report. "Undertakers say that a sufficient amount of gas cannot form to cause it to rise."[16] Most experts agreed on that point. If a human head is thrown into the sea, it will sink rather quickly to the bottom, its flesh stripped to the bone by hungry fish.

9

Faurot

Investigators from the Hudson County Police Department were dispatched to the city of Newark to interview employees of Robinson-Boders Company, the manufacturer of the pillowcase found at Weehawken. After the company was asked to review its sales receipts for the year, police learned that only twelve items of this style of bedding had been sold. The sale had taken place during the previous summer and the stock shipped to a furniture dealer in New York City. Detectives contacted NYPD inspector Joseph Faurot, chief of Manhattan detectives, who agreed to meet with the Hudson County Police on Wednesday, September 10. It seemed more likely than ever that the murder of the dissected woman had taken place on the New York side of the Hudson.

Joseph Faurot joined NYPD in 1896. He proved to be a fearless street cop and received several commendations during his rookie years. Promoted to detective sergeant on April 28, 1903, Faurot, like many of his contemporaries, learned investigative procedures as he went along and evolved into a talented, persistent investigator. Faurot was one of the few police officers in the city to recognize the value of fingerprint identification in law enforcement. Though Scotland Yard had adopted the new method by 1901, America lagged far behind. Faurot began to assemble his own collection of fingerprints and became a tireless crusader for the adoption of that method in the NYPD. In 1907, he was promoted to lieutenant and later became chief of detectives in Manhattan, one of the most prestigious posts in the department. In 1911, he became the first law-enforcement agent in the United States to obtain a conviction using fingerprint identification when he testified in *People v. Crispi*.

Charles Crispi, a known burglar, was accused of breaking into a garment manufacturer on Wooster Street in Lower Manhattan. Faurot had used his fingerprint knowledge to make an arrest and declared that a fingerprint found at the scene belonged to Crispi. At trial, when the judge asked Crispi to admit to the crime, the defendant confessed. In exchange, the judge gave Crispi a reduced sentence. Thereafter, the use of fingerprint identification became a valid law-enforcement tool.

Faurot worked the Times Square beat, better known during that era as the Tenderloin District. No other area of New York City better epitomized the opportunities and dynamic energies of the United States. It was big, brash, and gaudy, and overwhelmed the senses with a dazzling array of sights and sounds that were unlike any other in the nation, or even the world. It had hundreds of vaudeville shows, live theaters, movie theaters, gambling casinos, restaurants, and saloons populated by every type of thug, gangster, and lowlife of the era.

At the epicenter of all this activity, the intersection of Broadway and Forty-second Street became the symbolic crossroad of a cultural earthquake. Its image was indelibly projected in the public mind by electric signs, a new art form invented solely for the purpose of display along the crowded streets of the Tenderloin. By 1913, Broadway had more than twenty city blocks of these spectacular moving advertisements that drew massive crowds each night when they were turned on by excited technicians. Using a simple off-on sequence of colored lights, a technology perfected at the 1901 Pan American Exposition at Buffalo, designers were able to create the illusion of motion in their signs. Once the technology was perfected, dozens of these gigantic displays, some of them hundreds of feet long, were installed on the skyscrapers along Broadway and its intersecting streets.[1]

Led by a visionary showman named O. J. Gude, who coined the phrase "the Great White Way," these signs came to define Times Square's image all over the world. At night, the streets were lit up brighter than day and populated by hordes of muggers, pickpockets, prostitutes, gamblers, and criminal opportunists. They were drawn to the Tenderloin by the allure of a never-ending party, which began at sundown and ended at daybreak, attended by tens of thousands who drank, danced, and gambled through the night. It was like an amusement park in the street, a vast palace of overindulgence and unbridled hedonism to which people were drawn as bees to honey. "The rules of self-restraint and delayed gratification that had been drilled into generations of Americans had been lifted, if not quite obliterated. . . . The only moralists on Broadway are fools."[2] It was here, in this sea of sin, that Lieutenant Joe Faurot learned the ways and means of the New York City detective.

Leonard Marcy, chief of police of North Bergen, presented Faurot with the evidence gathered by his men and the other New Jersey departments. Though there were indications that the murderer could be a doctor or a surgeon, the evidence was not conclusive. The cuts on the recovered body parts were neatly performed, but they could have been done by a layperson as well. Identification of the body might still be possible, for there were several birthmarks on the upper torso that could be recognized by someone who knew the victim. Faurot felt that the next step should be to contact the furniture dealer who received the linens from Robinson-Boders.

George Sachs of 2782 Eighth Avenue, located near West 147th Street, was the only dealer in New York who purchased bedding from the Newark company in the preceding year. The pillowcase in question had flowers embroidered on its fringes and a price tag attached to an inside hem when it was found wrapped around the upper torso in the Hudson River. The item was the cheapest grade of linen produced by the Robinson-Boders Company. On the morning of September 11, Faurot dispatched two of his men, Detectives James O'Neill and Frank Cassassa, to the Sachs Furniture Store. "The police investigation became confused as soon as Mr. Sachs was interviewed," said one press account. "Only two of the twelve pillows he had used in his stock were missing. One of them he thought he sold to a woman of whom he gave a part identification. The other he was unable to account for at all."[3] The detectives insisted on seeing his business records. They examined each sale made by the company in the past six months. Buried in those records was a sale made on August 26 that sparked their interest.

The receipt indicated that on that day, a bedspring, mattress, and pillows were sold to a Manhattan buyer for twenty-one dollars and sixty-eight cents. All the items were secondhand except the pillowcases. When the receipt was shown to Mr. Sachs, he remembered the sale. "The party that bought these things bought two fifty-nine-cent pillows and I made a mistake when I delivered them," he later said. "I delivered two eighty-nine-cent pillows."[4] He recalled that the man, who identified himself as A. Van Dyke, paid in cash and asked to have the items delivered to his apartment. The receipt indicated that the delivery was made to a third-floor apartment located at 68 Bradhurst Avenue, only a few blocks from the Sachs Furniture Store. The items were shipped by the Amsterdam Van Express Company, the only trucker used by Sachs.

Detectives James O'Neill and Frank Cassassa then made their way over to 68 Bradhurst Avenue to look for the superintendent of the building. Since the day's weather was clear and the location was nearby, the two men chose to walk the short distance. Bradhurst Avenue runs north and south, parallel with Eighth Avenue, between 145th and 146th streets on the Upper West Side. Building number sixty-eight was a six-story walk-up with five apartments on each floor. Directly opposite the building, Bradhurst Park, a vacant expanse of undeveloped land replete with maple trees, running streams, and tall, unkempt grass, stretched from 145th Street all the way up to 155th Street. O'Neill located the superintendent, an elderly black man who lived in the ground-floor apartment. His name was Carlton Brooker, an Alabama transplant who, like a lot of other black Americans during that era, fled the South in 1910 one step ahead of a lynch mob.

When detectives questioned him about the delivery, he told them he remembered it took place on August 26 and watched the men carry the items up to the third floor. Brooker said he had rented the apartment only one day before to a man who had walked in off the street. "I was outside and I came in the hallway," he said, "and when I came in the main hall, I seen a gentleman walking up and down the hallways and he was looking from door to door. So I says, 'Well, sir, what is your business?' He says, 'Have you any apartments?' and I says that I did. He was dressed in plain clothes but he had a light grass hat on. It was not a Panama hat but something like it, a straw hat."[5] Brooker also noticed that the man spoke with a heavy German accent.

Brooker told the stranger that he had only one apartment, which was in the rear, up on the third floor. The man requested to see the flat, and Brooker took him upstairs. "I opened the door and showed it to him," Brooker said. "He stood right by the door and he walked from one end of the room to the other and then came back to me. He said to me that he would take these rooms. I told him he had to pay five dollars deposit. So I gave him a receipt for five dollars and he paid me right there."[6]

There was more. Brooker said the man wanted to move in right away with his wife, but at that time the painters were on strike and the apartment could not be painted. The janitor made arrangements to have the flat cleaned that very day. The man also asked that Brooker receive any deliveries that arrived for him. "So it must have been about five or six o'clock," he later said, "somewhere around there, a bed came, and a spring and mattress and two pillows. So I went up, opened the door to the apartment and received them myself and the driver put them in."[7] On the next day, August 27, the man returned. "He wanted the keys and I told him if he wanted the keys he would have to give the balance of the rent. I told him it was nineteen dollars. I had this conversation in my room. He gave me the money and I sat down to my dining room table and I wrote him a receipt. He said his name was H. Schmidt."[8]

O'Neill wanted to go directly up to the flat and search the rooms, but Cassassa insisted on relaying the new information to their office. The two detectives returned to the precinct house, where they briefed Inspector Faurot. A decision was made to return to Bradhurst Avenue with a full team of investigators and attempt to locate the occupant of the apartment. Detectives began to canvass the tenants in the building. "They questioned E. J. Keefe, who had the adjoining apartment, and he said he had heard no noises or disturbances of any kind in the flat. Mrs. Keefe remembered seeing a man on occasion, sneaking out of the apartment early in the morning. He always held his head down, so he could not be recognized."[9]

Police soon discovered that no one knew the occupant of the third-floor apartment. Neighbors had observed the man come and go, but it was always late at night. A woman frequently accompanied him, but other tenants were never able to get a good look at her. They heard voices in the apartment but, again, it was always after midnight and on very few occasions. Detectives Cassassa and O'Neill knocked on the apartment door for several minutes with no response. Since there were no other leads, Faurot ordered his men to stake out 68 Bradhurst and wait for someone to show up.

For the next three days, the detective squad sat on the house twenty-four hours a day. Cassassa and O'Neill took up residence in the janitor's apartment, watching the street from the front window. Detectives Kevin McKenna and Bill Connolly took turns waiting in a grocery store at 72 Bradhurst where the men drank coffee all day and napped in the rear office with the blessing of the owner, who was glad to have the police around to protect him. Faurot made frequent appearances during the night, reassuring the men and providing encouragement for the boring assignment, which he knew could not go on forever.

By the third day, Commissioner Rhinelander Waldo was asking how much longer Faurot would keep the squad on the case. Murders happened every day in Manhattan. There were pressing issues and more demanding cases waiting to be solved. On the night of September 13, with no apparent activity inside the apartment and no visitors so far, Inspector Faurot made a pivotal decision. "During these three days, no one visited the apartment," the *New York Times* later reported. "This circumstance aroused suspicion more and more and when other clues had been investigated and one by one proved false, Inspector Faurot grew impatient and on Saturday night, decided to break into the apartment."[10]

Cassassa went around the back of the six-story building and climbed the fire escape. He looked in through the bedroom window and saw nothing but darkness. After he was convinced there was no one inside, he pried the window open with a knife. "Only a short survey of the kitchen and the bathroom was enough for Cassassa to press the button that admitted Faurot and his detectives."[11] Within minutes, the men were searching through the apartment.

On a kitchen shelf was a large bloodstained knife. Next to the knife was a carpenter's saw with ominous staining along its teeth and dried blood on its wooden handle. The bedroom rug had noticeable signs of recently washed areas that were darker than the rest. "All around them the squad of searchers saw unmistakable signs that the crime had been committed there," said the *New York Herald* the next day. "Stains were everywhere on the floor and marked the route over which the murderer had dragged his dying victim to a bathroom where he dismembered the body."[12]

Faurot noticed signs of blood on the walls and on the frame of the bed. "I saw blood spots on the foot of the iron bedstead, on the westerly wall of the dining room, on the door leading from the dining room into the small hallway leading to the bathroom, and several spots of blood on the bathtub."[13] It was obvious that efforts had been made to clean up the apartment. "All about was evidence that someone had tried to wash away much blood," said the *New York Press* the following day, "but so hurriedly had the job been done that the corners of the room, especially the bathroom, had been overlooked."[14]

In the living room, the team found bits of underwear that matched those wrapped around the torso found at Weehawken on September 7. Even more significant, however, was what was lying next to the clothing. There were several pages of the *New York Times* dated August 31, which was part of the same paper wrapped around the body part found at Cliffside Park. At the opposite end of the room, Detective Cassassa discovered a spool of wire that, at first glance, seemed to match the wire that tied the same bundle. "In the kitchen were found six empty ginger ale bottles, a sack of granulated sugar, part of a loaf of bread, a bread knife, a glass water pitcher and two drinking glasses. In the cupboard, there was also a glass inkwell and a stamp-moistener. The refrigerator contained nothing but an empty milk bottle."[15] On top of the refrigerator was a handwritten receipt from George Sachs, 2782 Eighth Avenue for a bed, mattress, and sheets totaling twenty-one dollars and sixty-eight cents.

In a closet, police found a man's jacket, the only item of clothing in the apartment. When they examined the garment, they discovered the words "A. Van Dyke" sewn into the lining—the name used by the man who purchased the pillows at Sachs. "Hey, look at this!" called out O'Neill. In the same closet, he had come across a small metal box. When he opened it, he found dozens of handwritten letters. Some of the notes were in German; others were in English. Faurot handed out the letters among the detectives to screen for names and addresses. They seemed to be from different women in Germany, but all of the envelopes were addressed to Hans Schmidt. Many were from an Anna Aumuller at several addresses. The most recent address was 428 East Seventieth Street.

Faurot, along with detectives Cassassa and O'Connell, decided to go to that address while the others continued their search at the Bradhurst apartment. When they arrived at the new location, Faurot found a Joseph Igler and his wife living there alone. Igler was a boatman who worked at Central Park. "I know Anna," he said. "My wife knew her from Germany and she lived with us there for three years. She came to America some time ago and lived with us here as well."

Igler told the police that Anna was twenty years old and was born in Oedenburg, Hungary, where she lived until she came to America. Her father died unexpectedly when she was a child and Anna was later raised by an aunt who sent her to a Catholic school at a very early age. As a teenager, Anna was very bright and very pretty; she had little trouble attracting boys, who noticed her sparkling blue eyes and pouting lips. She had a pleasant disposition and a fun-loving personality that made her one of the most popular girls at school. Anna had musical talent as well and learned to play the piano. Shortly after Anna graduated, her aunt decided to send her to America, where she imagined Anna could continue her musical training in New York City. Igler explained that his wife and Anna's aunt were best friends, so Mrs. Igler arranged for Anna to work at the Church of St. Boniface as a housekeeper.

"Where is she now?" asked Inspector Faurot.

"I don't know. I got the girl a job at the church and I never heard from her again. That was about two years ago."

"St. Boniface on Second?"

"Yeah, that's the one. Father John took her in as a housekeeper."

With that, Faurot and Cassassa climbed back into their car and drove to Second Avenue and Forty-seventh Street. In 1913, a police car was still somewhat of a novelty, though the NYPD had dozens of cars in use, most of them assigned to the Manhattan precincts. They cruised down Third Avenue past blocks and blocks of dingy taverns, ill-concealed gambling casinos, and neighborhood saloons that occupied almost every storefront.

Faurot had spent nearly his entire career on these streets. There was little that he had not seen before. On each corner, small groups of men gathered under the lights to pass the time, play cards, or shoot craps.[16] Everywhere were crowds of faceless people, milling about or hurrying to their chores, dodging the never-ending mixture of horse-drawn wagons and noisy automobiles, a city in motion, a metropolis that never rested and never slept. It only charged forward, like a wild bull, oblivious to all limits and restraint, fueled by a kind of self-confidence and surety that the rest of the world, especially Europe, which was unaccustomed to such energy, interpreted as arrogance.

Faurot marveled at the tremendous change that had taken place in the city since he came on the job in 1896. New York had grown by leaps and bounds, a growth unlike any other city in America. Its population was greater than that of Switzerland, Denmark, or Greece. Manhattan was a kaleidoscope of diversity, language, and customs that was unrivaled anywhere in the world. Not even London or Paris could compare to New York's whirlpool of nationalities. One out of every three residents in the city had been born in a foreign country, and Manhattan alone had over one million immigrants, more than the entire population of Philadelphia. Each day, Ellis Island was crammed with thousands of refugees, a never-ending avalanche of humanity, who prayed every waking minute that they would not be sent back to the old country, and dreamed of the moment when they would walk free on the streets of America. Through all of its changes, New York depended on its beleaguered police force to maintain the peace, enforce laws, and present some type of order to a metropolis that often seemed to be on the verge of pandemonium. This was how Faurot visualized his job as a police officer—a guardian against chaos. For without the police, there was little doubt that New York City, even with all its improvements and all its technological advancements, would still plunge back into the medieval jungle with blinding speed.

It was almost midnight by the time Faurot and Cassassa arrived at St. Boniface, at 882 Second Avenue. The doors were locked, and both the church and the rectory were dark. The men pounded on the front door until they saw someone turn on a light inside, on the first floor. In a minute, the parish priest, Father John Braun, opened the door and greeted Faurot.

"Sorry to bother you, Father," he said, "but may we speak to you on an urgent matter? I'm Inspector Faurot from the police department, and this is Detective Cassassa."

"Of course, come in, please," said the priest. At first, Father Braun thought someone had died and they needed a priest for the last rites, because that was why the police usually came to the rectory door at midnight. Faurot explained that they were trying to find a missing girl and showed Father Braun Anna's photograph. The priest immediately recognized her as a girl who once worked for the church as a housekeeper, but she had left St. Boniface some time ago. Faurot then asked if he had ever heard the name Hans Schmidt. Father Braun stated that he was a priest who was assigned to St. Boniface in

1910. He had come with a written recommendation from another priest whose name Braun did not remember.

"Schmidt, I might call an average priest," he told Faurot. "Although he performed his duties here acceptably, there was always something about him that seemed mysterious to me. Usually, his face bore an expression of mock piety, but at other times, he would glare like a lion."[17] Father Braun said that he had not seen Father Schmidt since May 1912 when he left to go to St. Joseph's parish up on 125th Street. It was better that way, the priest explained, because he could not get along with the strange man. "I was mystified by these constant changes of expression," Father Braun explained. "I tried to understand him, but I couldn't. The only way I can describe him was he was like Stevenson's Jekyll and Hyde."

"And what of Anna?" asked Cassassa. "Where did she go?"

"Oh, she decided to go to St. Joseph's as well. She told me she didn't want to stay here anymore after Father Hans left."

Within minutes, Faurot and Cassassa were back in their car speeding up Second Avenue toward 125th Street.

10

The Rectory

Several hours before, Father Hans Schmidt sat quietly inside the confessional booth at St. Joseph's; the darkness was like a warm cloak to keep out the numbing effects of sin and despair. Over and over, he listened to the endless complaints through the one-square-foot opening that was covered by a flimsy screen to present the illusion of anonymity. It was believed that if the parishioner had the assurance of not being recognized, he or she would be more forthcoming. However, the screen did not hide the sinner; it only made it harder for the priest to see. With a little effort, he could identify the person in the confessional. Of course, at other times, the person would volunteer an introduction. Some people felt that by naming themselves, the process of forgiveness and atonement became more personal.

"Bless me, Father, for I have sinned," were the words that began the confession. What usually followed was an endless litany of sin and transgression. Every offense, no matter how trivial, was confessed in the hope of forgiveness. This was the Catholic way and, in the eyes of the believer, the only path to redemption. The sin had to be recognized and confronted. The power of forgiveness was a cornerstone of church dogma and a vital function of the Catholic clergy. Father Schmidt knew that and accepted his duties willingly in the confessional. As a priest, he felt it was up to him to act as a conduit to the Lord. And if those offenses happened to revolve around sexual matters, it was all the more interesting to him. Carrying the burden of sexual sin for most of his life, it was much easier for him to understand the temptation of flesh and desire that many in the parish seemed to face every day.

He was especially interested in the young and how they dealt with their sexual feelings, of which they understood little, but were shamed by their power. Day and night, they filed into the confessional with lurid stories of sexual stimulation and sensations they had never experienced before. Overcome by guilt and sure that they would be punished for such sinful thoughts, they longed for understanding and forgiveness. Instead, they met Father Schmidt, who long ago learned that the confessional was a convenient tool to identify young men and women with adolescent problems that could be exploited and, later, enjoyed. Discovering who was having difficulties or who might be open to experimentation was simple. Every detail, no matter how personal, was open to discussion. And if a particularly attractive young man was receptive to a personal meeting later on, to continue a discussion, then Father Schmidt would be more than willing to comply. Using his finely tuned perceptions to determine who was receptive to his advances was a skill he practiced for years. He became quite good at it. The result was a never-ending supply of sexual opportunities that even a king could not buy.

After he finished his confessional duties for that night, he decided to go up to his room. He walked through the old church, which was completely dark except for rows of burning candles at the altar. He passed through a side door that led to the rectory and proceeded up to the second floor. His apartment consisted of two comfortable rooms with a private bathroom. He lit his lamp on the table, collapsed on the bed, and within a minute plunged into a deep sleep.

At the same moment, Inspector Faurot and Detective Cassassa were already driving up Second Avenue toward 125th Street. Though they had some theories about the case, they still had doubts as to who had killed Anna Aumuller. "We were still bothered by the fact that no one in a priest's garb had ever appeared at the apartment," Faurot later told reporters. "We were by no means certain that Schmidt was implicated. It seemed rather unlikely, as a matter of fact. We expected however, that Schmidt would know something about it, especially if it was he who rented the apartment."[1] At 1:30 A.M., the men knocked on the front door of the Church of St. Joseph of the Holy Family rectory. When no one immediately answered, Inspector Faurot removed his blackjack from his rear pocket and pounded on the wooden frame. Father Quinn, the pastor of the church, opened the door.

"Evening, Father," said Faurot. "May we talk to you for a moment on an important matter?"

"Yes, certainly, come in. Please."

Faurot introduced himself and his partner. He then asked Father Quinn if he knew a Hans Schmidt. The pastor, visibly concerned, replied that yes, he did. As far as he knew, Father Schmidt was up in his room on the second floor. "The policemen followed into the rectory parlor. They sat down and waited while the priest went upstairs to the room for his sleeping clergyman."[2]

Father Quinn knocked on Schmidt's door and called out. "Hans! Hans! Are you awake?" The priest called out several times until a voice answered from behind the door.

"Ja, was wuenschst Du? [Yes, what do you want?]"

"Hans, please come downstairs. We need you," said Father Quinn.

Father Schmidt imagined that someone had died or was about to die. "All right, I'll be there in a moment," he said as he rolled out of his bed and began to dress. He slipped into a black cassock and turned up the lamp on his desk. He glanced at his reflection carefully in the mirror, smoothing out his hair and straightening his garment. He stepped out into the narrow, darkened hallway and walked down the single flight of stairs. There was a long passageway that led from the dormitory area into the church. He opened the door and proceeded into the corridor, his steps making a loud rapping sound on the smooth marble floor.

Always conscious of maintaining a proper appearance, he continued to adjust his cassock, and buttoned his white collar snugly around his neck. As he passed the Stations of the Cross, which lined the corridor walls, Father Schmidt was careful to recite the prayer associated with each panel. Those that he could not recall, he simply skipped over. His mind wandered to the ascent at Calvary and the suffering of Jesus as he was crucified. He wondered, as he had many times in his life, what it all meant. There were some difficult concepts in Catholicism, some too complex for him. "Es ist mir ein Raetsel [It is a mystery to me]," he often said. But he had learned that if he could not grasp a certain aspect of the religion, he could safely ignore it and nothing would happen. If he had to lecture to the flock on a subject of which he knew little, such as the Trinity or the Immaculate Conception, he could say almost anything because parishioners did not know any more than he did. He just had to speak in ambiguous terms, and the other priests would simply nod their heads in approval. Priesthood, at least to him, was a life full of questions and doubts which no one could explain, not even his sacred mother.

He paused for a second to look out the hallway window. Outside, the moonlight cast its spell on the open courtyard, its delicate light causing shadows to shift gently and suggest the perception of movement. The moonlight touched his face for a moment and he pulled back instinctively into the obscurity of the darkened corridor. He continued on his way to the rectory door. But as he neared the end of the hallway, he was able to see inside Father Quinn's office through its side window. He saw two men he did not know standing with the pastor. For some reason he did not understand, Father Schmidt felt a chill that resonated deep into his bones.

When he entered the office, Faurot and Cassassa identified themselves as the police. Schmidt remained standing and asked what he could do for them. Faurot then showed a photograph of Anna Aumuller and asked Father Schmidt if he knew her. He denied that he did. "For half an hour the inspector and the detective quizzed Schmidt with little success."[3]

"No, I don't think I recall the name," he said. "Is she a member of the parish?" The men studied Schmidt for a moment. He seemed confident and unafraid. He smiled as he clasped his hands together in front of his chest. But they knew that Schmidt had lied when he said he did not know the girl. Investigators had found numerous letters signed with Anna's name in the Bradhurst Avenue apartment and Schmidt and Anna had worked together at St. Boniface's Church the year before. Faurot decided to get aggressive.

"Father Schmidt," Faurot said, "we've come here to tell you something of the utmost importance." His voice was firm as he moved closer to the priest. "There was still the smile on his face and his attitude was interpreted by the police as being the same as it would have been had he been expecting his callers to inform him his services were needed hurriedly in the room of a person who was ill."[4] Suddenly, Faurot took the photograph, threw it onto a table, and stood directly in front of Schmidt and yelled, "Why did you kill that girl?"

The color drained from the face of Father Schmidt and his hands began to tremble. "Whatever trace of bravado might have remained in the priest fluttered out before the face of the girl as it looked up at him from the table. The priest's body seemed to convulse. He swayed and would have fallen had not Inspector Faurot and the other policeman jumped to his side and held him to his feet."[5] Hans covered his face with his hands. Sobs broke the sudden silence in the room, but Faurot did not ask any more questions for the moment. Cassassa helped Schmidt over to a chair and he collapsed into the seat. Faurot came over and placed his hand on Schmidt's shoulder.

"Don't lose your nerve," urged the inspector. "Brace up and tell us the truth. You murdered Anna Aumuller. Tell us what happened."

"I killed her!" he cried out. "I killed her because I loved her!" In between sobs, Father Schmidt said he had married the girl several months before her death. He said that he was thinking of leaving the priesthood to establish a new life. On the morning of her murder, he said, he went into her room and cut her throat with a special knife that he bought the day before. After he was sure she was dead, Schmidt told Faurot, he dismembered the body. He said

he packaged all the pieces and dumped them into the Hudson River, one by
one. Each time he went out of the house, he went to an empty lot at 144th
Street and picked up some heavy rocks. He later used those rocks to weigh
down each bundle. He could not say how many times he took the ferry that
night but it was several trips. Later, he noticed that the mattress in the
apartment was covered with blood and realized it was not safe to leave it
there. He tied it up and carried it to the same lot where he had picked up the
rocks and burned it. While it was burning, he said, a group of neighborhood
children gathered around and watched.

"What did you do with the head?" asked Faurot.

"Into the Hudson also, the same night," Schmidt said.

Faurot took the priest up to his room and the two officers searched the
premises. While Schmidt began to pack a few garments into a bag, Cassassa
discovered hundreds of business cards in a large wooden trunk. The name on
the cards was DR. EMIL MOLIERE, FORMERLY ASSISTANT SURGEON, MUNICIPAL
WOMEN'S HOSPITAL, PARIS, FRANCE. The bottom line of the card read: REPRE-
SENTATIVE OF THE CHEMICAL HYGIENE MANUFACTURING COMPANY OF DEMORALLE,
FRANCE. Schmidt said he sometimes used the name for non-church-related
business, but he would not elaborate to Faurot. In the same trunk, Cassassa
also found a marriage license in the name of Hans Schmidt and Anna
Aumuller dated February 1913. Faurot asked him where and when he was
married.

"I'm a priest," replied Schmidt, "so I married us myself."

"You married yourself?" said Cassassa.

"You wouldn't understand."

"I don't understand any of it," said Faurot. "On the way in to the station
house, I want you to show us the vacant lot on 144th."

"If you look in that closet, you'll find some of her clothes," Father Schmidt
said to Cassassa. On the wooden rack, the detective found a woman's coat
that matched a skirt found in the Bradhurst Avenue apartment. On the shelf,
Cassassa also found a key and a rent receipt. "A number of bottles of medicine were found in the room," the *Times* later reported. "These, detectives
learned from Schmidt, were manufactured by a company he was interested
in and their use was condemned by law. A number of stock certificates in
corporations manufacturing patent medicines were also discovered in the
room."[6]

"She never knew what happened," said Schmidt as he waited for the search
to end. "I carried her into the bathroom and finished the job there. I didn't
want to make such a mess in the bedroom."

"That was considerate of you, Father," said Cassassa.

"What happens now? I mean, do I get a lawyer?"

Faurot picked up all the items from the room and placed them in a bag. He then went across the hall where Father Quinn and the other priests of the parish had gathered and watched the police search the room. They all held rosaries in their hands and prayed silently as the drama unfolded around them. Schmidt stood in the hallway and asked the monsignor to step outside the room. One newspaper account described what happened next. "As Father Huntmann entered [the hallway], Father Schmidt turned toward him, extended his arms and made as if to embrace his rector. Father Huntmann's face was blanched, his body was shaking nervously but he revolted from the touch of the accused man. Father Schmidt struggled, however, to entwine his arms about the head of the church and the rector forcibly thrust him away."[7] Faurot said that he was taking Schmidt with him to the station house where he would be charged with murder. Cassassa placed handcuffs on the prisoner and escorted him to the car parked outside on 125th Street. As he watched Schmidt climb into the police vehicle, Father Huntmann began to cry.

"Oh God! How did such a thing happen? Did he really do it?" he said.

"You heard him, Father," said Faurot. "He did it all right. I'll be in touch with you at a later time, Father."

In the meantime, precinct detectives were dispatched to Bradhurst Avenue, where the superintendent, Carlton Brooker, was picked up. He was taken to the station where he waited for further instructions. It was nearly 5:30 A.M. by the time the car arrived at the station with Father Schmidt, Faurot, and Cassassa. They brought Schmidt in through the back door and took him to the second floor. Detectives quickly canvassed the precinct house and obtained five officers to participate in a lineup. They were ordered into civilian clothes and told to respond to the detective division. Schmidt was asked to remove his cassock and collar and was given a blue suit and tie. Once he had changed into those clothes, detectives O'Neill and Cassassa brought him into another room where the five police officers in civilian clothes had already assembled. Brooker was then called in.

"That's him!" said Brooker as he pointed to Schmidt without delay. "Brooker immediately picked out Schmidt as the man who had rented the flat where Anna Aumuller was killed."[8] That was the man, Brooker said, who had given him $5 as a down payment for the rent on the apartment on August 25. Schmidt returned a few days later with the balance of the rent and the very same day, August 27, the bedding, including the pillowcases, was delivered. After he was identified by Brooker, Schmidt was questioned again. "I produced a diagram of the body," Faurot later told reporters, "and showed it to him and he identified it as the way he had cut the body to pieces in the bath tub. He severed the head, then the upper part of the body, then the arms, the stomach part and the legs."[9] Father Schmidt had committed many other crimes as well, Faurot said. The police would continue their investigation into the complex life of the suspect. "There are some very important questions to be investigated concerning this case," he said. "Schmidt was reluctant to talk about his remedies and his medical cards and his stocks. There may be much more to be said about that later."[10]

As the Manhattan morning rush began to build, Faurot and his team of detectives took Schmidt down to police headquarters to be booked and processed. They drove by Center Street where Father Schmidt pointed out the shop where he had purchased the knife and the saw he used to cut up Anna. The store, H. S. Sterns and Company, was located at 116 Center Street, directly across from the courthouse where in all likelihood Schmidt would be tried for the killing.

The district attorney's office was notified and sent over Assistant District Attorney Deacon Murphy and Coroner Feinberg. While Schmidt awaited paperwork at the booking station, Murphy questioned him about the events leading up to the murder. Schmidt confessed to the killing once again and provided additional details as well. At each retelling of the story, he seemed to sink deeper into depression and despair. "Schmidt, whose age the police recorded as thirty-three years, is sallow-faced with glassy eyes whose general appearance and actions... caused many to think that he is addicted to drugs."[11] After he was fingerprinted, Schmidt was transported over to the city jail and logged in. "The priest was assigned to cell #136 in the 'murderer's row' in the Tombs prison. According to keepers in the prison, as soon as the door of his cell was closed behind him, Father Schmidt removed his coat, made an impoverished pillow of it, laid down on his coat and went to sleep."[12]

Later that day, Inspector Faurot met with Assistant District Attorney Murphy at the 152nd Street station house. The detective squad met for a full briefing on the case and reviewed the details of what still needed to be done. Murphy, Faurot, and several detectives went over to the Bradhurst Avenue apartment to conduct another search.

In the meantime, the newspapers were already reporting the arrest in the Hudson River Mystery case, and photos of Father Schmidt appeared on the front pages. "While Inspector Faurot, Assistant District Attorney Murphy, and several detectives made a minute examination of the apartment, a crowd of 3,000 persons gathered in front of the place and reserves from the West 152nd Street Station were called out."[13] Measured by contemporary standards, some newspapers, like the *New York Times* and the *New York Herald*, were subdued in their coverage of the arrest. Others, such as the *New York Press*, the *Evening Telegram*, and the *Sun*, tended to be more sensational. Under the headline "River Murder Traced to Priest Who Confesses," on

September 15, 1913, the *New York Times* began its lengthy coverage on Father Hans Schmidt. In a front page story, the report described the fast-breaking developments in the case, including the spontaneous confession made to Inspector Faurot at St. Joseph's Church the night before. "Inspector Faurot put more questions to him about the girl and about the apartment at Bradhurst Avenue. The priest shook his head or answered in the negative each time, but finally, when the questions revealed how much the detectives knew, he sank into a chair and began to weep." Police officials spoke freely with reporters, often to the point of revealing privileged information or sharing details that may have impinged on the defendant's civil rights. The *Times* story also noted, "Schmidt admitted his relations with the young woman while he was a priest and she was a domestic servant at St. Boniface's rectory. He told how he and the young girl obtained a marriage license in February and he had performed the marriage ceremony. Schmidt told the police that he considered this a legal marriage and that he had officiated at it himself because he would be expelled from the church if the fact became known."[14]

As the search of Father Schmidt's various residences continued, more incriminating evidence was discovered. Dozens of letters to and from Anna were discovered in his mattress at Bradhurst Avenue. Offering envelopes, which were torn open and the cash removed, were found in a pile in the closet. "Men working under Inspector Faurot have learned that many petty crimes can be traced to Father Schmidt's door," said another press report. "Several hundred dollars of Easter Sunday collections among the people of St. Joseph's parish are said to have been confiscated by the priest. It also has been discovered that the mysterious robbery of a clergyman visiting the St. Joseph's rectory some time ago was the work of Anna Aumuller's murderer. That robbery was traced when the missing wallet was found among Schmidt's effects."[15]

In the living room, detectives found another interesting item. In the corner of the darkened room, lying on a chair, was an ornate, newly knitted jacket for a child. Before she had her throat cut, Anna was putting together a wardrobe for the baby she would never have.

11

Muret

The public was fascinated with the seemingly brilliant work of New York City detectives and especially Inspector Faurot, who was already famous thanks to the *People v. Crispi* case in 1911. Faurot's use of fingerprint evidence in that case became a sensation and opened the door to a new era in police science. But rarely had a criminal case so captured the imagination of armchair sleuths and mystery buffs as the Hudson River Mystery. "Clever Detective Work Solves Case," said the headline in the *Evening Telegram*.[1] "Working on the tiniest of clues, Inspector Joseph Faurot completed the most brilliant piece of detective work seen in many years," said the *Telegram*. "Twelve hours later, he had placed under arrest the Reverend Hans Schmidt and had obtained from him a confession to one of the most brutal murders known to New York City." The police basked in glory, eager to compensate for the endless stream of scandals and corruptions that were usually on the front page of the city's newspapers. the *New York Herald* said, "As startling almost as the crime itself was the manner in which the mystery was brought to an abrupt and dramatic termination yesterday morning. The solution was forged out of a clue that had been in the hands of the police almost from the moment they began their investigation."[2]

The *New York Press* was supportive of the detective squad as well and published a story on September 14 praising Faurot's investigative team. "Crime's Solution a Police Triumph," said the headline. "Lacking the spectacular methods of the detectives of fiction, by infinite patience the chief of New York detectives added bit by bit to the structure he was building up from the disconnected pieces of evidence. At first, the case looked hopeless. Students of police methods shook their heads and said the mystery would never be solved," said the *New York Press*. Coroner Feinberg of Manhattan said Faurot's work was "something that puts the best work of Scotland Yard or Paris to shame."[3] But there was still more work to be done.

At the time of Father Schmidt's arrest, police confiscated papers found in his room at the rectory of St. Joseph's Church. Among these documents was a rent receipt written to a George Miller on June 3, 1913, for twenty-three dollars. The address for the rental was 516 West 134th Street. During the afternoon of September 15, detectives O'Neill and McKenna went to the location to investigate the lead. It was a typical five-story walk-up tenement in west Harlem between Broadway and Riverside Drive, a thirty-minute walk from St. Joseph's. After they located the landlord, Jim Duffy, he was questioned about the receipt.

"Why do you want to know?" Duffy said. He was a chubby, pie-faced man with a large scar across his left cheek. His gray, stringy hair constantly fell in front of his eyes like a blanket. Every few seconds, he ran his pudgy hands through his locks, pushing them back.

"'Cause we do, that's why," McKenna replied. He placed his arm above the man and leaned it on the wall. "What's it to you, anyways? You in with these guys?"

"No, naw, no way. I was just wondering is all."

"Well, stop wondering and start walkin'. We want the key."

The man fumbled in his pockets as if he did not know where it was. Within three seconds, though, he had the key in his hand.

"Oh, here it is, yeah. This is it, yeah." O'Neill grabbed the key out of his hand.

"Which apartment? And when was it rented?"

"A few months ago, in the summer it was. Two men. His name was Miller. Yeah. Miller. George Miller. He was with another guy. Looked like his brother. They were decent men. I can tell you know. I can tell. They was good people. Paid me all in cash, too. Twenty dollars it was."

"Twenty-three it was," said McKenna. He looked up the narrow staircase, but it was too dark to see. "What floor might it be?"

"Oh, it's up on the fourth floor, first door on the left, 4B it is. Oh yeah, right, twenty-three."

"Let's go." The two cops drudged up to the third floor and unlocked the door with the key.

"Can't see a damn thing," McKenna said. The door creaked open. The light from the hallway was barely enough to see inside. They slowly walked in and went to a window on the opposite side of the room. Heavy, thick curtains had been nailed to the top of the window frame. O'Neill yanked on the drape and pulled it off the nail, flooding the room with sunlight.

A few feet away, on a table in the center of the room, was a large metal machine. Next to it was a stack of paper, all cut to about three inches by five inches. On a large shelf behind the table, O'Neill saw a dozen bottles of what appeared to be a dark liquid. He walked over and read the label.

"Black printer's ink. What the hell is this place?" In a metal can next to the table was a mound of discarded paper. When O'Neill grabbed a handful, he saw that it was crumpled up ten-dollar bills.

"Counterfeit," he muttered. "The priest is a God damn counterfeiter, too. I'll be damned!" Along with the hundreds of ten-dollar bills in the waste can, they also found a copper twenty-dollar engraving plate, which contained the serial number 1234567829A. "It was complete in every detail, from the dark photographing room to the heavily carpeted floor, so covered to prevent the sound of the running presses from attracting the attention of the tenants in the house. Partly burned counterfeit bills were found. The camera, presses, photo-engraving equipment and other outfits found there were taken to headquarters."[4] All the twenty-dollar bills recovered from the apartment had the same serial number. The paper was of high quality, though not perfect. The floor was covered with ripped and burned pieces of the same paper. In the adjoining room, O'Neill found another printing press that had apparently been set up for ten-dollar bills. Stacked along the walls in the kitchen were dozens of bottles containing chemicals and ink. There was a large set of repair tools on the floor but not a stick of furniture in the bedroom.

"I don't think it was a one-man shop," Inspector Faurot told the press later. "All the rooms were given over to a workshop. The bathroom was used as a darkroom for developing photographic plates, the kitchen for the storage of chemicals, the dining room as a drying room and the parlor as the pressroom. In the bedroom were stored the paper."[5] A search of the bedroom also turned up mail and several cards addressed to a Dr. Ernest Muret at 301 St. Nicholas Avenue. McKenna and O'Neill decided to pay a visit to that office as well. They locked the door and kept the key.

When they arrived at the Nicholas Avenue location, which was on 125th Street, they parked their car around the corner and walked to the front door of the building. They entered the four-story brownstone structure and located the office of Dr. Muret on the third floor. Again, the door was locked and no one answered their persistent knocking. They started down the stairs.

As they walked down the narrow staircase, an older woman was climbing up. She carried some groceries and the packages seemed heavy. O'Neill passed her. McKenna stopped to offer a hand.

"I'll help you with that, ma'am," he said.

"That's right kind of you," she said. The lady ignored O'Neill, who waited on the next landing. She looked over both men with a knowing eye.

"Cops, eh?" She smiled.

"Maybe."

"Looking for those two slugs up on the third floor?"

"Maybe," replied McKenna again.

"I figured. Strange people, them two."

"Yeah, why's that?" he asked as they reached the second floor and the woman stopped at the door to her apartment.

"Oh, just some things," she said. "A woman can see things." She placed the groceries on the floor and placed the key in the lock. "I'm gettin' too old to climb these damn stairs anymore, you know?"

"What things, lady?"

"I told my daughter that I'm comin' to live with her up in the Bronx. She and her husband got a wonderful farm up there, cows and horses and all that. It's very peaceful there. She'll take me, too. She was always a good girl. I saw them two many times, you know? That man would come and visit the dentist. It's shameful, I say."

"What's shameful, ma'am? Lots of people visit the dentist."

"I told her give me till this winter, then I'll be there. Yeah, lots of people visit the dentist. But how many stay in the office for three days at a time?"

"Three days?" said McKenna. "What's he doing up there for three days?"

"What's with your partner?" said the lady. "He don't like to help old ladies up the steps?"

"Oh, he don't mean nothing. He's just got a lot on his mind," said McKenna.

"Next time, help an old lady, damn it!" the woman yelled after O'Neill. "I tell you, them two got something going on and I don't mean business neither. Them's boyfriends, I say."

"Really?" said McKenna who was genuinely surprised. The woman began to close the door.

"Thanks much, I do appreciate the help of a gentleman."

"You're welcome, ma'am," he said and began to follow his partner down the cramped hallway.

"Oh, I forgot to tell you," she yelled out, "the one that comes to visit, I think he's a God damn priest!" The door shut and a bolt slid loudly into place.

The two detectives returned to the ground level where they sat outside the building and waited. For six hours, they lingered about the doorway and across the street, drinking coffee, smoking cigars, and trying not to be conspicuous. It was to no avail because within thirty minutes, virtually everyone in the neighborhood knew the police had staked out the apartment building. Shortly before midnight, a trim, well-dressed young man appeared. He entered the building and walked quietly up to the third floor. The cops followed at a safe distance. When the man placed his key in the door to Dr. Muret's office, McKenna and O'Neill grabbed him.

"Police!"

The man nearly jumped out of his suit. He dropped his key on the floor and turned to face the detectives.

"What? What do you want?" he asked, his eyes wide with fear.

"Who are you?" said O'Neill.

"Why, I'm Dr. Muret. This is my office. I'm a dentist."

"Oh yeah, Doc? Tell me, you keep midnight hours, I guess? Let's go in and talk about it," said McKenna. Once inside the office, the two detectives began to rummage around while they spoke to the nervous doctor who fidgeted with his coat and brushed his dark hair away from his eyes.

"How long you been here, Doc? Do you know Father Hans? Where you been today?" They asked question after question, barely giving him a chance to answer.

"Father Hans?" Muret replied. "Well, I don't think I know that man. I've been here for a year."

"Well, he knows you!" McKenna lied. While Dr. Muret struggled to answer the rapid questions, Detective O'Neill picked up some photographs from the desktop drawer. The first photo was of a bearded man wearing a hat. It looked very much like Hans Schmidt. Other photos were of the same man in different poses.

"Sure you don't know him, Doc?" O'Neill said as he went through the photos.

"Father Hans?" Muret said. "Father Hans, you say? Wait a minute, yes, oh yes, I think he was a patient of mine once. Yes, Father Hans Schmidt, that's him." At that point, O'Neill found a burned piece of paper in an ashtray by the couch. When he picked it up and saw that it was a partially singed twenty-dollar bill. The serial number was still easy to read. It was number 1234567829A, the same as all the bills found at the 134th Street apartment.

"Now this is interesting," he said as he held the bill up to the light. The color in Muret's face seemed to drain. McKenna looked over. "Want to tell us what's going on Doc? Unless you want to go to the federal pen. Counterfeiting is a federal rap, you know. They'll lock you up and throw away the key."

Muret grew noticeably weaker and seemed to be unsteady on his feet. "I had nothing to do with the murder," he said suddenly.

"What murder?" said O'Neill as he glanced at his partner. "Who said anything about a murder? What murder you talking about, Doc?"

"I heard Father Schmidt was arrested for that murder of the girl. I had nothing to do with it." No sooner had he finished the sentence than Detective McKenna came out of the adjoining room holding a .38 caliber handgun.

"This yours?" he said holding the weapon up to the dentist's face.

"Yes, it's mine. What of it? I need it for protection. This is a rough neighborhood. So what?"

"By the way, Doc, you're under arrest," said O'Neill. "Possession of a weapon." Dr. Muret wavered on his feet and grabbed the edge of a chair to steady himself.

"I knew it wouldn't last. I told him so."

"Who? Who did you tell?"

"Father Hans. But he is a stubborn man. Very stubborn. I told him counterfeiting was a bad business. But murder? No, gentlemen, no murder for me. Whatever he did, he did on his own, believe me." Muret admitted to the counterfeiting plan and that Schmidt had been the one to secure all the equipment. He also said that he was never actually licensed to practice dentistry but did attend school for two years in Berlin. When he arrived in America in early 1908, he got a job working with established dentists to learn more of the trade. In December 1908, he rented the St. Nicholas Avenue space and set up a dentist's office. One of his first patients, he said, was Father Hans Schmidt. He paid fifty-eight dollars on his first visit for work done on his teeth. After that initial treatment, they became friends. But the two detectives noticed a strong facial and physical resemblance between Muret and Schmidt.

"Are you two brothers?" asked McKenna.

Muret did not seem surprised by the question. "No, we are not brothers. But some people think we are. I know we sort of look the same."

"Yeah, I think you look a lot alike. Well, let's go. Inspector Faurot will want to talk to you down at headquarters." Muret buttoned up his coat and brushed back his hair. He smoothed the front of his clothing with his hands right down to the cuffs of his pants. He pulled his cuffs down so that his white shirt protruded just the right measure from his coat sleeves. As he walked to the door, he placed his hat squarely on his head, tilting the brim fashionably to the left at a modest angle.

"All right, gentlemen, let's proceed. I'll be happy to talk with the inspector." Muret opened the door and led the two detectives into the hallway. As they reached the first floor, a young woman entered the vestibule. She glanced up at the men and said. "Ernest, are you going out?" She was an attractive, dark-haired woman with warm, expressive eyes. Dr. Muret did not answer and pretended not to hear the remark.

"Who's this, doc?" asked McKenna. Muret just shook his head and said he did not recognize her.

"I'm Bertha. Who are you?" she said to McKenna.

"We're the police. Bertha who?"

"Bertha Zech, I'm his friend," the woman said, pointing to Dr. Muret.

"And now you're ours. You're coming with us, too." McKenna grabbed her on the arm and pulled her toward the car.

"Dr. Ernest Arthur Muret, dentist, was arrested at one o'clock this morning," said the *New York Herald*, "and according to the police, confessed that he had been making counterfeit twenty-dollar bills as the partner of Reverend Hans Schmidt, the Roman Catholic priest now in the Tombs as the confessed murderer of Anna Aumuller, the victim of the Hudson River Murder mystery."[6] At the precinct house, Muret told Inspector Faurot that Schmidt had purchased all the printing presses and seemed to know how to print money. He said he did not know who had burned the money that detectives had found in the West 134th Street apartment because he had not visited the flat for several days. Bertha Zech said she knew nothing of the counterfeiting plot, and though she heard mention of Anna Aumuller's name, Bertha had no idea she was murdered.

"I knew of her, but I know nothing of her death, God help me!" she said to investigators. She said she worked as a housekeeper to Muret and, on occasion, to Father Schmidt as well. Though investigators felt she knew more about the killing, Zech insisted that she had told them everything. She was released later that day. In the meantime, detectives returned to the West 134th Street apartment and Dr. Muret's office at St. Nicholas Avenue and removed everything they could carry. Included in the items were numerous photographs of Father Schmidt in his priestly attire and civilian dress as well. Many of the photos were partially scorched, as if someone had tried to burn them.

Late that night, Inspector Faurot received a tip that someone had tried to burn parts of a human body in an empty lot on the night of September 5. The caller said the lot was located "on Seventh Avenue between 137th Street and

Macomb's Place...where a man bearing a strong resemblance to Father Schmidt appeared at the lot carrying a tightly wrapped bundle in one hand and a small can in the other. While children looked on...the man entered the lot poured the contents of the can over the bundle and then lighted it."[7] Investigators from the West 152nd Street station hurried over to the lot to look for evidence. As they searched through the debris in the lot, Detective O'Neill found a large piece of bone and several partially burned photographs. One of the photos was an image of a man wearing the garments of a priest. Parts of packing material, which resembled the similar packing found in the West 134th Street apartment was also recovered. It, too, was partially scorched. Inspector Faurot later told reporters he believed the burned package contained the head of the victim.

In the morning, police had located a housekeeper who worked for the St. Boniface Church at the same time as Anna Aumuller. Annie Hirt told investigators that she knew Anna well and they were good friends. She said that if she saw her body she would be able to identify her, even if she did not see the face. Hirt said that Anna had a brown birthmark on her breast that was easily recognizable. Detectives decided to let Hirt view the remains at the Hoboken morgue. "Before she went to the morgue in company with Detective Cassassa," the *New York Herald* reported, "Miss Hirt described in detail to Inspector Faurot and Deacon Murphy, Assistant District Attorney, the marks she knew were upon the body of Miss Aumuller. She also gave a minute description of the article of clothing owned by Miss Aumuller, which she would be positive to identify."[8]

By 10 A.M. on September 15, Miss Hirt was at Volk's morgue in downtown Hoboken, New Jersey. Detective Cassassa waited with her in the lobby while Dr. King prepared the viewing. First, he carried out the upper torso, which was found on September 5 by Mary Bann and her brother Albert. He placed the item on a metal table on its back. Dr. King then brought in the bottom half of the torso, which was found on September 7 by Joseph Hagmann at Weehawken. He placed it on the same table just below the first piece. The two parts fit together almost perfectly.

Then Detective Cassassa brought in Miss Hirt. At first, she gasped when she saw the body parts. But she already knew what to expect and soon regained her composure. "As she had promised, she made the identification," reported the *New York Herald*. "She went even further, however, and proved her previous description of the body was correct by displaying to the police and the morgue attendants a faint brown spot in the skin of the dead woman, on the left breast. This mark had escaped detection before but was easily discernible after Miss Hirt had called attention to it."[9]

Miss Hirt told Cassassa that Anna had talked about her relationship with the priest. "She often spoke about him," she said. "After she had been out the day before, she always, the following day spoke about him. She once said that in two weeks, she was going to get married. She also said that she had been to the flat with her intended and to the moving pictures and she told me how the rooms were in the flat."[10]

The chemise that had been located near the bottom half of the torso was also identified by Miss Hirt. "It had not been too long back when Miss Aumuller purchased it at a bargain sale and had been turned up so it had a hem six inches deep. The hem was found on the chemise and also prominent was the clumsy stitching Miss Hirt had said would be found on the garment."[11] The police were satisfied. The body was Anna Aumuller and the Hudson River Murder mystery had been solved.

12

Stigmata

As the police continued their investigation into the murder, Father Schmidt remained locked up in the Tombs, New York City's bleakest prison. Alphonse Koelble, a prominent Manhattan lawyer, agreed to represent Schmidt in the criminal proceedings. Koelble was also a popular lecturer who delivered speeches throughout the city on legal issues. Some of the lectures took place at church meetings and on one occasion, at the St. Boniface parish. "I went to see Father Schmidt in the Tombs," he told reporters from the *New York Herald*, "and we recognized each other immediately . . . he greeted me in the counsel reception room with a strained face, pale and emaciated."[1] Koelble had a long conversation with Schmidt who told him that he killed the girl because of a command from God. "There is left in my mind no doubt that the man is crazy," Koelble said. But the Tombs warden, John Fallon, had a stronger opinion. "I think he is the most dangerously crazy man I have ever seen in my forty years as a prison warden," he told reporters.[2]

An alienist, as a psychiatrist was called at that time, was brought in to study Father Schmidt. Dr. Carleton Simon, who was frequently called upon by the district attorney's office as an expert in such matters, was also a believer in phrenology. Developed during the mid-nineteenth century by pseudo-scientists who wanted to believe that physical characteristics could reveal personality traits, phrenology had many supporters. An Austrian physicist, Franz Gall, popularized the "new science," as it was called, and published several academic papers that claimed a nexus between the shape of the human skull and deviant behavior. He claimed that each human emotion—aggression, hostility, loyalty, love—had a corresponding location in the brain, and therefore if that part of the head was more physically pronounced, that particular trait would be more pronounced in the person. Depending on which expert was quoted, there were between twenty-seven and thirty-eight regions on the human head that were closely associated with personality traits. Skull maps that indicated these regions and their exact locations were produced by the hundreds. However, many of the charts were developed by amateurs, who simply invented the details to suit their own needs. They followed no accepted criteria and were vastly different from each other.

Physicians, psychiatrists, and other scientists soon joined the fad and phrenology became a sensation. Journals on the "new science" were published all over the world, especially in Europe, where plans were made to add phrenology to many university curriculums. Even politicians and world leaders became enamored with the exciting possibility that human behavior could be accurately predicted using a skull map. As a result, phrenologists branched out into other areas of society. They were hired as consultants in business, politics, and medicine. Some became famous and demanded huge fees for their startling insights into human behavior.

Unusual machines were invented that claimed to measure and determine a man's personality by the size and shape of the bumps on his head. A criminal was thought to possess a damaged brain, which generated hostility and aggression that could not be controlled. Though American judges rejected the introduction of phrenology into the courtroom, it was still used on occasion to either support or deny existing testimony, especially as it applied to a defendant's psychological background.

Dr. Simon performed an examination of Father Schmidt's head while he was at the Tombs and arrived at some astonishing conclusions. Dr. Simon said that the excessive length of Schmidt's jaw and his high cheekbones indicated "brutality and instability of mind." Furthermore, the doctor said, "the lack of symmetry is shown the length of the lower jaw, a jaw such as is seen only in persons who are given to brutality and crime. There are also many other abnormalities about this man's countenance. He has a contour not unlike that of an American Indian, although of German extraction." Dr. Simon found that the narrowness of his forehead designated "him at once as of unstable mind, one whose physical desires would often outweigh his moral attitude." The facial details also displayed "an inherited duality . . . as well as a mental stigmata." He took careful measurements of Father Schmidt's skull and made detailed diagrams of the shape of his eyes, nose, and forehead, and their relationship to each other. "To criminologists and alienists," Dr. Simon reported to the district attorney's office, "the mouth is one of the most significant features of an individual. In the case of this man, it is strikingly expressive of animality. While many persons may live an uneventful life having features similar to those of this individual, they nevertheless tend to a similar mental bias and it is when reason becomes dethroned in such persons that the greatest cruelty is shown. This man is of Slavonic type, which would tend to make him preponderantly emotional. His would be a mind that would suffer from contrition and remorse for an act committed but this would not be in ratio to the harm done."[3]

Coroner Israel Feinberg of Manhattan also gave his interpretation of Father Schmidt after a brief conversation that took place on September 15 at the city jail. He claimed to observe marks of both good and evil in the prisoner's face. "Israel L. Feinberg, coroner, called attention to the asymmetrical face of Father Hans Schmidt," said the *New York Herald*. "The coroner observed when talking to the slayer of Anna Aumuller that one side of the priest's face present[ed] a sanctified appearance, 'a look such as a priest might have. But the left side of his countenance is totally different. There are marks of a devil on that side of his face. I noticed that about the mouth on one side brutal instinct seems to be marked. Looking at his left eye and cheek, he has the cunning look of a fox. I turned suddenly so that I could see the better side of his countenance and the difference was remarkable. Even about the eyes one could see it. One had a diabolical leer, while the other had a beatific expression.' "[4]

Another phrenologist hired by the state, Dr. Charles W. F. Horn of West Eighty-seventh Street, had a slightly different opinion. "Father Schmidt," he told reporters, "does not possess a criminal head or face, but his bumps show he is very secretive, cautious, constructive, and combative. He is not an insane man but a shrewd and cunning one."[5] Horn was of the opinion that Schmidt's demeanor to the police and public was a sham. He said that Schmidt was faking a psychosis in order to escape responsibility for his crimes and to avoid the electric chair.

But Koelble protested and asked for more examinations. He knew he would eventually find a doctor who would see it his way. Any psychiatrist who could get up on the stand and swear that Schmidt was insane was a plus for the defense. It could help save his client from the electric chair. "While indications were becoming more plentiful that such a line of defense would be offered to save the cleric from the electric chair, the priest himself, ranting in his cell, almost savagely denied he was mentally unbalanced," reported the *New York Herald*.[6]

Schmidt told anyone who would listen that he was definitely not crazy and whatever he did, he did so on the orders of God. "Well, there isn't much to say about this," Hans told Koelble on his first visit with his client. "God in his own time will clear it up. Perhaps the people will never understand this thing. But God and Abraham know why I killed her. Policemen tell me they question my right to say I am a priest. I held a double order to the priesthood, for I was ordained in diocese of Mainz and I was reordained by St. Elizabeth. What's the use of talking about it anymore? I married her. I performed the ceremony myself, as I had a right to do. I was commanded to marry her by St. Elizabeth, my patron saint."[7] When asked if he had any remorse over her death, Father Schmidt denied any regrets. "Why should I?" he told Koelble. "I was commanded to do it."

On Wednesday, September 17, Manhattan District Attorney Charles S. Whitman had just returned from a vacation. He sat at his desk on the fifth floor of the Criminal Courts building and felt ready for the new challenges ahead. Educated at Amherst College and New York University, Whitman began his illustrious career as a public official in New York City when he was hired as assistant corporation counsel in 1901. He later was president of the board of city magistrates until 1907. Governor Hughes appointed him judge of the court of special sessions during the following year and he served on the Manhattan bench until he became district attorney in 1910.

Whitman was a staunch Republican and a vociferous supporter of the death penalty. "I consider capital punishment for murder necessary in this country," he said during an interview in 1911, "although there is a strong prejudice against it."[8] Whitman was politically minded and aspired for bigger and better things. He made no secret of his ambitions and never shied away from public attention. Astute when it came to prosecuting high-profile cases, he maintained friendly relationships with several of the city's major newspapers. He cultivated that relationship often, such as when he told the *New York Times* on December 3, 1911, "In my opinion, New York newspapers as a whole are mighty powers in favor of public morals. I cannot agree with those who so condemn their constant minute examination of our daily life. I believe that, in the main, it is a good thing for the city and the nation. Crime can almost never be hidden here . . . for this we have to thank the newspapers. The mightiest detective force in all this world exists in the United States and its members are the men who make our newspapers."[9]

One of Whitman's assistants, Deacon Murphy, kept him informed of the ongoing developments in the Schmidt case. Each morning, while he rested by the Jersey shore in a rented Victorian at Cape May, Whitman read the *New York Times* and the *Evening Telegram* from the night before. He was well aware of the story of the Catholic priest who may have committed a murder and dumped his victim into the Hudson River. Even New York City did not get too many cases like that; and at times, it seemed as if New York was the nation's most violent city.

In recent years, the infamous *La Mano Nera*, the Black Hand, had wreaked havoc in Manhattan, especially among the immigrant population. In 1913, police arrested just one *Mano Nera* gang member, who admitted to 125 bombings in the previous ten months.[10] Though the street wars between the Plug Uglies and the Dead Rabbits during the 1890s were long over, their reputation lingered and the slum neighborhoods below Houston Street could be relied upon to produce a new harvest of criminals and deviants every few years. Public outcry against crime was at a feverish pitch. The jails were full and Sing Sing's Death Row was overcrowded.[11] Each day brought more depressing revelations of corruption and murder. The future of the city looked dim.

No one could be trusted, not even the police. The public's fear of crime was intensified by the belief that the police were just as bad as the criminals. It was common knowledge, supported by a succession of scandals during the previous decade, that the police department was in bed with Manhattan's criminal underworld. Ever since the 1890s, political commissions and official inquiries into secret police affairs occurred every few years. The revelations offered at these hearings became headlines in the city's tabloids and convinced a weary public that a change had to happen. But people also knew that the bribery and graft that occurred each and every day on Centre Street could never exist without the knowledge and cooperation of the police department. The Lexow Committee of 1894 was the flagship of the corruption inquiries. The parade of sordid characters, straight out of the Tenderloin depths, who testified at the proceedings recited endless litanies of police payoffs, graft, robbery, and murder that extended into the highest levels of police management.

Investigators discovered that a young man in New York had to pay a $300-bribe just to be appointed to the police force. Police Commissioner James Martin, who testified at the hearing, told the committee that it cost a patrolman $2,500 to be promoted to a sergeant. A captain's position was worth about $10,000 in bribes and an inspector's title was going for at least $12,000. These prices were the standard rates for the late nineteenth century and became higher after 1910.[12] "The Lexow Committee revealed such a mass of filth and robbery, oppression and blackmail as made the entire nation gasp!"[13]

At City Hall, the situation was even worse. No city permit could be obtained, no business could open and no building could go up unless a payment was made to the proper recipient on Centre Street. Graft and bribery permeated every level of the bureaucratic structure and dictated who would succeed and who would not.[14] And at its foundation was the New York City Police Department, rotten to its core. This sort of arrangement had been going on for years. The illegal gambling casinos were everywhere and it was plain to see that they could not remain in business unless the police ignored their responsibilities and looked the other way. One city judge told reporters, "Policemen, instead of being looked upon by citizens as a protection against lawbreakers and as guardians of the peace are too often looked upon with undistinguished suspicion . . . the evil reputation of the American police has often clogged or wholly misdirected the whole course of justice."[15]

More than any other period in its history, the police department was now seen in some parts of the city as an occupying army, an evil branch of government that seemed unstoppable and all-powerful. Even worse was the prevailing attitude of the police who considered themselves above the law and were nonresponsive to the public. "Insolent, arrogant and vicious, they produced a reign of terror as cruel as that of Cossacks during Old World pogroms."[16] This may help explain the almost hysterical reaction to the story of Lt. Charles Becker, NYPD's most corrupt cop, whom Whitman himself had sent to death row.

Charles Becker was raised in Sullivan County in upstate New York. He was of Bavarian heritage, outgoing, cocky, and had boundless energy. Tired of the quiet country life, he moved to Manhattan in the 1890s. Even as a young man, Becker was big and intimidating, and proved to be a fearsome fighter. He got his first job as a bouncer for one of the gambling joints in the Tenderloin District where it was estimated that there were more than 200 such establishments in operation every day of the week. There were hundreds more below Forty-second Street extending directly into the heart of the financial district surrounding Wall Street. They wielded a certain political power at City Hall as well, because they had as their representative a domineering, charismatic, and thoroughly corrupt politician known city wide as "Big Tim" Sullivan, the overseer of all graft and bribery in Manhattan.

Nothing could get done in New York City without his stamp of approval. "No matter who was head of the local Democratic machine at Tammany Hall, Big Tim had, for two decades, been the man to see if you wanted to do business in the Tenderloin."[17] His rule over the criminal empire in Manhattan was so complete, that he was considered more powerful than the mayor, and everyone knew it. "If a fellow was short of the specified payoff money, he could still qualify if he was one of the boys from Big Tim's old East Side clubhouse for whom the politician felt a sentimental attachment."[18] Sullivan took a liking to the young brawler and gave Becker more responsibility in the illegal clubs on 42nd Street. In 1892, under the guidance and supervision of Big Tim, Becker joined the NYPD.

Over the next decade, Becker rose through the ranks, increasing his wealth and power by his alliance with Sullivan and his friends at City Hall. By 1910, Becker was probably New York's wealthiest cop and he exerted an iron grip over the Tenderloin's illegal casino empire. Club owners paid thousands each week to the police department to keep their doors open and their customers out of jail.

When one casino owner, Herman "Beansy" Rosenthal, threatened co-operation with District Attorney Whitman, Becker became enraged. On the night of July 16, 1912, Rosenthal was shot and killed outside the Cafe Metropole on West 43rd Street. His killers, Harry "Gyp the Blood" Horowitz, Frank "Dago Frank" Cirofici, Louis "Lefty Louie" Rosenberg, and Jacob "Whitey Lewis" Seidenschmer, were caught and confessed to the crime. They also implicated Lieutenant Becker as the man who had ordered the killing. After a sensational trial, which generated international headlines, all the defendants were convicted and sentenced to death. But Becker's conviction was later overturned. Whitman led the prosecution a second time and won another conviction.[19] Becker was sentenced to death, the first city police officer to receive the death penalty. It was a tremendous achievement for Whitman, who would eventually be elected governor of New York State based on his reputation as a corruption fighter.[20]

It is difficult to exaggerate the level of press coverage given to the Becker case. His case was front-page news for over three years and was written about in Europe and Asia as well. The Rosenthal murder came to symbolize big-city corruption and the abysmal failure of the police to effectively combat this evil in their own ranks.[21] Though many people believed Becker was innocent, and the evidence that convicted him was far from conclusive, he received little sympathy from the media. Not surprisingly, the police department supported Becker, who was well liked and respected by the average cop on the street. Of course, since many police were immersed in the web of bribery and graft themselves, they may have had little choice but to protect one of their own.

Whitman was shrewd enough to know that the public was repulsed by the shocking story of Father Hans Schmidt. The daily disclosures on the case intensified the need for a speedy conviction and swift justice. But already, defense counsel announced that they would plead insanity, which could help their client escape the death penalty. Alphonse Koelble informed Whitman that he would be willing to drop an insanity plea in exchange for a second degree murder conviction. Whitman refused. The District Attorney's office "insisted that Schmidt must either go to the electric chair or to the State

Hospital for the Criminal Insane at Matteawan if it was established that he was or was not legally responsible."[22]

A panel of psychiatrists was appointed to examine Father Schmidt and report back to Whitman with their results. "Dr. William Mabon of the Manhattan State Asylum for the Insane and Dr. Carlos F. MacDonald, one of the alienists who judged Thaw insane, were appointed by Charles S. Whitman, District Attorney. A third expert will be selected soon."[23] The initial examination took place at the Tombs, in the absence of Mr. Koelble, who chose not to be present during questioning. But Father Schmidt proved to be a difficult patient and one who seemed to be very cautious of what he said to doctors. "Schmidt answered readily most of the questions put to him by the alienists. He showed reluctance to talk only when the examination involved the details of the immoral life which the priest confessed that he had led for several years."[24] It was an odd reaction for someone whose lawyer claimed he was insane.

"Priest in Insane Ward as Slayer of River Victim," declared the *Evening Telegram* on September 15. The story went on to say that, "Father Schmidt, who admits killing Anna Aumuller and dismembering her body, said to be the worst lunatic in Tombs prison in years." The insanity angle, so prevalent in the press reports, was promoted endlessly. One doctor told reporters that, "he was convinced that Schmidt was suffering from a paranoiac type of dementia praecox."[25]

The fact that Schmidt was a priest was a source of never-ending speculation on the obvious contrasts of good and evil. "The incredible hardness of heart of Schmidt was revealed more than ever today when it was learned that at the moment he was aroused from sleep to face the accusing eyes of Inspector Joseph Faurot, he was tired out from listening to a long line of communicants who were relieving their conscience by telling their faults into his ear in the confessional of St. Joseph of the Holy Family."[26] Many explanations were offered in the city's press for this departure from the goodness of religious faith. Many reports blamed Schmidt's evil on his lineage, a popular target during that era, thanks to Darwin's much-publicized theories on genetic destiny. But some press reports offered other explanations as well. The *Sun* wrote, "Schmidt, whose age the police recorded as thirty-three years, is sallow-faced with glassy eyes, whose general appearance and actions yesterday caused many to think he is addicted to drugs."[27]

On September 23, a federal Grand Jury indicted Hans Schmidt and Dr. Ernest Muret for counterfeiting and other related charges. "Three counts for counterfeiting and one for conspiracy are included in the indictments," said the *New York Press*. "The vote followed the exhibition to the jury of plates for making twenty-dollar bills and other counterfeiting paraphernalia found in

Formal photograph of Anna Aumuller taken in New York City in 1911. (Court Record, New York State Court of Appeals, 216 NY 324; 1913.)

the apartment in West 134th Street and in the rooms of the two prisoners."[28] Each count carried a penalty of fifteen years and a fine of $5,000. The conspiracy charge could mean a ten-year sentence and a $10,000 fine. But it was doubtful that Schmidt would ever be prosecuted on the federal charges as the police announced the same day that they had enough evidence to convict the priest on a murder charge. "The prosecution is ready with its case," Whitman told the press. "The evidence is now in shape to be placed before the Grand Jury. The Coroner's Inquest is set for October 2nd."[29] As for Muret, he would soon be turned over to federal authorities.

13

Bellevue

On the evening of September 19, three men assembled in the busy lobby of Bellevue Hospital on First Avenue and Twenty-eighth Street. They were Dr. Menas S. Gregory, chief psychiatrist for the psychopathic ward; Dr. Smith Ely Jeliffe, an expert in mental diseases; and Dr. Morris Karpas, assistant director of psychiatry. The Manhattan District Attorney's Office had asked the team to assess Father Schmidt's mental state of mind on the night of Anna Aumuller's murder. The New York *Sun* said that Koelble "had a talk with the prisoner in the afternoon and came away from the interview more convinced than ever that Schmidt was insane."[1] He later told reporters, "I interested myself in Schmidt at the request of a number of German Catholic laymen who had been friendly to the prisoner. I have talked with the man and am certain that he is insane. I do not see how anyone hearing him talk could escape that conclusion."[2] But the defendant disagreed. "That is absurd," he said to reporters. "If there is anything you can be sure of is that there is no trace of insanity in me."[3]

However, the *New York Times* also questioned Schmidt's claim of insanity. "If Schmidt were truly insane," one story said on September 21, "his delusions would certainly have found their way into his sermons. He would have mentioned his belief that he was under the direction of St. Elizabeth and his

Father Hans Schmidt as he appeared in 1907 shortly after his ordinationan at Mainz Seminary, Germany. (Court Record, New York State Court of Appeals, 216 NY 324; 1913.)

views on human sacrifice while he was a free man, instead of developing them immediately upon his arrest for murder." But Alphonse Koelble continued his campaign to convince anyone that his client was insane and not responsible for the death of Anna Aumuller. He ridiculed the police who claimed that Schmidt was a cunning criminal who was trying to get away with murder. "They would give the impression that Schmidt was a shrewd man who deliberately started out on a criminal career and expected to get rich by it. But on the contrary, as far as I can find out, he is penniless. If he had money he could get little enjoyment out of it because most of his time had to be spent on his calling as a priest, and the life of a priest is a hard one."[4] Koelble boasted he would have little difficulty convincing a jury that his client was insane. He planned to have an alienist of his own choosing visit the

Tombs to examine the defendant and report back to him. Newspapers quickly seized upon the issue of insanity as the dominant theme of the case.

But in order for an insanity defense to be successful, it would have to be demonstrated conclusively that Father Schmidt did not know that it was wrong to cut the throat of his wife, chop her up, and drop the pieces into the Hudson River. It did not matter that his past behavior tended to show that he acted irrationally. It did not matter that he rode his bicycle almost nude in Germany and he liked to cut off the heads of geese when he was a child. According to New York State law and the criteria established by the M'Naghten rule in the nineteenth century, none of that mattered.[5] The crucial aspect of any insanity defense in American courts was that the defendant did not appreciate the wrongfulness of his act and the consequences of his actions.

The three psychiatrists were escorted to the ninth floor of the hospital where they were taken to a wide, empty office, save four chairs and a wooden coffee table that held a small electric light. The only window in the room faced the East River and was framed by one-inch-thick steel bars. The men settled into the three chairs that were arranged in a semicircle facing the fourth chair. They placed their copious notes on the table, which was soon covered with an assortment of papers and folders. It was decided that Dr. Gregory would be the lead interviewer while the others would assist and make corresponding notations of what was said during the meeting. Dr. Jeliffe, who had performed research in the Royal Clinic of Mental Diseases in Munich, would act as an observer of the prisoner's behavior. None of the doctors had met Father Schmidt before and most of what they knew about the case they surmised from the newspapers.

After a twenty-minute wait, there was a loud pounding on the door and the sound of bars being shifted into place. The door swung open and two guards entered the room. Behind them, Father Schmidt, hunched over with his hands clasped in front of his waist, shuffled into the room. He wore a gray suit, a white shirt, and no tie. His clothes were badly wrinkled and it was obvious that he had slept in them. His wrists were chained in front of his body and attached to a thick leather belt that ran around his abdomen. One of the guards removed a key from his pocket.

"Sit down here!" he commanded and pointed to the one empty chair. Father Schmidt sat quietly while the guard fumbled with the key to unlock the handcuffs. Dr. Gregory studied the prisoner. He was a handsome man, appeared to be about thirty-five years of age, with dark brown eyes and very light skin color, almost pale. His facial features were classic Nordic, balanced, neatly defined, and somewhat appealing. He wore his long, unwashed hair straight back and had not shaved in several days. His left eye twitched noticeably.

Mug shot taken of Father Hans Schmidt on September 15, 1913 by the New York City Police Department. (New York City Municipal Archives.)

"He had on a loose shirt, which was open at the trousers," one of the doctors, later said, "a handkerchief loosely tied, rather untidy, his trousers were unbuttoned, and he gave the appearance of indifference and carelessness. There was a general slovliness [sic]. His hands were dirty and at times there would be particles of food on his beard."[6]

"Which one is the doctor?" asked one of the guards.

"I am and . . ." replied Dr. Gregory.

"If you need us, we'll be right outside that door, doc," said the guard who appeared to be in charge. All the uniformed men walked out of the room and locked the door behind them.

"Have you a cigarette?" asked Father Schmidt. He adjusted his ill-fitting clothes and settled into the chair facing the three men.

"I have one," said Dr. Jeliffe, as he removed a cigarette from a package in his pocket and handed it to the priest.

"Freundlichen Dank, [Thank you kindly]" he replied. He glanced about his surroundings. "It's dark in here."

"Well, there's only that one light, but we'll have to make the best of it." Dr. Karpas adjusted the position of the lamp until it was centered upon the table. But the light barely touched upon Father Schmidt, who leaned back in his chair, fading, at least temporarily, into the corner of the room. When Dr. Karpas looked up to talk with the prisoner, he had to squint his eyes slightly in the glaring light between them. Father Schmidt struck a match, which lit the room in flickering brightness for just a moment. He puffed on the cigarette and blew out the match, holding the cigarette between his inverted thumb and forefinger in the manner of the European smoker.

"I'm Dr. Gregory. This is Dr. Karpas on my right and Dr. Jeliffe on my left. We have been asked by the district attorney's office to talk to you this evening about the case and report back to Mr. Whitman of our findings. We intend to . . ."

"You want to see if I'm crazy?" asked Father Schmidt.

"Well, Father, not quite like . . ."

"They used to call me crazy when I studied in Munich, you know. They teased me constantly. They couldn't understand how a man could be so close to God such as I."

"And do you still feel close to God now, Father?" asked Dr. Gregory.

"Certainly. Even closer than before. A man in my position can't help but feel spiritual."

"Father, I would like to ask you a few questions about your childhood in Germany. Would you mind?"

"Not at all. I have lots of time."

"What kind of life did you have as a child? Were you happy with your mother and father as you were growing up?" The doctors looked up from their note pads and studied the prisoner. He sat back in the chair and puffed on the cigarette.

"You know, I always wondered about that myself. Was I happy? Did I receive the love and attention that I deserved? I don't think so. Since I had nine brothers and sisters, there was a lot of commotion in my home. My father was away most of the time working for the railroad and the task of raising us children fell mostly upon my blessed mother who tried very hard. But to answer your question, was I happy with my mother and father, I can't say because I don't feel like I knew my father very well. He was a stern man, always demanding much from his children. Maybe too much. Maybe that's why I wound up here. I lacked the love and understanding other children received. Yes, I can see that now. It's his fault. My damn father, he was always too busy for us. Es ist Schade [It's a shame]."

"I am sure, Father. But what about your mother? Was she responsive to you?" asked Dr. Jeliffe.

"Oh, most definitely. She was a blessed woman, very devoted to the church. I mean she is responsible for what I am now, in every way. She always wanted me to become a priest, you know, a holy man. She is very proud of me." Schmidt sat back in his chair as if he were proclaiming a truth that everyone should take for granted. He puffed on the cigarette slowly and exhaled from the side of his mouth so as not to blow smoke directly in the faces of the others.

"I'm sure she is," replied Dr. Jeliffe, "but how do you feel about the predicament you find yourself in now? Do you feel that you have done anything wrong?"

"Wrong?" Schmidt said as he turned his palms upward, "How could anything be wrong if it was ordered by God? This sacrifice was the will of God and as such, can be considered a holy thing. I don't think God would take a human life in such a frivolous manner without having some sort of higher purpose."

"But what purpose could there be for such a brutal killing?" said Dr. Gregory.

"I don't know. I'm not privy to all of God's intentions," said Schmidt. "I'm not that holy."

As Dr. Gregory spoke to the prisoner, he used his hand to make a point, or to follow his notes. He noticed that Schmidt seemed to pay a great deal of attention to his movements. The day before, Dr. Gregory had suffered a small scratch on the index finger of his right hand. Father Schmidt seemed to become fixated on that tiny spot. After several minutes, he attempted to hide his interest by forcing himself to look away. But his gaze would soon return to the same injured finger. Dr. Gregory excused himself from the group and went into an adjoining alcove. He decided to try a psychological experiment. "I went to the corner of the room away from the place where they were conducting the examination," he said later, "and I drew a large drop of blood on the index finger of the left hand."[7] He had taken a small knife and made a small incision on his finger causing the blood to flow. He pressed a handkerchief over the wound, placed his hand in his coat-pocket and returned to the interview.

When he sat down in his chair, he kept his hand hidden in his pocket. Suddenly, he removed it and brought it to within inches of Schmidt's face. "While they were examining and talking to him," Dr. Gregory explained later, "I approached him and I put my finger between Dr. Karpas, who was on his left side, and Father Schmidt's back was turned to me—and I suddenly put my finger with the drop of blood on it in front of his eyes."[8] The prisoner

Montage of Anna Aumuller and Father Schmidt, which appeared in the *New York Telegram* on the morning after his arrest. The saw and knife that were used in the dismemberment of Anna Aumuller are in the foreground. (*New York Telegram*, September 15, 1913.)

became excited as his dark eyes went wide with passion. "He immediately became flushed, his face became red and his eyes dilated, became large—the pupils, I should say."[9] With that, Schmidt abruptly jumped up from his chair, grabbed the doctor's finger and tried to pull it into his mouth.

"The blood! The blood!" he screamed.

"My God!" yelled Dr. Gregory as he fell backward, his chair crashing to the floor. In an instant, Schmidt was upon him, knocking over the small lamp on the table. The room plunged into chaotic darkness. With both hands, the priest held the doctor's left wrist and succeeded in getting the bloody finger past his lips and began to suck. "A drop of blood fell on his lip, which he licked with his tongue and said, 'Allus blut ist mein! [All blood belongs to me!]'[10] Dr. Jeliffe and Dr. Karpas grabbed Schmidt around his neck and tried to pull him off their terrified friend. But his grip was powerful and he held the doctor's wrist with both his hands.

"Guards! Guards! Help! Help!" Dr. Gregory screamed.

Schmidt lapped up the blood from the finger while Dr. Karpas managed to get his arm around the priest's throat and pull him back. His arms reached for the bloodied finger as Schmidt growled for more. Dr. Gregory, flat on his back on the floor, struggled to get to his feet. Father Schmidt sputtered curses and continued to fight as the door swung open and the uniformed personnel rushed in. They jumped on top of the wailing priest and pinned him to the floor. After the guards handcuffed the prisoner, they lifted him up to his feet. In the meantime, Dr. Jeliffe located the lamp, but it was inoperative. The men stumbled around in the darkness bumping into one another and falling over the upended chairs.

"Sorry about that, Doctor," said Schmidt, "but the blood is mine. It should be for the sacrifice!" The guards hauled the prisoner out by his elbows, the back of his heels scraping the wooden floor. As he disappeared through the door, he grabbed the doorframe and held on. "I hope you're all right, Doctor. I'm not such a bad man," he said. The guards gave a mighty pull and Father Schmidt finally disappeared down the darkened corridor. His screams turned to maniacal laughter as he called out to Dr. Gregory, "I'm home, where the hell are you?" He kicked the guards while they struggled to control the raging prisoner. They dragged Schmidt down the hallway while Jeliffe and Karpas assisted Dr. Gregory to his feet.

"Are you all right, Doctor?"

"Yes, thank you, I'm fine," he said as he slowly got up.

The men helped Dr. Gregory to a chair. He looked at his bleeding finger, which displayed visible teeth indentations from Schmidt's mouth. As they picked up the furniture, they could hear the strange noises from Father Schmidt, off in the distance, while his grim laughter echoed through the halls, into the barren recesses and alcoves, around each corner, and into every room and cell.[11]

"Bless St. Elizabeth, too!" Schmidt yelled before he vanished into the darkness. The men heard a door slam loudly and then, complete silence. A sudden and inexplicable fear enveloped the three doctors. They glanced at one another briefly, recognizing something in each other's eyes, impossible to put into words, and yet a tangible presence, a feeling shared that maybe something unspeakable had happened in the room. Something terrible. Something evil.

14

In the Tombs

Throughout the next few days, Father Schmidt spoke freely to reporters who were allowed to visit the cell-block with permission from the warden. Sometimes, they passed notes to the guards containing questions for the prisoner, who then wrote his answers on the reverse sides and returned them. "I can't explain this to you," he told one reporter, "because you would not understand it, but God in his own time will clear this up. The people will never be able to understand it, but God and Abraham will eventually clear it up."[1]

While Schmidt languished in the forgotten recesses of the city jail, a coroner's inquest was scheduled by the district attorney's office.[2] It was customary at that time to appoint leading citizens to serve at a hearing that would ascertain the cause and manner of death of the deceased. The more publicity a case received, the more famous the jurors tended to be. When Coroner Israel L. Feinberg sent out subpoenas for the inquest, some of the most famous people in New York were asked to serve. "John D. Rockefeller, Jr., Cornelius Vanderbilt, George Gould, August Belmont, and Vincent Astor have been subpoenaed," said one press report, "along with thirty other men, all of whom are almost if not quite as well known, to attend the inquest into the death of Anna Aumuller."[3] It was thought that if the jury consisted of men who had the finest reputations in the community, there would be less chance of bribery or jury tampering.

"In the list of thirty-five men to be impaneled, from which twelve will be chosen, will be several of New York's leading bankers, business men, railroad officials, and merchants, the coroner says. Among those his servers could not locate yesterday was J. P. Morgan."[4] Coroner Feinberg also told reporters that the fact that Hans Schmidt was a priest should not be a consideration in court. "I shall ask no man his religious belief," he said. "I am convinced that any man, be he a Catholic, Protestant or Jew will be overwhelmed by the enormity of the crime as shown by the quantity and the quality of the evidence."[5] It was expected that the defense counsel would demand proof that the body parts found in the Hudson were in fact Anna Aumuller's, and challenge whether she was legally identified. The hearing was set for 10:00 A.M. on Friday, October 2, 1913, at the Manhattan Criminal Courts building.

Thanks to the daily reports in the tabloids, Father Schmidt became an immediate celebrity. Photographs of the handsome priest, replete in a black cassock and white collar, appeared in many of the dailies. His angelic facial expression in these images, which was in stark contrast to his alleged crimes, depicted a sturdy, confident-looking young man who displayed a certain level of sex appeal. The *Evening Telegram* reported, "five girls between the ages of sixteen and eighteen years and all richly dressed visited the Tombs today and asked to be shown through the prison. They refused to leave until they had seen Schmidt. Warden Fallon finally permitted them to be led past the priest's cell but not until they had promised not to speak to the prisoner. The warden is besieged daily by many women who want to take just one look at Schmidt."[6]

During late September, information had been leaked by the detective squad that during the second search of Schmidt's apartment, police found dozens of blank death certificates. When they asked the priest about the documents, he told a curious story. He said the world was full of cripples, infirm, and elderly who did not deserve to live. The world could be a better place without them, he added. He intended to kill those in his parish by poison and then forge their death certificates. But first, he planned to obtain life insurance on his victims so that the poor could share the profits. Under the headline, "Schmidt Purposed to Kill For Money," the *New York Times* reported the bizarre plan and said, "Hans Schmidt, the suspended Catholic priest who murdered Anna Aumuller and attempted to make counterfeit money, intended to commit a series of murders for the purpose of defrauding life insurance companies... a prominent physician told Inspector Faurot yesterday that Schmidt approached him with this plan."[7]

Inspector Joseph Faurot was Chief of Manhattan Detectives in 1913 and one of the pioneers of fingerprint technology in America. (New York City Police Museum.)

Coroner Feinberg began the inquest as scheduled on October 2. The press quickly took to calling the jury panel, "the millionaire jury." When the parade of some of New York's most famous citizens settled into the jury box that morning, "Hans Schmidt was led in by Detective Cassassa, one of the men who had aided in his capture. Glancing around the room with apparent unconcern, Schmidt walked rapidly to the counsel table and after shaking hands with Alphonse G. Koelble, took a seat with his back to the crowd."[8] Father Schmidt's appearance had changed since his arrest. Some of the people who knew him were surprised at his physical condition. He had lost weight and walked with a noticeable crouch. "His hair was tousled and his beard, scrubby and reddish, made him look unlike the dapper, young priest who was led into the Tombs almost three weeks ago," said the *New York Press.* "He wore no collar and his suit was unpressed."[9] The hearing was attended by a diverse group of observers. "Lawyers, physicians, sociological students and many persons from literary walks of life were present along with the morbidly curious," reported the *New York Press.* "There were several women in the courtroom."[10]

Testimony began with Mary Bann, who found the partial torso of Anna Aumuller on September 5. "A little after one o'clock in the afternoon," she told the court, "I saw something in the river. I sent my brother down to pick it up and see what it was. I went down myself and found it was a pillow and in the pillow was part of a woman's body."[11] Annie Hirt, who worked at the Church of St. Boniface and knew Anna Aumuller, took the stand next. "I first met Miss Aumuller at the rectory," she said. "She was employed there and I was also. I had occasion to go into her room and saw her partially undressed. I noticed a brown spot she had on her bust. I went to Volk's morgue in Jersey City and identified portions of her body by the brown spot on her right breast."[12]

Dr. George W. King, the county physician for Hudson County, New Jersey, testified to his autopsy findings. "The body had been cut in two portions," he told the court. "It was cut in the center of the body and the legs were cut off, and the head was cut off. I fitted those two portions together and found they were portions of the same human being. At a later time, I came into possession of the right leg and fitted the right leg to the lower portion of the woman's body. In my opinion, death was due to hemorrhage."[13] The jury panel, not accustomed to such graphic descriptions of murder, squirmed in their seats. They were much more at home attending board meetings, discussing the financial markets, or watching the changing numbers at the stock exchange. When Dr. King left the stand, there was an audible sigh of relief in court.

During the afternoon testimony, Coroner Feinberg commented to the room that the victim would have to be buried at New York City's Potter's Field because she left no estate and apparently had no surviving relatives. Feinberg expressed his hope that some of the wealthy jurors would step forward and assume responsibility for her burial. When none did so, some spectators made comments about rich people, which caused a lengthy period of sarcastic laughter. Father Schmidt became indignant. "Standing erect at the counsel table, he hurled two strings of rosary beads and a handful of money among the spectators in the crowded courtroom," the *New York Press* reported. "Schmidt's anger was caused by snickering among those directly behind him who thought they saw something humorous in the coroner's appeal for money to keep the murdered girl's body from Potter's Field."[14]

Inspector Faurot was sworn in after the lunch break. The panel was eager to hear exactly what Father Schmidt had said to the police at the time of his arrest. The distinguished-looking Faurot, his reputation already the stuff of legend, was sworn in by the jury foreman. Thanks to the daily press reports, which hailed the detective's rapid solving of the so-called Hudson River Mystery, his skills as an investigator were unquestioned and his judgments accepted as fact. As a result, he became something of a celebrity and was easily recognized on the streets of New York. "I arrested the defendant, Hans Schmidt, on the night of September 13, 1913, and afterwards took him to 68 Bradhurst Avenue," he said. The Inspector stated that he told Father Schmidt anything he said could be used against him and then questioned him about the murder. "He stated that he killed Anna Aumuller first in the rectory," Faurot told the court. "Then he said it happened in the house at 68 Bradhurst Avenue. He said he had cut her throat, carried her body to the bathroom, dismembered it there, and took it by the Eighth Avenue surface car, through 125th Street to the ferryboat at Ft. Lee and thrown the body overboard."[15]

Testimony concluded in the late afternoon and deliberations began immediately. Led by juror foreman, Theodore P. Shonts, president of the Interborough Rapid Transit Company, the celebrity jury retired to the adjoining room while spectators began to assemble in the hallways. Included on the panel were such luminaries as Marcus Loew, Vincent Astor, George W. Fairchild, and Jacob B. Prager. Though the jury decided within the hour, their decision was not announced until the following morning. "Upon the oath and affirmation of twelve good men of the State of New York, duly chosen and sworn, or affirmed, and charged to inquire, on behalf of said people, how and in what manner the said Anna Aumuller came to her death, do, upon their Oaths and Affirmations say: upon the evidence submitted, that the said Anna Aumuller came to her death on the 2nd day of September, 1913 at 68 Bradhurst Avenue by hemorrhage caused at the time and place aforesaid at the hand of Hans Schmidt."[16]

Father Schmidt listened to the decision without comment. Rumor swept the courtroom that consideration would be shown to the defendant's profession by releasing him to the custody of the church, pending future court appearances. But Coroner Feinberg declined, "It appearing to me from the within Inquisition, that the crime therein mentioned has been committed and there is probable cause to believe, Hans Schmidt, the defendant herein, guilty thereof, I hereby order that the said Hans Schmidt be committed to the city prison to await the action of the Grand Jury."

Known everywhere as the Tombs, the prison was New York City's most crowded detention center. Of its 450 cells, only 425 were available to actually house prisoners. The others were in wretched condition, unsuitable for human habitation. At the end of the summer that year, there were 727 men, women, and boys in those 425 cells. Fewer than 100 inmates had a cell completely to themselves. Most prisoners were doubled up and in some cases, even tripled up inside the cramped cells, which were designed in the mid-nineteenth century to house only one person. Inmates in the Tombs were usually angry and resentful since no prisoner was convicted of any crime. They were only accused of a crime, waiting for paperwork, or pending a trial.

Conditions were much worse for female prisoners, who were sometimes assigned the leftover cells in the basement or mixed in with the males, on a higher level, where they were subjected to constant harassment and sexual assault. "So dark are the women's cells and so uncleanly their appearance in the bottom tier that one does not marvel at the reek of disinfectants that permeates the whole prison. That is the smell of smells, though there are other forceful odors to be detected," said one newspaper report.[17]

The wretched conditions inside the city jail were widely known, thanks to the city's tabloids and especially the reports published in *Frank Leslie's Illustrated News* and *Harper's Weekly*. "I was put into a cell with ten other boys, most of them older than myself," one inmate later said. "The rats used to eat through our pockets to get at the waste crumbs of bread and sometimes we would place large pans of mush on the floor just to keep the rats from us."[18] The public was particularly repulsed by the often-repeated story of one teenage girl who was arrested for the crime of stealing a small sum of money for food. It was common at that time to place all prisoners, whether they were teenagers, male or female, together in the same cell-block, even the same cell. Placement was dictated more by availability of space than by common sense. "Police caught her one day and while awaiting trial in the Tombs, where prisoners often had to build their own fires to keep themselves warm, the helpless girl apparently froze to death."[19]

Part of the problem was the construction site of the prison. It was built originally in 1838 over an unstable tract of land known as the Collect, a large pond situated in the area now known as Lafayette and Mulberry Street.[20] Soon after its completion, the building began to sink into the mud. This caused the foundation to crack and allowed water to seep into the basement walls. For many years, this ongoing seepage resulted in a dank and damp condition that intensified the facility's medieval atmosphere. Originally called the Halls of Justice, it quickly picked up the nickname of the Tombs because it was modeled after an ancient Egyptian mausoleum.[21] Many people believed that water still flowed under the prison, which caused the bone-chilling dampness and provided a comfortable breeding ground for all sorts of vermin. "Of course, it is impossible to keep parts of the Tombs free from vermin under these conditions," the *New York Times* reported. "Doubling up in the cells, too few keepers, cells that never get the light of day, a constant come and go of all sorts of persons, including the most uncleanly, all these things make vermin a condition always to be reckoned with. The most that can be done is to fight it and keep it down."[22]

Disease was also rampant in the Tombs because only the most rudimentary sanitation procedures were in effect at the jail. With so many people entering and leaving the facility each and every day, it was impossible to maintain an acceptable level of cleanliness in a jail that was notoriously understaffed. Once a man entered the Tombs and remained incarcerated for any length of time, no one knew what would happen to him. He could be bitten by rats, assaulted by other prisoners, contract any number of diseases, or suffer the effects of contaminated food, a very common problem at the facility. "When a prisoner is put in the Tombs overnight," the *New York Times* said, "he cannot know that the next morning will find him vermin infested; when he lies in the Tombs for as long as four months waiting trial, he runs a very serious risk of contracting disease. And if a boy goes to the Tombs, no one can foresee what vices he may learn."[23] Simply put, when a man was banished to the Tombs, it meant imprisonment in horrendous conditions where he had a better than even chance of succumbing to pneumonia, tuberculosis, or an endless list of other diseases that were rampant in city jails and whose methods of transmission were poorly understood.[24]

"Schmidt spent a quiet day in the Tombs yesterday," the *New York Tribune* reported. "He arose shortly after 1 o'clock, had a light breakfast and went to mass. He read the newspapers before dinner and complained of not feeling well. He ate little and seemed moody. He took a short walk at 2 o'clock, the time when prisoners exercise, and then returned to his cell. He lay down, telling one of his keepers that he felt exhausted."[25] Schmidt continually wrote secret notes to reporters who published his comments in the next day's newspapers. "Father Schmidt changed his attitude so far as the newspapers were concerned," reported the *New York Herald*, "and yesterday in his cell at the Tombs, he answered a long series of notes sent to him by reporters."[26] He implicated Muret in the counterfeiting scheme and also in the murder.

Already imprisoned in Atlanta, Georgia, on counterfeiting charges, Muret became enraged. When he realized he might be brought back to New York to stand trial as an accessory to murder, he contacted his attorney and later wrote a letter to Schmidt on December 25, 1913. He begged his friend to tell the truth and exonerate him for the killing of Anna Aumuller.

Dear Sir,
The enclosed newspaper clippings compels me to direct these lines to you. You are the only
person in the world who knows how untrue and unfounded the things said in this, as
well in probably other papers are and I beg you in the name of fairness and justice to
have the newspapers correct these statements.

I never had even known that woman the paper refers to and the rest is untrue too. The
only time you ever spoke to me about this case was when you had me called to the tier
where you were incarcerated on the day before I left for Atlanta. . . . What have I done to
deserve all this? Do you not feel sorry that I have been torn out of my peaceful life only
because I have known you?. . . I do not ask you to have heart because I do not want
mercy; but I ask for justice. I am not a free man now. . . . If I do not get justice I shall
fight for it step for step. Up to now I have considered my being here as the will of God
and put up no fight, but I begin to see that it is the will of man and my indifference to
defend myself properly. I do not care to suffer even if unjustly but I desire to have the
truth known and to keep my name. My days are counted and it is only a short time that
I may have to live longer but if I die I want to die having it known that I am a victim of
circumstance and if possible I want to die not a convict but a free man. Therefore please
tell the truth!

I have to write this letter in English because it has to pass the sensor.

Very truly,
Ernest Muret
Atlanta, Georgia

On the night of October 3, Father Luke J. Evers, the prison chaplain of the
Tombs and pastor of St. Andrew's Church at City Hall Place, went to visit
Father Schmidt. Through the darkened corridors and twisting halls of the
city's bleakest jail, Father Evers made his way to the cell-block where Schmidt
was being held. The prison keeper took the priest down two levels to an area
of cells and rusted doors where forgotten men languished in the frigid
shadows of darkness and neglect.

"Help me, Father! Help me!" a voice called.

"I want to see my mother!" another pleaded.

"Go to hell, Father! There's nothin' here for you!" The men screamed
and cursed, banged on the steel bars with cups and wooden stakes broken from
their benches. They laughed, cursed, and spat on the priest as he passed.

"Hey, tell the coppers to drop dead!" one man said. The guard who
escorted Father Evers was a twisted old man who had spent many years in
the dungeons of the Tombs. He knew its corridors well. He also knew never
to turn his back on a prisoner, for some of them would kill in an instant with
little provocation, especially the gang members from the West Side like the
Whyos, the Dead Rabbits, and the dreaded Swamp Angels. Immersed in
the bitter hatreds inspired by the Five Points street wars a generation before,

St. Joseph's Church as it appears today on West 125th Street, Manhattan. The rectory is to the left in the photograph. (Courtesy of the author.)

the gangs still claimed their own territories, and the mere appearance of a rival gang member was enough to provoke a killing.

Father Evers arrived at the front door of the cell where he could see the silhouette of a man sitting in the rear of the concrete room. The single light hanging from a wire in the center of the ceiling was broken and the priest could not be sure it was Father Schmidt. He strained his eyes to get a better look as he grasped the cold steel bars with his hands.

"Hans?" he said meekly. "Hans? Is that you?"

The figure stirred slightly. He moved his feet and his arms folded across his chest, but he did not look up.

"Hans? I say, Father Schmidt?"

"Who's there?" a voice finally answered.

"It is I, Father Evers." He could barely see the man in the dark. There was little light in the dungeons because the cell-block was located on the lowest level. Only a single gaslight located 100 feet away, at the edge of the corridor, provided any light.

"Go away," he said. "I don't need you."

"Hans, I want to help you. Is there anything we can do for you?"

"Yes, you can leave me alone!" He turned his back to the door and rolled over.

"Hans, we only know what we are told by the police. We can help if you let us." The priest shifted his body slightly to get a better view. "Hans, did you do it? Did you kill Anna?"

There was no reply at first. From some unknown depth of the Tombs, a man screamed. There was a loud banging sound, then silence. More screams followed in the distance. A metal door slammed shut.

"I know you," Schmidt said, "I've seen you before. You work with the jails don't you?" For the first time, he rolled over on the wooden bench and Father Evers could just about see his face.

"Yes, I'm the prison chaplain here." Father Evers said calmly, "Hans, did you kill this poor girl?"

Father Schmidt rolled his eyes and folded his arms on his chest. He sat on the edge of the cot facing the older priest. He cleared his throat almost as an afterthought, before he whispered in a very low tone.

"Well, I think I did. Yes, I think I may have done it."

"But why, Hans? She was a fine girl! She couldn't . . ."

"No!" he said abruptly. "She was not what you think. St. Elizabeth implored upon me to sacrifice her. I had a visitation. She compelled me to sacrifice Anna. It was in her name I did it. Like the sacrifice of Abraham. I have a clear mind, Father, for this was holy work and it shall be done."

"Hans, people say you are not a priest, is it true?"

"Ha! I have them on that one. I was ordained just like you. Just like you, I say. In Mainz, Germany, by Bishop Kierstein."

"Why did you leave Germany, Hans?"

"I had a misunderstanding with the bishop," Schmidt said. "He did not like me. So I came here, but Father Braun took a dislike to me as well. And then St. Elizabeth told me to love this girl." The prisoner shifted around in the rear of the cell. He sat on the cot, rocking slowly to the right and left as he spoke. He ran his hands through his hair. It felt clammy and unwashed. "Es ist kalt hier, [It's cold in here]" Schmidt whispered. He wrapped his arms tightly around his chest. "The dampness gets into the bones of a man."

"Hans, we want you to cooperate, please. The police, they want to know everything, the printing press in the apartment, the letters, the papers, all the articles at 134th Street. The dioceses are very concerned. Cardinal Farley is very upset. He wants to. . . ."

"Cardinal Farley is not a higher authority than God!" Schmidt shouted. "It is Him I must answer to." He buried his head in his hands. Then he suddenly looked startled. "By the way, has the girl been located?"

"Yes, at least parts of her. Horrible! Horrible! How can we face our people, if we have a priest who has done such a terrible thing?" Father Evers shook his head. "The shame will be so great. How?"

"I wondered about that myself. And I am in sympathy with the church as you can imagine." His voice took on a conciliatory tone. "If there's anything I can do Father, please let me know. Maybe I could write a sermon to soothe the troubled parish. After all, the work of God is not easy to understand." He nodded his head mechanically while he made the sign of the cross.

"Not easy? God's work? It is not the work of God here, Hans. It is the work of the devil!"

"I didn't think so."

"Who would do such a thing?"

"I'm not sure. Except, I am thinking that it must be God's will. St. Elizabeth and all that."

"Hans, Hans!" Father Evers wrung his hands together. "Do you listen to what you say?"

"Sure."

"Then how can you believe it? Anna was such a sweet girl, a devoted Catholic, too. Why, many times . . ."

"Very devoted."

"I saw her in the church, in confession . . ."

"Me, too."

"Cleaning the aisles also. A good worker. She was always . . ."

"Ja, es ist Schade. [Yes, it's a shame.]" Father Schmidt clasped his hands together as if to pray. "A damn shame."

"Such a fine girl," Father Evers said. "And who is this Dr. Ernest Muret the police are talking about? Does he have anything to do with it?" He pulled his coat tighter around his body and buttoned it all the way to the collar.

"Muret?" Schmidt sat up rigid. "He's just a dentist, I believe."

"But why are they so interested in him?"

"I couldn't imagine. Maybe because of who he is. Nobody likes dentists."

"Such a horrible place here," Father Evers said, as he shook his head. "I have appealed to the city council so many times to repair this building."

"Oh, it's not so bad. There's a lot of time for reflection and prayer. I feel comfortable here."

"Hans, the cardinal wanted me to ask you about Louisville . . ." Schmidt began to unbutton his shirt. "He said that the police in Louisville have spoken to the New York police and they . . ."

"There's no air in here! Can you feel it?" Schmidt pulled his shirttails out of his trousers. "God, I need better air!"

"...want to talk to you about a little girl who was killed some years ago..."

"Louisville!" he shouted, "I never liked that city. The people were unfriendly there. They didn't like Germans, I can tell you that. I never felt such hostility as I did in Louisville." He rubbed his palms in a circular motion across his bare chest and breathed deeply, sucking in all the air his lungs could bear.

"Hans, what about the little girl?"

"What little girl are you talking about?"

"They said her name was Alma Kellner, a student at the St. John's Church on Clay Street. She was eight years old."

"I never heard of her! What are they talking about? I never hurt anyone, why is everyone against me? I'm just a priest who tried to do good. Father, you know me. I wouldn't hurt a little girl. Louisville!" he said with disgust. "I'll never go back there. I can't recommend it, Father."

The guard returned suddenly. "Time's almost up!" The man shook his keys, making a loud metal rattling that pierced the clammy silence in the hallway. He was responsible for the security in the jail, though his dedication was usually motivated by how much money he could extort from visitors. Since he could expect no such motivation from a priest, he would show no courtesy. "Let's go," he added.

"Hans, I have to leave. I might be back to talk to you later, all right?" The old priest rose to his feet.

"Well, that's okay with me," replied Father Schmidt. "But can you bring me something to eat? The food here is unacceptable."

"I'll try, but the guards are very strict—and corrupt as well."

"I know," said Father Schmidt. "They can't be trusted. Nobody in this place can be trusted. Think how I feel being here with all these criminals."

"See you later, Hans." Schmidt leaned back onto the bench in the recesses of the cell. His face blurred into the darkness.

"It's not so bad," he said as he rolled over on the cot to face the wall. "Really."

Father Evers walked through the dreary corridor, not daring to lose sight of the keeper. They were mindful to walk on the opposite side of the hall to avoid the prisoners who sometimes spit on visitors or threw objects as they passed by. When the keeper unlocked the first iron gate, the old priest hurried through, eager to get away from the cell-block and all its pandemonium. The heavy door slammed shut with a loud, sudden bang. In his cell, Father Schmidt sat up instantly.

"Father?" he called, "Father, have you gone?" He stood up and wrapped his hands around the metal bars. He listened for any sign of the old chaplain.

But there was only the shrill noises of the other inmates cursing, wailing, chattering on with each other, and their awful, unrelenting pleas for salvation. He felt a sudden stab of panic. On the floor of his cell, he noticed a large cockroach, its copper skin reflective in the dim light, crawl out between the bars and into the corridor. The insect made a sudden right turn and slithered down the hall toward the door. Schmidt went to the edge of his cell and pressed his cheek against the cold steel to get a better view, following the bug as far as he was able to, until he lost sight of it. He shook his head ruefully with a bitterness that brought bile to his throat and chilled the blood in his veins. The other prisoners called out to him but he could not respond, for he was indelibly fixated on the thought that even a cockroach had more freedom than he, a holy man. Tears welled up in his eyes.

"Has God abandoned me?" he cried.

15

Trial

The Manhattan Criminal Courts building was completed in 1885 and almost immediately the exterior walls began to bulge outward. Corruption of municipal inspectors during construction, which allowed the use of lesser quality materials, was suspected but could never be proven. The new building was a persistent eyesore that dominated the landscape at Franklin and Centre Street. City officials condemned the courts building from time to time but other than using some strong verbal diatribes in the press, nothing much was done about it. Smoky soot, the fine residue from home-heating fires in lower Manhattan, accumulated daily on its towering roof, especially when the temperature dropped and the fires burned all day long. Sometimes, it would build up to several inches thick. When it rained, it would mix into a sort of black mud that flowed down its sides in a river of grime that streaked the walls like paint. "It is one of the gloomiest structures in the world . . . tier on tier it rises above a central rotunda, rimmed by dim mezzanines and corridors upon which the courtrooms open and is crowned by a glass roof encrusted with soot through which filters a solid and viscous light. The air is rancid with garlic, stale cigar smoke, sweat, and the odor of prisoners' lunches. The corridors swarm with Negroes, Italians, blue-bloused Chinese, black-bearded rabbis, policemen, shyster lawyers and their runners, politicians big and little."[1]

All the Five Points crimes, and there were many, were prosecuted at the Manhattan Criminal Courts building. It had been the legal venue for many of the murder trials of the 1890s, the place where all the killers from the legendary street gangs like the Whyos, Bowery Boys, and the Plug Uglies met justice for the final time. In 1891, professional baseball player Jim Slocum was convicted of murder there, despite public pleas for leniency due to his abilities on the playing field.[2] A suspect in London's "Jack the Ripper" case, Carl Feigenbaum, received a death sentence at the Courts building for the 1894 mutilation murder of his landlord, Juliana Hoffman.[3] For many residents of the lower Manhattan region, the trial procedures of the city's courts provided a source of spectacular entertainment. It was a show that rivaled anything in the Tenderloin District theaters and, most important of all, it was free.

The trial of Hans Schmidt was scheduled for Monday morning, January 19, 1914. Charles Whitman, still basking in the glory from the Becker case, guided the prosecution team from opening statements to closing arguments. Though he did not attend court every day of the trial, he chose his most trusted assistant, James Delehanty, to handle the proceedings.[4] The case had lost none of its public appeal, and the bizarre details of the murder were still being published in the city's tabloids. Whitman realized the outcome of the trial could be a pivotal event in his political career. He knew a "not guilty" verdict would not be good for his crime-fighter image. "I'd like to be Governor," he told a reporter for the *New York Post* in 1912.[5] It was no secret that Whitman had always aspired for bigger and better things in the political arena. When he was not prosecuting high-profile cases in Manhattan that got his name in the daily newspapers, Whitman attended testimonials and formal dinners where he could plead his case for the Governor's mansion.[6] It was essential to him that the Schmidt trial close with a "guilty" verdict.

As Whitman assembled the final pieces of evidence for the trial, Koelble lined up his psychiatric testimony to support an insanity plea. Though he had several depositions from Schmidt's family in Germany and the favorable reports of three alienists who had examined the defendant in late 1913, Koelble knew that the plea was still a gamble. Thanks to the M'Naghten Rule, the criterion for an insanity defense was already well established by the turn of the century. However, a jury could still be persuaded by testimony of expert witnesses. Sometimes a defendant seemed so crazy that a jury would vote for insanity simply because they felt they had no choice. In other cases, some prosecutors failed to demonstrate to the court the essential elements of an insanity defense. It was not enough that the accused did horrible things. It had to be shown that he did not understand his action was wrong and that he did not appreciate the consequences of his act. In the case of Father Hans Schmidt, that was a major obstacle for Koelble to overcome.

The defendant had given many statements to the police, beginning at the moment he was arrested. His confession to Faurot at St. Joseph's rectory was particularly damaging. He also supplied written depositions on several occasions and spoke freely with the alienists at the Tombs. There was also the manner in which the victim's body was disposed. If Schmidt did not know what he did was wrong, why did he cut up the body and throw it into the river? Why did he try to clean up the Bradhurst Avenue apartment and burn the bloodstained mattress? There could be only one conclusion. He knew that if he left things as they were, he would be arrested and prosecuted. Therefore, he was aware that killing Anna was wrong. In spite of those factors, Koelble decided to show the jury that Schmidt was a deeply disturbed individual since he was a child and was not responsible for the murder because he was mentally ill. It seemed to be the only defense that had a chance of success.

Jury selection began on the morning of Monday, January 19, and moved fairly quickly, thanks to the continuous prodding by Judge Vernon Davis, a magistrate known for his fondness for quick trials. Many of the prospective jurors had to be disqualified immediately when they admitted to reading about the case in the newspapers and to having already formed an opinion about the defendant. There was also a general belief that married men were better for the defense since husbands tended to take their responsibilities seriously. Consequently, Delehanty objected to bachelors and would accept only those men who were married. On the other hand, Whitman believed that tall men were better for the prosecution because he thought shorter people were angrier and more hostile toward the world. After both prosecution and defense exhausted their challenges, they settled on their last choices by Tuesday afternoon. "The two men chosen yesterday to complete the jury were George C. Whitworth, a clerk of 138 West 104th Street, and Joseph C. Hogue, a wholesale wine dealer of 121 East Eighty-second Street," reported the *New York Times*.[7] By trade, most of the panel were businessmen and white-collar workers, such as accountants, bankers, and a few laborers. Traditionally, females were not selected to serve on juries.

On Wednesday morning, January 21, prosecution and defense delivered their opening statements. Delehanty told the court that the state would prove beyond any reasonable doubt that not only did Father Hans Schmidt murder Anna Aumuller, but cut her up into pieces and dumped her remains into the Hudson River. He disposed of her body for only one reason, Delehanty said, to escape detection and arrest for what he had done. That fact demonstrated that Father Schmidt not only knew what he did was wrong, but also showed that he knew the consequences if caught by the police.

Alfonse Koelble countered the prosecution by declaring anyone who would do what Father Schmidt did must be crazy. Koelble planned to introduce evidence and additional testimony from Germany that would prove that Schmidt was mentally ill and had been for many years. When Delehanty and Whitman heard the defense plans, they were pleasantly surprised. Though depositions from family members might help to show that the defendant was not mentally stable during his childhood, it would do little to show his state of mind during the killing. Under the requirements for the insanity defense, that was all that mattered.

The courtroom was filled to capacity. Reporters gathered in the press section, which was inadequate for the number of people who showed up each day. Those citizens who could not get seats knelt down behind the last row so as not to disturb the judge, who had a reputation of banishing anyone who did not obey his rules. Testimony was expected to be salacious and therefore unfit for young people or women. The *New York Times* said on January 22, "Few women were present yesterday. All who were about to enter the court room were informed of the nature of the testimony and although they were not ordered to stay outside, the doorkeeper told them that Justice Davis warned them that the testimony was such that no woman should hear."

The first witness to be called to the stand was little Mary Bann. The eleven-year-old girl repeated her Grand Jury testimony, which described the morning of September 5, when she and her brother, Albert, were playing in the waters of the Hudson River off Cliffside Park, New Jersey. She told the court that it was she who first saw the floating bundle they later dragged to shore. When she tore the paper off the strange package, a partial human torso rolled out, she said. At first, they did not realize what it was.

"I never saw nothing like that before," she told Assistant District Attorney Delehanty. "I ran and got my mother." After Bann's testimony, Irving Broander from Keansburg told the court how he found a human leg in the river. Delehanty then called upon Michael Parkmann of Weehawken to describe the bottom piece of the torso he found on September 7. As soon as Parkmann left the stand, Delehanty called for Dr. George King, the medical examiner from Hudson County who performed the autopsy on the body parts.

Dr. King was the medical superintendent of the Hudson County Hospital for the Insane for over thirty years. He had been associated with the county physician's office during that time as well and in 1911 became the county coroner. During the course of his duties, he performed over two thousand autopsies and became New Jersey's foremost expert on postmortem examinations. Dr. King was a distinguished and gregarious man who possessed a razor-sharp memory. Always confident of his opinions and articulate on the witness stand, his testimony made a noticeable impression on the jury.

"What conclusions did you arrive at after your examination of the Hudson River body parts?" asked Delehanty.

"The first observation I made, that dismembered part of the upper torso, the breasts, the mammary glands were enlarged and bulging, indicating that it was that of a female, the soft texture, the velvety feel of the skin and absence of hair, all indicated it was a female."[8] Dr. King went on to describe the other parts brought to him by the Hudson County Police. Even before he examined the lower torso and the thigh, he had his suspicions that all the parts were from the same body. After he and his assistant had a chance to study all the specimens, he was convinced.

"Can you say whether or not those portions of the body were from the same human body?" asked Delehanty.

"They are, unquestionably."

"Oh, and what leads you to that conclusion, Doctor?"

"They were severed between what is called the second and third lumbar vertebrae, spinal bones in the lumbar region. Between each vertebrae there is cartilaginous tissue, which is hard, but will permit a knife or sharp instrument to go through. The cut was right through that disc, as it is called, the intervertebrae disc. The knife went as far as it could until it met the resistance of the spinous process of the bone, the spinous process that bends down. Then that was cut through. Those parts put together fitted so approximately, so neatly, that they could not have come from any other person but the same individual."[9]

When Dr. King put all the parts, including the thigh together, it was obvious the pieces belonged together. "When we returned to Hoboken from the river," he continued, "we completely separated the bone from the fleshy part of the thigh and we found that it was an oblique saw cut serrated. It was obliquely cut and there remained on the thighbone, a splinter of bone. There was a corresponding depression in the stump. They both fitted exactly. And furthermore, the oblique of the cut and the circumference of the broken fragments corresponded so exactly that they could have come from no other place but from that one particular individual."

The witness then described how the head was severed from the neck, "between the fifth and sixth cervical vertebrae," and the condition of the internal organs. "The liver was attached to the diaphragm. That was intact. The stomach was there, the spleen was there and some of the large and small intestines were cut through. The pancreas could not be found."[10]

When Dr. King finished his testimony, which repelled the jury and spectators alike, Delehanty called on Annie Hirt, a friend and co-worker of the victim, who was also a housekeeper for the Church of St. Boniface. Hirt was a crucial witness because it was she who made the identification at Volk's morgue on September 15.

"Did you at anytime see Anna Aumuller when the upper part of her body was unclothed at the rectory of St. Boniface?" asked Delehanty.

"I did," replied Miss Hirt.

"Did you notice on her body any mark whatever?"

"I did."

"Describe it to the jury, please."

"It was a little brown mark on the right breast," she said as she held her hand up and held her forefinger and thumb apart to show its size. (Although earlier newspaper reports indicated this mark was on the left breast, sworn testimony says it was actually on Anna's right breast.) Delehanty asked if she had gone to the Hudson County morgue in Hoboken for the purpose of seeing a body. When Miss Hirt replied she had done so on September 15, Delehanty asked the witness what happened there. She said the coroner had displayed a portion of a female human body, the upper torso, which had been found in the Hudson River.

"I saw a little brown mark on the right breast." Delehanty showed the witness a photograph of the torso. "It was right there," she said, as she pointed on the photograph.

"And are you able to say whether or not that portion of the female body which you saw at Volk's morgue is a portion of Anna Aumuller's body?"

"Yes, sir. It is."

The witness placed her hands on her lap and glanced at Father Schmidt, who did not acknowledge her. Hirt also told the court that she had embroidered a linen blouse for Anna at her request. Miss Hirt said she hemmed the garment and identified the item of clothing found with the torso as the same one. She also said that during her last conversation with Anna, she had asked Hirt to be a godmother for her baby.

"I said 'maybe.'" Miss Hirt added that she was not sure how she felt about Father Schmidt since she did not know him. He left the parish before she was hired as the housekeeper.

"As a matter of fact," asked McManus during cross-examination, "had you ever seen Father Schmidt?"

"No, sir. Never." At the end of Annie Hirt's testimony, Judge Davis called a halt to the day's proceedings. He congratulated both sides for the speedy manner in which the day's proceedings moved along. Reporters hurried out of the courtroom and headed for their respective offices, eager to file the latest developments in the city's most lurid murder trial.

On the following morning, Delehanty called Inspector Faurot to the stand. The spectators anticipated Faurot's testimony because his reputation, already impeccable in the press, had grown to heroic proportions after it became known how he solved the Hudson River Mystery. Faurot was a stoutly built man with a square jaw and piercing dark eyes. He wore his mustache in the common manner of the day, which was broad, thick, and trimmed neatly below his upper lip. Dressed sharply in a fitted jacket with button-down vest, he projected a sense of professionalism and confidence as he took his seat to the left of Judge Davis and was sworn in.

"You are an inspector of the police department of this city, are you?" asked Delehanty.

"Yes," was the immediate reply.

"And were you in charge of the investigation into the supposed crime in connection with the finding of a portion of a female body in the Hudson River on September fifth and seventh?"

"I was."

Delehanty went on to inquire what steps were taken by the detective squad under Faurot's command in that investigation and how they came to be at the apartment at 68 Bradhurst Avenue on the night of September 13. The witness described the pillowcase wrapped around the female torso found at Weehawken. He outlined the sequence of events that led detectives to the Robinson-Boders Company at Newark, the Sachs Furniture Store on Eighth Avenue in Manhattan, and finally to the rectory at St. Joseph's Church. Delehanty asked Faurot to describe what he later found in the Bradhurst apartment.

"The dining room was used as a bedroom. There was an iron bedstead, bed spring, steamer trunk, two pillows, a coat on the radiator, a spool of wire, and a box on the bed spring containing fancy work, materials and needles and thread."

"What was the condition of the floors, Inspector?" asked Delehanty.

"Very clean. As though they had been scrubbed," Faurot replied.

"Did you see any blood spots on any of the walls or woodwork of the apartment?"

"Yes. On the foot of the iron bedstead, on the westerly wall of the dining room, on the door leading from the dining room into the small hallway leading to the bathroom and several spots of blood on the bathtub." Faurot said his team took some photographs of the apartment and the suspected blood stains. After searching the closets, hundreds of letters and postcards were found. Most of them, he said, were addressed to Father Hans Schmidt at various addresses. All of the letters were from an Anna Aumuller who listed her return address as St. Boniface Church on Second Avenue and Forty-seventh Street.

"What did you do then, Inspector?"

"We took some of the postal cards and two photographs we had found and went by automobile to the St. Boniface Church on East Forty-seventh Street."

"Photographs? And whose images were on those photographs, Inspector? If you know?" asked Delehanty.

"Yes, I know. They were photographs of Anna Aumuller."

"And what happened when you arrived at the church?"

"Well, we got to the church, me and Detective Cassassa. We found Father Braun and his sister there and we questioned them about Anna Aumuller and Hans Schmidt. Father Braun told us that Anna once worked there as a housekeeper but had since moved on. He said that Father Schmidt had been reassigned to another parish on 125th Street." Faurot told the court that Father Braun directed them to Marie Igler who lived at 331 East Seventy-seventh Street. She was a housekeeper at the rectory who brought Anna to work there in the summer of 1912. Marie would know where Anna went after she left St. Boniface's Church. Faurot said that Marie Igler and Anna Aumuller knew each other from the old country.

When Faurot and Cassassa located the address and woke up Marie Igler, it was after midnight, he told the court. Igler said that she had not seen Anna Aumuller in months, but that soon after she left St. Boniface's, she found another housekeeping job at St. Joseph's rectory on West 125th Street. Faurot, Cassassa, and O'Connell then went to that location where they found the rectory dark and closed. By then it was past 1:00 A.M. They knocked on the door for several minutes until someone answered, he said.

"Father Quinn admitted us," he told the court.

"Did you have some conversation with him at that time?" asked Delehanty.

"I asked him, at least I told him, that I would like to speak with Father Schmidt. He went upstairs and left us waiting. Cassassa followed him up the stairs. A few minutes later, Father Schmidt and Father Quinn came into the reception room."

"Tell us what transpired there?"

"As Father Schmidt came into the reception room, I requested Father Quinn to leave the room. As he left the room, I could see that Father Schmidt was in a nervous condition. I introduced myself and Detective Cassassa. At that time, there was a noticeable shudder or tremor and he clenched his hands." Faurot said they sat down in the office while Cassassa warned Schmidt that anything he said could be used against him. They questioned him about Anna Aumuller and Schmidt at first claimed he knew nothing of her. After a few minutes however, Faurot said Schmidt became extremely nervous. Faurot showed the photographs from the apartment and asked Schmidt if he killed her. Father Schmidt did not answer the question.

"I arose and patted him on the back," Faurot said. "I says, 'Speak up, tell the truth, Father!' He raised his head and said, 'Yes, I loved her! I killed her!' "
After Father Schmidt blurted out the admission, Faurot said he and his men

decided to search Schmidt's room. They all went to his bedroom where they found a large trunk by his bed. When they opened it, they found a receipt for the 68 Bradhurst Avenue in the amount of five dollars and a marriage certificate in the name of Johann Schmidt and Anna Aumuller. At the bottom of the certificate, where there should have been a minister's name who presided over the ceremony, there was none. "He admitted to me that he married her himself. In other words, he performed his own ceremony," said Faurot.

"What else was there, if anything?" asked Delehanty.

"There were four bank books, two in the name of Schmidt and two in the name of Anna Aumuller. There were two rings, a gold wedding ring in which there was a blood spot on the inside of the ring and a small ring with an opal. He admitted they were Anna's rings." Later, Faurot said, Father Schmidt took him to a vacant lot on 144th Street and Eighth Avenue where Schmidt said that he burned a bloody mattress on the day of the murder. "He pointed to a burned-out fire and he said that's where he burned it. He also said it was where he got the rocks which he placed in the bundles of body parts."

While Faurot testified, Father Schmidt stared straight ahead, never once looking at the witness. He tapped his right hand on the table impatiently while he waited for the testimony to finish. Occasionally, he would lean over to whisper in Koelble's ear and then sit upright as if he were preparing for a response. He seemed indifferent and at times appeared to be drifting off. By the time McManus began his cross-examination, Schmidt seemed removed from the proceedings.

"Inspector, is it true that you and your men broke into the apartment at 68 Bradhurst Avenue?" McManus asked.

"Well, we made an investigation and found nobody was in and nobody had come or gone."

"But you did break in, correct?"

"In the course of my duties as a detective. . . ."

"But you broke in, did you not?"

"Well, I guess so, yeah, I guess we did. After a surveillance of several days." McManus asked a series of questions to highlight the break-in and focused on the property that was seized from the apartment.

"Do you know whether any photograph of the defendant was found in the Bradhurst Avenue apartment?"

"I don't think there was. I don't remember any," replied Faurot.

"With respect to the trunk in the rectory, were there any marks on the outside of the trunk?"

"No, I don't think there was any. No."

"In other words, you can't really be sure that the trunk actually belonged to Father Schmidt, can you?"

"Well, it was found in his room."

"But did it have his name on it?"

"No, I don't recall."

"Interesting," said McManus. "So we have no way of knowing if the trunk was his?"

"Well, his marriage certificate and bank books were in there."

"Your honor, I move that the witness's answer be stricken from the record as being unresponsive to the question."

"Denied," said Judge Davis. "Come on, Mr. McManus, let's continue."

McManus returned to the defense table where he conferred with Koelble and Father Schmidt. After a minute's conference, he said, "No further questions at this time!"

When Faurot left the stand, Judge Davis concluded the day's proceedings. By then it was nearly 5:00 P.M. on Friday. Court was adjourned until 10:00 A.M. on Monday. Prosecution and defense had two days to rest and prepare witnesses for the following week's testimony. Koelble and McManus knew the case was going poorly. Because Delehanty's presentation was strong, it placed additional pressure on Koelble's medical testimony, which he had planned for Schmidt's defense. The entire case depended on the psychiatrists he would call to the stand the following week. It was up to them to convince the jury that Father Schmidt was insane.

16

Close Union

On Monday morning, January 26, 1914, Koelble delivered his opening statement for the defense. Afterwards his assistant, Terence J. McManus, told the court that the defendant was seeking an insanity verdict and described Schmidt's childhood experiences for the jury. He said that he planned to introduce testimony that would show beyond a reasonable doubt that his client was insane. For his first witness, McManus called the defendant's sister, Elizabeth Schadler, to the stand. She had traveled from Germany to support her brother during the trial. Elizabeth was ten years older than Hans, though she appeared to be younger. She wore a blue printed dress with a collar buttoned to her neck. Her dark hair was tied up on top of her head, which accentuated her strong facial resemblance to her brother.

"You are the daughter of Heinrich Schmidt, are you not?" asked McManus.

"Yes, I am," she answered.

"Are you related to the defendant?"

"He is my brother."

Elizabeth Schadler said that her brother's religious character was derived from their mother. "He was and always became more so. Our mother always prayed and always asked us not to say one more word than necessary, because she said every word that you utter which isn't necessary you have to give account for. To everyone, she was known as a religious woman."[1] Church was the focus of her life and she tried to make it the center of her children's lives as well. "When she was well, she went several times during the day."[2] The witness told the court that even when sick, her mother got out of bed to attend church services, leaving the housework and chores to the children.

Of Hans, she said, "He was very pious, very devout. He built altars in his room and wore the vestments of a priest. He would go through the motions of a priest saying mass. He knew it very well."

"How old was he when he did that?"

"He was very young, in age ten years, and even before that. He always studied day and night and went to church most of the time."[3] She said that Hans had told her about the voices he heard. He was thirteen years old when he said the voice told him he should become a priest. When she asked him who this voice was, he told her, "Die Stimme Gottes! [God's voice!]." Once, when Hans was sick, she had to take care of him while he was confined to bed. She noticed a strange birthmark on his left abdomen. "I said, 'What do you have on your side there?' He said, 'I am a special birth. Here blood and water flows.' As a young boy, he walked around the house with his hands joined at the palms as if in prayer, even if he wasn't praying."

"What about an incident at a shrine in the village of Wertheim? Will you tell us whether he spoke of seeing blood on that occasion?"

"We went to the Wertheim shrine that day when he was very young and when he returned, he told me, 'Now I have seen the place where a priest had dropped a cup of blood, holy blood. The cup fell over and the blood was changed and the head of Christ was the blood, which came out of this cup. I am happy now. When I become a real priest I will see the right blood."[4]

"Did he say he saw the head of Christ in blood on the altar at Wertheim, is that what he meant?"

"Yes," Schadler replied, "on the cloth covering the altar. It is preserved there since 1802 at the shrine. A holy relic, it is said."

"Was it the head of Christ, Mrs. Schadler?"

"I could not see it myself. But many people have. It was a miracle, God's message to the people of the village to hold their faith, to believe in Him and the blood of his only son."

"And Hans believed it as well, didn't he?" said McManus.

"Yes, he did. He saw it, the face of God. Er war ein heiliges Kind!"

"I'm sorry, Mrs. Schadler?"

"He was a holy child, I said."

"Thank you, Mrs. Schadler," said McManus as he returned to the defense table.

Delehanty rose from his chair to approach the witness stand, sensing that the dignified woman had made a favorable impression on the jury. "You love your brother, don't you, Mrs. Schadler?"

"Yes, I do. Always love him." She looked over at the defense table where her brother sat. "Hans, ich habe Dich lieb. [Hans, I love you.]" she said softly.

"You helped your mother bring him up, didn't you?"

"Yes, I did."

"And you, along with the neighbors in the town, called him 'little chaplain' isn't that right?"

"Yes, we did that. Der Kleine Pastor. I encouraged his religious behavior. I thought because he prayed so much it was the course of God, that God taught him to do that, you see."

Delehanty picked up his notes from the table and walked across the room in front of the jury. He scanned the faces of the panel quickly, trying to look into the eyes of each juror. "When he came home and told you that he hoped someday to be a priest and he hoped himself to see the blood of Christ on the altar, you didn't think that was strange, did you?" he asked.

"I thought as I always thought, that through this piousness and constant praying that God is more graceful, or giving more grace, and showed him that."

Mrs. Schadler was unperturbed and kept her arms folded on her lap. She explained how Hans thought of nothing else as a boy except religion. He went to sleep praying and woke up praying. Their mother thought it was a wonderful thing and could not wait for Hans to grow up so he could become a real priest. Although the family saw Hans as pious, they also thought him as strange as well.

"Was there a slaughterhouse near your home?"

"Why?" replied the witness.

"Please answer the question if you know, Mrs. Schadler," said Judge Davis.

"Yes, there was."

"And did the defendant go there as a child?"

"Yes, often, every day, in fact."

"And you never saw him kill an animal, did you, Mrs. Schadler?"

"That I don't remember. But he would not hurt an animal. Of that I'm sure."

"Only a person, then, perhaps?"

Koelble jumped to his feet. "Objection, your honor! There is no need for that. If counsel has a pertinent question, then let him ask it as such."

"Granted," said the judge. "Mr. Delehanty, no similar remarks, please."

"I'm sorry, your honor," he said as he looked over at the jury, but the point was made.

"Thank you, Mrs. Schadler, for your insightful testimony."

McManus then introduced the deposition of Heinrich Schmidt, the defendant's father, into the record. He still resided in Germany, and his statement was taken in the city of Frankfurt before Mr. H. W. Harris, U.S. Consul General, on November 8, 1913, upon request by the defense. Koelble himself had prepared the questions to be asked. He wanted to show that the defendant had serious psychological problems even as a child.

Heinrich Schmidt said he was sixty-five years old and resided in Schweinblein, Germany. He described his work with the railroad company where he was employed for over thirty-eight years. "I was away from home very much," he said.[5] He said Hans was a studious child who displayed an interest in philosophy at an early age. When the boy was only seven years old, he noticed that his son was unlike the other children and did peculiar things. "He killed geese belonging to my wife and played with their blood. He then took their heads and hid them in his pockets. When I asked him why he did that, he said, 'I like to see blood!'"

By the time Hans became a teenager, Heinrich said, he was distant and uncommunicative. The boy had few friends and became more engrossed in religion with each passing year. "He was absent-minded constantly," he told the court. "He couldn't give prompt answers at any time. He ran back and forth and then stood still, quietly, and gazed into nothing. No one could get a response from him. He was always secretive and said very little . . . and he was always very distant to me."[6]

Heinrich described the mental problems in his own family that caused the death of several relatives. Part of the defense strategy was to demonstrate that insanity existed in the Schmidt family and therefore could have been passed on to the defendant. Insanity was thought to be inherited and the idea that there was some type of gene that was passed from generation to generation grew in popularity during the late nineteenth century. These principles of inherited insanity were partly derived from a set of theories first published in 1859 that became one of the most influential books ever written.

Charles Darwin's *The Origin of Species* impacted upon the scientific world with all the subtlety of a hurricane. Many of the theories presented in Darwin's book concerning human evolution were carried over into areas of the social sciences. "Natural selection," "survival of the fittest," and "genetic destiny" became common phrases in psychology, sociology, and, later, in medical science as well. Contemporary scientists, captivated by Darwin's innovative research, applied modified versions of his theories into their own fields. Despite little or no academic support for these new applications, this practice continued well into the twentieth century.

One branch of the social sciences that experienced a dramatic transformation of thought and generated a dazzling litany of untested theories was criminology. Many psychologists began to believe that deviant behavior was genetic in origin. They became convinced that insanity was a biological defect that was passed from one generation to the next. Researchers, like Dr. Cesare Lombroso and Richard Dugdale, published huge volumes of uncontested observations that seemed to confirm theories of genetic destiny.[7] If just one person displayed mental problems or insanity, they said, his descendants might succumb to the same fate because the causal gene could be passed from parent to offspring. For this reason, Koelble felt it was important to demonstrate that mental illness existed in Father Schmidt's family.

Heinrich Schmidt told the court that his grandfather, Nicola Schmidt, died from alcoholism and insanity. He said that his mother's brother, Conrad Seppler, hung himself in 1901 and his sister, Margaret, also committed suicide by throwing herself into a river. Heinrich witnessed her death and watched the police pull her body from the water. He also described the death of his nephew, Otto, who shot himself in 1912 in Frankfurt. A niece was later confined to a mental institution, unable to cope with the family tragedies. Heinrich's wife, Gertrude, also had similar problems in her own family. Her brother, Lorenz Miller, hung himself in Gonsenheim in 1903. His daughter, Babette, hung herself a short time later as well. But whether these traits were inherited by the defendant remained an open question.

Heinrich said he had tried to help his son when he was arrested for forgery in the seminary. "I gave him at the time about 3,000 marks and also hired a lawyer for him," he said. "After he appeared in the Munich court, I took him to Jordanbad for the treatment, the Kneipp cure and the cold water cure." It was shortly after his stay at the spa, Heinrich told the court, that in 1909 Hans decided to travel to America. Since then, he never saw his son again.

Immediately after reading the words of Heinrich Schmidt, Koelble introduced the testimony of the defendant's brother, Karl. His deposition was also taken at the American Embassy at Frankfurt in November 1913. Again, Koelble's questions sought to portray the defendant as mentally disturbed. "He was an extraordinary man, never smoked or took alcoholic drinks," Karl stated. "A further account I must mention that he wasn't mentally normal was firmly impressed in my mind when I visited him at Engelberg. He wore under his priestly clothes a light pair of trousers and when he went walking with me, he left his cassock unbuttoned so far that his underclothing could be seen."[8]

When asked if he noticed that Hans performed any irrational acts, Karl replied, "When he came back from Munich, I then thought his behavior was such that he should not become a priest and told him so. He asked me not to make any difficulties for him and he was happy when he was taken back into the seminary."[9] Karl also said that despite his brother's request, he told a Catholic priest in Mainz his feelings about Hans. The priest indicated that he would notify the diocese in America about Hans' mental condition.

Next, the deposition of Katrina Schmidt, a twenty-seven-year-old cousin who lived in Frankfurt, was read into evidence. Her brother, Otto, had shot himself on January 4, 1912, in the downtown section of the city. She too, had noticed the strange behavior of her cousin on many occasions while she lived at Aschaffenburg. "He was so timid in his conduct, he ran so here and there in the street. One could not tell from looking at him what and where he himself wished to go."[10]

Koelble then introduced the deposition of an attorney who represented Father Schmidt in the forgery case in Munich. Johann Georg Boxheimer said to the court that he was hired by Heinrich Schmidt in January 1909 to defend his son against the criminal charges. During this time, he took notice of Schmidt's eccentric character. "I was of the conviction that he did not conduct himself as a mentally normal man and I incorporated this conviction in a motion to the court."[11] But when cross-examined, Boxheimer had to admit that he was not an expert in mental illness.

"I had the impression only as a layman," he answered, according to the deposition.

The next deposition to be offered as evidence was that of Father Jacob Sieben, age 30, a chaplain at Darmstadt, Germany. He knew Father Schmidt since 1903 and had served with him at Gonsenheim in 1908. During that time, Father Sieben lived with Schmidt at the rectory and they frequently had meals together. "I made the observation that Chaplain Schmidt must be a kleptomaniac," Father Sieben said in his deposition. "Regularly in the afternoon, I placed a tray with the coffee utensils outside of the door in the hallway. When I stepped out of the room a few minutes later the sugar and the bread which I just left there disappeared."[12] When Father Schmidt left on an errand one day, his room was searched and large quantities of the same bread and sugar were found in his dresser drawers. "The food was very plentiful and good and he never made any complaint. I can only add that he also had this mania in the seminary, in fact. After the meals he frequently came back to the servers and ate with them and also took bread and rolls with him."[13]

Koelble then read the testimony of Father Johannes Seebacher, age 34, into the court record. He said that he knew Father Schmidt since 1901 and was always perplexed by his behavior, especially at the church in Germany. "His confused look and his wild answers always impressed me," he said. "He often times seemed to wander in another world entirely and on being reproached concerning his faults he gave the most evasive answers. He also seemed to have a wild manner and on various occasions when he should have been at the church, he was away."[14] Father Seebacher also said that Schmidt was not knowledgeable of church customs and mass protocol. "In this he showed great ignorance in the liturgical parts most necessary," Seebacher testified. "On my rebuke, he gave an unconcerned answer."

After Seebacher's testimony, Judge Davis called an end to the day's proceedings. In general, both McManus and Koelble were satisfied. They demonstrated to the court that Father Schmidt had a long history of odd behavior, which was corroborated by family members and several priests who knew him before and after his time at the seminary. But Koelble knew there were risks to his defense. Once his witnesses took the stand, there was no way to control what they may say about Father Schmidt. Insanity was a difficult concept to some people. It was hard to understand how a man could behave in such a crazy manner and still be considered sane by the courts. They had to show that Father Schmidt did not understand that it was wrong to kill Anna and did not know what would happen if he did. And to demonstrate that, he had to bring in testimony that could be extremely damaging to his client. The jury would have to know how and why Father Schmidt killed Anna and what his actions were after the murder.

The following morning, Koelble called Dr. Frank A. McGuire, the city prison physician, to the witness stand. Though his office was located on West Eighty-fifth Street, Dr. McGuire maintained a separate practice in Lower Manhattan. Licensed as a doctor since 1877, he had been the Tombs physician for nearly ten years and was a familiar sight not only in the city's jail but in the courts as well.

"Doctor," asked McManus as he moved closer to the witness box, "do you remember the time when the defendant came to the city prison?"

"I think it was about the middle of September last year or thereabouts. I have not my notes with me now," he replied.

"And did you have any conversations with him?"

"I had him brought down in the office, where myself, Dr. Lichenstein, and Dr. Gregory had arranged for a meeting."

"Did he make statements to you?"

"He did."

"And what were those statements, doctor?"

The witness cleared his throat and glanced over at Father Schmidt who was sitting back in his chair, staring into space. He did not seem to hear or care what the witness said. Every few seconds, the defendant looked into the crowd of spectators to look for people he knew. If he saw an acquaintance, he would briefly smile or nod his head and join his hands together as if in prayer.

Dr. McGuire told the court that Father Schmidt gave his pedigree and a brief outline of his career as a priest. Then he began to talk about the insanity that plagued his family for generations. One by one, he described the suicides of his relatives in Germany, careful to list the deaths in chronological order.

"And from these statements, Dr. McGuire, and from what you observed of his conduct during these interviews, are you prepared to state whether or not the defendant was being rational or irrational?"

"Oh, irrational, I would say. Certainly."

"Thank you, Doctor," replied McManus, who returned to his seat. He knew that the prosecution would challenge the witness, but he was not concerned because the opinion of the witness was his own and could not be changed. Delehanty was already up on his feet.

"Let me ask you this, Doctor, how many interviews did you have with the defendant?"

"One or two meetings it was."

"And who made the notes at that time?"

"That would have been Dr. Lichenstein."

"All right, Doctor, and why did he say he killed her?" asked Delehanty.

"That he had an inspiration to commit the act from God, he said. I think I am quite sure of that."

"Where did he say he had that inspiration?"

"He had the inspiration in church after he prayed to God. Just before he went up there to kill her," said Dr. McGuire.

"I see. And after that, Doctor, what did he say about what he did after he finished praying?"

The witness fidgeted in his seat for a moment. He removed a handkerchief from his jacket pocket and wiped his brow. A look of discomfort passed over his face for a moment, and then he continued. "Well, he said he left the parish house, that is St. Joseph's, and went to the church, the sacristy, that he knelt down before the statue of Jesus Christ to pray. And he said he prayed there for quite some time. And that he felt the internal voices saying to him that the atonement had to be by love and blood, and after he was through with his prayers, he went to the house where Anna Aumuller, the wife, was and I forget now whether he said he turned up the gas, but his wife was sleeping, laying upon the bed and that he stooped down and kissed her on the lips, that he then had the instruments ready, which was a knife, he said, and he cut her throat. He then stooped down and partook of her blood as it flowed from the head, he then decapitated her, taking the head into the bath room, where he partook of more of her blood. He then came back to the bed. I then asked him did he do anything further."[15]

"And what did he say then?"

The doctor's voice lowered to a whisper. "He said 'yes.' I said 'what did you do?' "

"And doctor, what did he do?"

"He said that he had close union with the body."

"Close union? What did he mean by that?"

"Well, it meant that he had sexual relations with her." There were audible gasps from the spectators. Several women got up and began to walk out of the courtroom. Father Schmidt looked straight ahead, oblivious to the shame, indifferent to the reaction of the spectators.

"I asked him if he did anything else, too."

"Oh, and what did he say?"

"I saw that he did not care to answer the question and I had my ear close to him and then he said he committed sexual pervert acts upon the body. That was his statement—that he committed sexual pervert acts on the body."

"Doctor, what was the demeanor of the defendant while he told you these things?"

"Demeanor?"

"Yes, his demeanor, was he happy, sad, excited? What was the manner in which he told you?"

"Well, that's what struck me about him. His general indifference and his apathy. Even when reciting the revolting and gruesome details of the crime, he was perfectly indifferent, showing no responsibility, no reaction."

"Thank you, Doctor. That is all for now," said Delehanty.

"Anything, Mr. McManus?" the judge asked.

"No, your honor. I'm done with this witness."

Judge Davis called a halt to the proceedings and adjourned the court until the following day. As the guards surrounded Father Schmidt, he handed Koelble a piece of paper upon which he had scribbled a poem from memory. It was one he often recited to himself during times of stress or tribulation. The words comforted him and brought him solace in a world of confusion.

"Here, Alphonse, maybe this will help explain it," Schmidt said.

As the defendant was escorted from the room, Koelble read the words his client had written:

> The breeze—the breath of God—is still
> And the mist upon the hill,
> Shadowy-shadowy-yet unbroken,
> Is a symbol and a token,
> How it hangs upon the trees,
> A mystery of mysteries![16]

17

Jeliffe

Dr. Smith Ely Jeliffe was called to the stand as a defense witness. Along with Dr. Gregory and Dr. Karpas, Jeliffe was one of the alienists who had interviewed Father Schmidt on several occasions during November 1913. Though he had a wavering opinion of Schmidt's mental stability, he believed that the defendant did not know what he was doing when he killed Anna Aumuller. Koelble felt that Dr. Jeliffe's testimony was an important part of his defense because it would show that Schmidt had been mentally disturbed for many years and could not be held responsible for his actions. Jeliffe was a physician for over twenty-four years, a graduate of Columbia University and studied in Berlin and Paris with some of the best instructors in Europe. For the past sixteen years, Dr. Jeliffe had worked exclusively in the treatment of persons suffering from nervous and mental disorders. The district attorney's office had also used Dr. Jeliffe in past trials, a fact that would make it more difficult for the prosecution to discredit his testimony. After Dr. Jeliffe recited his résumé for the court, Terence McManus approached the witness stand.

"How frequently did you visit the defendant?" he asked.

"I saw him on eight occasions in November and on December 16. The shortest time was an hour; the longest was about four hours. I should say that on average, I spent about three hours each interview with him. At that time, I was with Dr. Gregory and Dr. Karpas at different times."[1] Dr. Jeliffe said that the defendant was very reluctant to speak at first and his manner was reserved. "He needed frequent urgings in response to our questions, either taking a few minutes before he would answer or frequent prodding."[2] But in time, Dr. Jeliffe told the court, Father Schmidt became responsive and talkative. During the interviews, Schmidt frequently arrived in a disheveled condition. "I would say that he was more careless or indifferent than anything else as far as dress is concerned," Jeliffe said.[3]

After the first few meetings, Schmidt spoke candidly about his childhood, his lingering sexual conflicts and his relationship with Anna and Dr. Muret. "Schmidt said that at the age of seven he had his first sexual experience with a friend of his by the name of Fritz Hugo," Jeliffe told the court. "This practice was carried on frequently between the two boys during the summer months. Later he masturbated excessively, he told us. It was about the age of twelve, and approaching his First Communion, that the sense of guilt entered into him. He became very sorry for what he had done; he frequently examined into his conscience. From the age of seven, however, to the age of ten the same type of act was carried on with his brother. He was constantly fighting the temptation and constantly failing."[4]

When Hans Schmidt was still a boy, Jeliffe explained, he visited a shrine near Aschaffenburg where, nearly 100 years ago, a miracle was said to have occurred. It was in the Wertheim chapel in 1802 where a priest had spilled a chalice of wine on the altar, causing a stain to appear that formed the image of Christ. That cloth had been preserved as a relic and pilgrims came from everywhere to see the holy cloth. When Hans visited Wertheim, the cloth had a tremendous impact upon the boy, Dr. Jeliffe explained. This was because his mother believed in the same miracle since she was a little girl, though she could not see the image of Jesus herself. But Hans saw the face of Christ very clearly. Her visit at the shrine with her son convinced Gertrude Schmidt that Hans was destined for the priesthood. It was at her urging that he decided one day to enter the seminary at the city of Mainz.

But Hans's later experiences at the seminary were not good, Dr. Jeliffe said. He was often ridiculed for his exaggerated pious attitude in church and his cavalier demeanor toward Catholic customs. After he came to America, he got into trouble at each parish to which he was assigned. Wherever he went, Dr. Jeliffe said, Hans found rejection and disrespect. It began at the Louisville parish in 1909 and continued right to the time he was assigned to St. Joseph's in 1913. These feelings of inadequacy hurt the young priest and he retreated further into himself, into a fantasy-like relationship with God, who Schmidt became convinced was the only one who understood him.

During Dr. Jeliffe's testimony, the defendant sat at the defense table next to Koelble, alternately wringing his hands and resting his head on the back of his chair. There were several priests seated among the spectators, including Father George Bruder of St. Joseph's and Father Braun of the church of St. Boniface. Whenever he saw the priests, even if it was every few minutes, Schmidt nodded gently in acknowledgment. To the amazement of many, the Catholic Church did not abandon Father Schmidt after he was arrested. Most clergy saw him as mentally disturbed but still deserving of their compassion and support. On January 23, the *New York Times* reported that the church had raised a substantial amount for a defense fund. "It was learned yesterday that the defense has raised a new fund to pay for the cost of the trial. This, it is said, totals nearly $10,000, the contributors being persons who believe that Schmidt is insane."[5]

"And tell us, Doctor, did Father Schmidt ever tell you that he had visions?" asked McManus.

"Yes, many times." Dr. Jeliffe looked down at his notes for a moment. "He said he first heard voices at the age of twelve and then again while in was in the seminary during his ordination. Again while he was in the church at Darmstadt. He said that he saw a vision of St. Elizabeth at those times."

"I see. And what about God Himself? Did he ever claim to see God?"

"Well, actually he did. He said that while he was in Gonsensheim he fell into a state of 'internal exaltation,' he called it. He said he saw Christ on the cross at that time bleeding and that He spoke to him and Schmidt spoke to Him back. He said it was very strange, almost dreamlike. The visitation took place when he was sick with rheumatism and he was very downhearted at that time."

"Doctor, did Father Schmidt ever talk about the man known as Dr. Muret?" When McManus asked the question, he noticed that the defendant jerked up in his seat and appeared to be very alert. The spectators became quiet and barely moved in their seats.

"Yes, he did."

"And what did he say?"

"He told me that he didn't like to talk about it. But with some reluctance, he said that he first met Muret in December 1912. He said he liked his appearance right away and that he liked his voice which was low and gentle."

"Was there any hesitancy when he told you this, Doctor?" McManus asked.

"Yes," Doctor Jeliffe said, "a great deal of hesitancy. Again, it was said in a very low voice. But I told him to go on, please. Don't be afraid."

"And did he?"

"Father Schmidt said he made the first advances, that he liked to hold his hand. He said that he used to hug him and then he kissed him. Muret told him that he did not like it at first. Then he would get into bed with him. Schmidt said that he loved him. He said that he liked Muret better than he did Anna. He said, 'There was never a grown-up man I loved as I did Muret.' Whenever Muret's name came into the conversation, he showed signs of suppressed excitement, like when he spoke of other sexual matters. He would sometimes blush. He would get up and go to the window and open his collar and take deep breaths. It was quite extraordinary."[6]

Dr. Jeliffe said that Schmidt was so in love with Muret that he even heard his voice during sleep, which he imagined to be the voice of God. Schmidt frequently had sexual dreams about Muret and fantasized about him when he performed mass. These obsessive feelings continued even during the time he was living with Anna and having sexual relations with her. "We then asked him, 'How did you feel during sexual intercourse?' And he replied, 'I felt in a state of exaltation, of being in communion with God.'"[7] Except for those times when the air was bad, Schmidt explained. He told Dr. Jeliffe that when the air was of poor quality, he "was always tired. It takes away all my power. When I get plenty of fresh air, then I am full of those powers." He claimed that he knew there was a way of transmitting thought and did it often when his powers were at their greatest.

When it came to Anna's murder, McManus wanted to show the jury that Father Schmidt acted under the belief that he was performing the will of God. If he believed the killing was a holy sacrifice, Schmidt might not be held responsible under the law. But McManus knew it was a difficult leap of logic for the jury to make. His only hope was to show the court that Father Schmidt did some crazy things in his life and, therefore, he must be crazy.

Schmidt had told Jeliffe that he first met Anna in 1912 at the Church of St. Boniface, where she worked as a housemaid for the rectory. Her job was to cook and care for the parish priests. During a period of sickness, Anna helped Schmidt back to health. "I wanted to love her from the very beginning. She took good care of me," he said. Over time, Schmidt fell in love with the pretty housekeeper, who had a warm and outgoing personality, just the opposite of himself. They had their first sexual intercourse in his sleeping quarters at the parish. "At first she ran away, but she came back," he had told Jeliffe. "To overcome her objections, I told her no one would know. At first we had sexual intercourse in the daytime, later she came nearly every night to me."[8]

"We asked him," Dr. Jeliffe told the court, "Did he feel any remorse? He said that it varied. Sometimes he would feel very guilty. Other times he thought it was God's will. He said to me, 'One day, I wanted to find out what God thought about me and Anna. At night I brought her before the altar and I had intercourse with her on the altar itself. I was very much excited; I was more worried about it than she. I kept looking at the Host all the time. There as no change. Either God would speak or show a light or something, some sign He would have given to express His disapproval. But towards the end, He made it known to me she was to be sacrificed.'"[9] With his last words, Delehanty was already on his feet.

"Doctor, are we to understand that the defendant told you he had sexual intercourse with Anna Aumuller on the steps of the altar at St. Joseph's Church?"

"Well, that's what the defendant said," came the reply. The spectators stirred in their seats, and audible grumbling could be heard in the room.

"And he saw nothing wrong with that?"

"If he did, he never expressed it to me." McManus walked over to the witness and asked him to continue. Dr. Jeliffe told the court that despite God's call for a sacrifice, Father Schmidt continued to see Anna. "He told me that he used to go to restaurants and plays together with Anna. He wore his collar at those times, to which she objected. He used to meet her in Bronx Park at night and have sex with her there on the ground." Sometime in August, Father Schmidt told Anna that God had asked him to sacrifice her.

"And what did she say to that, Doctor?" said McManus.

"He told me that Anna had used an ugly expression: 'Hans, du bist verucht! Hans, you are crazy!]' But he continued to tell her the same thing, over and over. 'I was thinking about it all the time,' he said. 'It would be with me from hour to hour. Sometimes I was able to forget it, and then I would wake up in the middle of the night and would hear the voice telling me to sacrifice her.'"[10]

"Doctor Jeliffe, is there any chance in your opinion, in view of the nature and scope of the examination that you made and the number of those examinations, that this defendant was shamming insanity?"

"Absolutely not," replied the witness, "absolutely impossible. A man cannot sham insanity such as he has any more than I can make an apple or an orange; it is a product of nature, not a product of artifice; no man can make it; it grows that way."[11]

"So then, Doctor, are you able to state, from the examinations you have made, from the statements made by this defendant to you and from all your observations of the defendant, whether or not at the time of the commission of this act charged in the indictment, to wit, the murder of Anna Aumuller, this defendant understood the nature and quality of his act?"

"In my opinion, he did not understand the nature and quality of his act."

"And was he in such a state of mind as to know that the act he committed was wrong?" McManus stood in front of the jury and stared at the panel as he asked the question.

"In my opinion," said Dr. Jeliffe, "he believed he was right and was not in the condition of mind to know that he was wrong."

"Thank you, Doctor." McManus turned to the judge. "Your honor, that concludes defense witnesses."

"Thank you, Mr. McManus," the judge replied.

Delehanty paced in front of the witness stand. "I only have a few questions, your honor," he announced. Delehanty surveyed the jury and came to the conclusion that they were thoroughly repulsed by the revelations of Schmidt's sexual promiscuity. "Doctor, I would like to address the physical examination of the defendant that took place in the Tombs on November 22. Can you tell us what happened on that day?"

"Objection!" yelled Koelble. "Your honor, there's no basis for that testimony. We never brought it in."

"I disagree," replied Delehanty. "Your honor, defense solicited testimony pertaining to this witness, and Doctors Gregory and Karpas, that they examined the defendant on eight occasions in November and December last. In fact, this witness's entire testimony concerns those examinations. We are simply asking about one of those exams to which the witness did not attest to until now."

"I think he's right, Mr. Koelble," said Judge Davis. "Proceed, Mr. Delehanty."

"All right, Doctor, can you now tell us about that exam of the defendant on November 22 last?"

Dr. Jeliffe put aside his notes for a moment. He took off his glasses as he spoke. "My best recollection is that on that date we made a physical examination of the defendant. We went over him systematically to determine the presence of any anomalies or abnormalities so far as the muscular or sensory part is concerned."

"And what did you find?"

"Well, there were certain little asymmetries in his body, that is, certain irregularities in the two sides of his body. There was a striking feature, that is striking to me at the examination, that I might say impressed me and that was the striking contrast between the man's face, which was somewhat aesthetic, finely chiseled, more or less, I might call it a beautiful face, with a body which was distinctly muscular, hairy, strong and massive and powerful, and I might say I had expected a more delicate type of bodily structure in looking at his face. Whereas the body was distinctly massive and stocky and gave the impression of a very powerful man from the standpoint of muscularity of the body, it was very hairy. But there was a striking anomaly, abnormality if one wants to so characterize it, at the base of the spine. There was a collection of hair, a very definite growth of hair just at the base of the spine. This occupied a triangular area of perhaps two inches by perhaps four inches, maybe six inches. It was a very striking anomaly, not unknown as a matter of scientific curiosity among those of us that have spent some time in studying abnormalities of this kind, if I may say, the animalistic features of the human body."[12]

"I see. Doctor, let me ask you this—did the defendant ever display to you that he did not know or was not aware of the fact that murder was wrong and against the law?"

"No, I don't think he did," Dr. Jeliffe replied, "but come to think of it, I don't think I ever asked him that."

"Well, did you ever ask him if he wanted to be alone with Muret?"

"Alone? You mean without Anna?"

"Exactly."

"We asked him, 'Did you not have the thought that Anna might pass from life so that you might be alone with Muret?' And he answered, 'I loved her always. I never ceased to love her, but one thing I noticed, though I was always good to her, but I was not as anxious to see her as before.' "[13]

"Interesting. And Doctor, did the defendant ever tell you about how he treated the deceased? For example, did he ever hurt her?"

"The impulse came and went, he told us." Dr. Jeliffe then read from his notes to the court. "He said that 'Anna often complained of my fierceness. I used to bite her sometimes; I liked to taste the blood. I would bite her on the arm, I would bite her on the breast. There would be teeth marks and it always made me feel better.' "[14] When Delehanty glanced at the jury, he saw several jurors wince at this last statement.

"Yes, Doctor, and let me ask you this. Did Hans Schmidt describe how he killed the victim?"

"Objection!" yelled McManus. "Your honor, the defense stipulates that the details of the event are such that they would upset the court and therefore prejudice my client. The court is aware that the victim was killed. That is enough." Judge Davis looked toward the prosecution table.

"Mr. Delehanty?"

"Your honor, we are simply asking what the defendant said. This witness was called to the stand by the defense and is testifying to statements made to him. In that spirit, we are now asking about those same statements. We can't allow only the parts of the conversation that are beneficial only to the defense, can we? Let's hear the entire conversation is all we're asking."

"I agree," said Judge Davis.

"So, Doctor, did the defendant describe what he did to the victim?"

"Yes, sir." Again, Dr. Jeliffe read directly from his notes. "He said to me, 'As I went in the moon was shining. There was no light. I was in such a state. I knelt on the bed. She slightly turned her arm. I kissed her for the last time. She had her nightdress on. That same evening I had bitten her and had tasted some of her blood. I had a desire to taste more. Then I did it. I cut her throat with the right hand. I cut almost through the neck. I did not close her mouth, I didn't think of it. As the blood ran all over her, it excited me greatly. I attempted intercourse with her while the blood was flowing. I was pressing against her. I felt perfectly satisfied. I was not frightened at all. I took some blood from the throat and mixed it with water and drank it. I then carried her out to the bathroom." When the witness finished the last sentence, he removed his glasses and looked up. Every person in the courtroom stared at Father Schmidt in shocked silence. Delehanty paused before he asked his next question.

"In other words, he had sexual passion? Even at this time?"

"He told me, 'When I saw the blood, it was a sexual passion. Before that it was religious ecstasy. During the act of cutting her throat I was overcome by sexual impulse. It's hard to analyze now. I thought I was acting on the will of God. I had prayed before leaving the parish house. I had spoken to God directly. I felt in a state of elation that I had been in communication with God. I fixed the blood and water and took it like in the saying of the mass. I said mass a few hours later.' That's what he said to me."

"Mass? The defendant told you he said mass that very same day?" Delehanty asked in a rising tone of voice.

"That's what he told me. A few hours later, he said the first mass of the day at St. Joseph's."

Some of the spectators yelled out from the audience. "Blasphemer! Heathen! Murderer!" A woman screamed and the men cursed. "Bastard!" one man yelled out. The police guards moved closer to Father Schmidt, who cowered in his seat. The uniformed men lined up behind him and faced the spectators. The judge slammed his gavel on the bench. "Order here! Order here! I will not have these outbursts in my court. I'll clear the room if I hear any more of it!" The room settled down but the atmosphere had changed. The spectators were angry. They saw a priest who had deceived his flock, murdered an innocent girl and performed acts upon her body that were repulsive, evil, almost satanic. And after the killing, Father Schmidt had presided over a mass and distributed Holy Communion as if nothing had happened.

"All right, Mr. Delehanty, let's push on," the judge ordered.

"Doctor, did you ever get a reaction from Schmidt while he told you this story? Did you take his pulse, for example?"

"Well, yes, we did. We had taken his pulse frequently on previous occasions and found that it ran from about seventy-two to about eighty, and the pulse while he was telling this story was also about eighty and mostly below."

"That is a perfectly normal pulse, is it not then?"

"Perfectly."

Delehanty nodded in approval so that the jury could see the look of satisfaction on his face. Then as he walked back to his seat, he shook his head slowly as if to indicate disgust.

"Normal?" he asked.

"Yes, normal," said Dr. Jeliffe.

"Thank you very much, Dr. Jeliffe."

Koelble and McManus were finished with the day's testimony. To some in the court, the point had been made that although Father Schmidt was mentally unsound, if not a raving murderous lunatic, he seemed to know what he was doing when he killed Anna. His family had testified to his mental problems, doctors had confirmed it, and the prosecution seemed unable to change the opinion of any of the defense psychiatrists. From the reaction of the jury, Koelble was confident they saw his client as mentally disturbed. But things were not going as well as he had hoped. Each day of the trial, the crowds outside grew larger and larger. Special squads of police from the First Precinct had to be called in just to maintain order. Dozens of spectators lined up each morning along Centre Street waiting for the doors to open so they could grab the few seats left that were not taken by the press, the celebrities, and politicians.

As guards escorted Schmidt from the courtroom, Koelble studied his client while he made his way to the door. Revulsion toward Father Schmidt had intensified for sure and the hostility in the courtroom was almost tangible. Koelble realized that a priest who kills an innocent girl, then commits horrendous acts upon her corpse was bad enough. But a priest who does all these things and then performs a holy mass while his hands are literally still dripping with her blood, well, that was something else.

⓲

Zech

On February 3, Koelble had planned to make his closing statements. But during the morning conference in Judge Davis's chambers, District Attorney Whitman informed him that he planned to call one final witness. "No way," replied Koelble. "You already closed your case! You can't reopen it now."

"What's this all about, Mr. Whitman?" asked the judge.

"Your honor, we only recently learned of a very important witness that is vital to the prosecution," he said. "The police only visited me last night to tell me that they have located the man and were able to produce him this morning."

"Your honor," interrupted Koelble, "this is very unfair. The district attorney's office had all the time in the world to do their work. I think it is inappropriate at this stage of the proceedings to bring in a witness for which the defense is totally unprepared." He pointed to Whitman and Delehanty. "They're only doing this because they know they're losing their own case!"

"Hardly," said Whitman. "The witness sheds new light on our assertion that the defendant is shamming insanity and always has been. It is essential, your honor, that the people be allowed to bring in all the evidence available. After all, we are after the truth, aren't we, Mr. Koelble?"

"What does this trial have to do with the truth?" interjected McManus. "Your alienists simply say what they know you want to hear. They're paid by the state, what do you expect? They don't examine in . . ."

Judge Davis banged his gavel on the top of his desk. "All right gentlemen, let's take a breath here. Everyone sit down, please." The men sat in the chairs around the judge's massive oak desk. As the lawyers grumbled under their breath, Judge Davis stood and lit a cigar. He took several puffs until it was lit and the end burned a fierce reddish-orange color. "I will allow the witness to testify as long as it applies directly to the prosecution's assertion that the defendant is faking insanity . . ."

"Thank you, your honor," said Whitman as he began to stand.

" . . . and the defense has ample opportunity to challenge the witness as well."

"I still think it's too late, your honor!" replied Koelble.

"Let's go, gentlemen," said Judge Davis. "Justice is waiting."

The courtroom was once again filled beyond capacity. Reporters wrote furiously on their paper pads as the court clerk announced the proceeding.

"All rise!" he shouted. The judge entered through a side door and sat at the bench while the spectators took their seats. Whitman had already made the decision to question his final witness. He rose from his seat and walked to the center of the courtroom.

"All right, Mr. Whitman, proceed," said the judge.

"Call Dr. Harold Hays!"

The rear doors opened and a slightly built man, wearing thick glasses and looking vastly uncomfortable, entered the courtroom. He stood by the witness chair and took the oath. After he sat, he unbuttoned his jacket and looked at Mr. Delehanty.

"Are you a physician regularly licensed to practice in the state?" he asked.

"Yes, sir."

"And licensed in the spring of 1913?"

"I was," Dr. Hays answered.

"Did you have any connection with the Postal Life Insurance Company at that time?"

"I was one of the insurance examiners."

Delehanty handed the man a piece of paper and asked him to look at it. The witness studied the document and then looked up.

"Have you seen that paper before?"

"Yes, I did. I put my signature on that when I was handed a check for $5 from a certain individual in payment for an examination."

"Objection!" yelled Koelble from the defense table. Father Schmidt stood up and tried to talk.

"Your honor, I am just trying to . . . ," Schmidt began.

"Mr. Koelble," said Judge Davis, "have your client take his seat!" Koelble whispered to Schmidt, who sat down, visibly annoyed.

"Your honor," said Koelble, "I really must object to this testimony. I think I know what Mr. Delehanty has in mind and he can't introduce this type of evidence unless it has a bearing on the case at trial. I don't see . . ."

"It does have a bearing, your honor," replied Delehanty. "I just need to finish my examination here."

"All right, let's continue. Next question," said Judge Davis.

"Dr. Hays, was that individual a man or a woman?"

"Oh, it was a man all right. And there was a woman with him. The woman to be examined."

Delehanty lifted a photograph from the defense table and approached the witness stand. "Dr. Hays, can you look at this photograph and tell us if this is the man who came to you that day?" He handed the photograph to the witness, who studied it for a few seconds.

"That certainly looks like the man," he said.

"Your honor, I want it placed on the record that it is a photograph of the defendant," said Delehanty. Father Schmidt shifted around in his chair and grabbed the arm of Terence McManus and whispered into his ear. "I also show the witness two other photographs, exhibits 20 and 21, and ask him if he recognizes either one."[1]

Dr. Hays took the photographs and studied them carefully. After a few moments, Hays said that he thought he had seen the woman before. "They both look like the woman that was with him that day when he applied for insurance. This man said his name was Hans Schmidt and that was his wife and the name on the application I remember was Mrs. Hans Schmidt." But the witness could not be sure. When pressed for a positive identification, Dr. Hays replied, "All I can say is that they look a great deal like her. I would think it is the same individual. I cannot swear positively."[2]

"Did you ask her name?"

"Yes, sir, I did."

"Objection!" yelled McManus, up from his seat in an instant.

Judge Davis looked over at the defense table. "You may have an objection to all this and an exception, Mr. McManus, if you wish," he said simply.

"Yes, your honor. I object as incompetent, irrelevant, immaterial, and not sufficiently identified."

"Very well, continue, Mr. Delehanty."

"She said her name was Mrs. Hans Schmidt," recalled Dr. Hays. He went on to describe the woman but was unable to say that it was Anna Aumuller. When the examination was over, Dr. Hays said, he filled out the application for a policy in the amount of $5,000. It went into effect in April 1913, and the beneficiary was Father Schmidt. During cross-examination, McManus tried to shake the identification by Dr. Hays, but the witness was emphatic. After his testimony was completed, McManus argued that there was nothing wrong about a man trying to obtain insurance for his wife. He moved to have the entire testimony of Dr. Hays removed from the record as immaterial, but Judge Davis denied the motion. Delehanty responded by pointing out that the matter applied directly to the defense's assertion that Father Schmidt was insane and that he received a command from God to kill Anna Aumuller.

"Your honor, again, there is nothing wrong with a woman obtaining life insurance for herself," declared McManus.

"If it was Anna Aumuller," added Delehanty.

"We have no proof it wasn't, judge!" No sooner had McManus uttered that statement, than Delehanty jumped at the opening.

"Judge, I would like to introduce one more witness in regards to this matter," Delehanty announced. As soon as the prosecutor made that request, McManus realized he had fallen into a trap. He said later, "I knew I made a mistake the moment I said there was no proof."

"I call Bertha Zech to the stand!"

"Objection, your honor! The prosecution already closed his case. How long is this going to go on? It's not fair if Mr. Delehanty can simply call anyone to the stand that pleases him."

"Mr. McManus, let's get to the bottom of this issue once and for all. I'll allow one more witness, Mr. Delehanty, that's all." Judge Davis turned to McManus. "Objection overruled," he said.

"Exception!"

"So noted."

"Bertha Zech!" said Delehanty. The guards held the rear doors of the courtroom open until a trim, neatly dressed young woman entered. She had a gentle face, framed by long, dark hair that fell upon her square shoulders, and she walked with the quiet assurance of a woman who was confident of her looks. Her dress was business-like and fit a well-formed body that showed ample curves and a sensuality to which every young man in the room responded. She stood quietly while the clerk read the oath.

"I do," she responded, and sat down gracefully.

"Miss Zech, do you know the defendant?" asked Delehanty. He saw Father Schmidt turn away when he asked the question.

"Yes, I do. I met him several years ago in a nightclub on the West Side."

"You are aware he is a priest, are you not?"

"Yes, I am. But the night I met him, he wasn't wearing a collar."

"I see. And Miss Zech, did you ever accompany Father Schmidt to the Postal Life Insurance Company?"

"Yes, I did. In April 1913."

"And what did you do while you were in that office?"

The witness looked over at the defense table, where Schmidt had his face buried in his hands. He was slowly shaking his head back and forth, but the witness felt no pity for the defendant.

Only the day before, she was hiding in New Jersey, trying to start a new life. She wanted to avoid the trial and the endless publicity. But District Attorney Whitman, aided by Inspector Faurot, found Bertha Zech and convinced her to testify, though at first she refused. Whitman showed her the statements made by Schmidt in which he said she had helped in the murder and disposed of some of the body parts. Zech became furious and agreed to testify. She never liked Father Schmidt anyway, even before the murder. Whenever he came to visit Muret, Schmidt always asked her to have dinner with him or to come to his apartment. In the office, when Muret was not around, he grabbed her breasts and kissed her neck. He offered her money to have sex with him and treated her like a whore. "Yeah," she told Whitman, "I'll testify."

"Well, Hans asked me to come with him to the insurance company to get some insurance for Anna. He said it was a surprise for her. He said that I would just have to say that I was Anna, that I was Mrs. Schmidt. It would be easy. He said that the doctor would examine me and it would be no problem."

"And did you do that, Miss Zech?"

"Yes, I did. He and Ernest were my friends. I honestly didn't think I was doing anything wrong. Ernest was so good to me, so good. I would do anything for him. I couldn't believe what happened . . ." Her voice trailed off. She went on to describe how she met Father Schmidt when she visited the West Side club with Muret in the autumn of 1912. Schmidt was a gentleman, she told the court, very polite and friendly. They all went out together on several occasions after that first meeting. Muret later confided in Bertha that Schmidt was a priest and that he had fallen in love with a woman named Anna. Then in the spring of 1913, Anna said, Schmidt asked her to go to the insurance company with him.

"And what name did you sign on the insurance application, Miss Zech?" asked Delehanty.

She paused for a moment and glanced over at the defendant, who never looked at her the entire time she was on the stand. "I signed it, Anna Aumuller Schmidt," she said.

"No further questions, your honor." At the defense table, Koelble and McManus discussed her testimony. They knew that the damage had been done to their client and little could be achieved by additional questions to which they did not know the answers. That could be a disaster. Who knew what else Bertha Zech would say? What other surprises did she have hidden? Koelble looked over at Delehanty, who had his hands folded on the table. McManus stood up.

"No questions for this witness, your honor," he said. "For the record, your honor, Father Schmidt has decided not to testify at this time." McManus shuffled some papers around on the desk. "The defense rests, your honor."

The next day under the headline, "Find Woman Dummy Who Aided Schmidt," the *New York Times* reported the story. "Assistant District Attorney Delehanty provided a surprise yesterday, just before the close of the trial before Justice Davis in the Criminal Term of the Supreme Court, by calling a new witness who gave testimony tending to disprove Schmidt's assertion that he killed the Aumuller woman because he felt that the Deity had ordered him to commit the act. Mr. Delehanty established the fact that in April 1913, long before Schmidt says he received the command from the Deity, he attempted to obtain insurance for $5,000 on Anna Aumuller's life."[3]

It was obvious to the jury that if Schmidt simply wanted to insure Anna, he would have taken her to the examination. Instead, he took Bertha Zech to pose as his wife. This indicated only one possibility: Schmidt did not want Anna to know that he was insuring her life because he was planning to kill her. The time of the application was months before Schmidt claimed to hear the voice of God demanding that he perform a "sacrifice." After the day's testimony, Koelble and McManus urged Father Schmidt to plead guilty and put himself at the mercy of the court. His life might be spared. But Schmidt would not hear of it. He was convinced that the jury would find him insane and later confine him to a mental institution where the church would use its influence to get him out.

At 9:30 A.M. on Thursday, the courtroom was, as usual, overflowing with reporters, lawyers, clergy, and spectators. Everyone connected with the case wanted to be present on this day because after the judge charged the jury, a verdict was possible at any time. Though a quick decision was not anticipated, the prudent approach was to be ready nonetheless. The last half of the trial turned into a battle of the alienists, with some experts supporting the notion that the defendant was faking insanity and others, like Dr. Jeliffe, taking the position that Father Schmidt was mentally unstable. It was up to the jury to sort it out. Judge Vernon Davis began his charge to the jury shortly after 10:00 A.M.

"The court now is about to submit for your final decision all the questions of fact in this case," he said. "None of those questions of fact is to be decided by the Justice presiding. The decision of those questions remains wholly with the jury. This case is a grave one. The issues are grave, not only to the defendant but to the administration of criminal justice in this state and the decision should be made by you after careful conscientious examination of all the evidence in the case."[4] Judge Davis said that both sides, prosecution and defense, had presented their case with clarity and attention to detail. He said that the defendant has the presumption of innocence and that presumption continues throughout the entire trial until it "is overcome by proof to your satisfaction beyond a reasonable doubt that he is guilty. The burden of proving his guilt rests upon the people."[5]

The jury had two issues to decide. First, it had to be determined if Father Schmidt actually murdered Anna Aumuller, by the evidence and testimony offered at the trial. Second, did the defendant kill the victim in a deliberate and premeditated fashion? If so, then the jury had to find him guilty of Murder in the First Degree. However, if the jury decided that Father Schmidt was laboring under such a delusion as to think that he had been ordered by God to commit the murder, and he believed that it was the right thing to do, then the defendant was insane and must be found not guilty for that reason.

"The law presumes that at the time the defendant deprived Anna Aumuller of her life, if he did so, he was sane and was responsible for his acts," Judge Davis explained. "That is the presumption. And when the defendant offers proof that he was not legally insane at the time he committed the act, that raises an issue in the case which has to be met by the People."[6] He reminded the jury that it was not enough that the defendant was an idiot or a lunatic. It had to be shown that "he was laboring under such a defect of reason as to not know the nature and quality of the act he was doing and not to know that the act was wrong."[7]

In arriving at their decision, the jury had to look at all the available evidence and draw their own conclusions. Expert testimony from the alienists was diversified and, at times, in complete disagreement. How was the panel to decide which expert's testimony was valid and which was not? "What they are doing here in court is to express their opinion as to his mental condition," Judge Davis announced. "You are to say what is the fact. So, it is opinion evidence, but you have no right to reject it arbitrarily. In fact, it is your duty to consider it along with all the other evidence, test it, examine it, bring as much of your thought to bear upon the consideration of evidence as you bring to bear upon all the other evidence."[8]

He said that if the jury found that the expert testimony was of no value, they were duty bound to reject it. Each expert must undergo the same scrutiny by the panel. In doing so, the jury was allowed to consider the statements made by the defendant to the examining alienists. They could be used to determine the sanity of Father Schmidt and provide additional insights to the defendant's state of mind. "If you are satisfied from this evidence," Judge Davis added, "that the defendant purchased the knife and saw and at that time was thinking upon using them as he used them on the body of Anna Aumuller, and if you are satisfied that in the middle of the night he went secretly to her chamber and entered, took off his clothing and cut her throat, and with this saw severed her body and he knew the nature and quality of that act and that it was wrong, and that he killed her from a deliberate and premeditated design to kill her, it will be your duty to find him guilty of murder in the first degree."[9]

At 12:25 P.M., the jury retired and broke for lunch. Most of the panel wanted to have something to eat before they began their deliberations. Jury foreman E. Howard Underhill, a thirty-five-year-old Wall Street banker, informed the judge that the jury intended to begin their discussion at approximately 2:30 P.M. that afternoon. Judge Davis called a recess while the spectators drifted out into the hallways. Alfonse Koelble and Terence McManus comforted Father Schmidt, who remained indifferent to the proceedings. But the defense was convinced that they had persuaded the court that their client was insane and not responsible for the killing. Schmidt was removed from the room and placed in the court's holding pen for the time being.

At 3:15 P.M., foreman Underhill sent word to Judge Davis that the jury wished to review a portion of the trial evidence. A rumor swept through the building that a verdict was in, causing hundreds of people to rush to the courtroom. Additional police responded to control the surging crowds. They piled into the corridors and stairwells, eager to get a seat before the room filled. The chaos continued until it became known that the jury had simply asked for court documents. Both prosecution and defense teams assembled in the courtroom to hear Mr. Underhill's requests. "If it pleases your honor," he said, "we, the jury, would like the following exhibits in evidence: Dr. Jeliffe's report, insanity chart, and a drawing made by defendant showing the manner in which the body was dissected." All the items were approved by Koelble and Delehanty and sent to the deliberations room.

Two hours later, a message was sent to Judge Davis that the jury had, in fact, reached a verdict. The crowds descended upon the first-floor courtroom within minutes. Traffic outside on Franklin Avenue came to a halt as police cars and taxis congregated on the site. Down on Chambers Street, attorneys at City Hall received notification and began the five-block jog to the Courts building. When parking space filled up, drivers simply drove their cars to a stop and raced up to the court. Inside, the defense and prosecution assembled at their respective tables while they awaited the arrival of the defendant. District Attorney Charles Whitman appeared and took his place alongside Delehanty. The side door swung open and Father Schmidt was brought in. He glanced around at the spectators and nodded his head to Father Huntmann of St. Joseph's.

"All rise!" shouted Court Clerk Penney. Judge Davis entered the room and took his seat at the bench. He cleared his desk of some papers and looked up at Delehanty and Koelble. When he was sure everyone who needed to be present was in court, he told the clerk to bring in the jury. The twelve men filed into their seating section and remained standing.

"Jurymen, look upon the defendant. Defendant look upon the jury," instructed Clerk Penney. Father Schmidt stared at foreman Underhill, who held a small piece of paper in his right hand. He handed the paper to the clerk who brought it to the judge.

"Have you agreed on a verdict?" the clerk asked.

"We have," replied Underhill. "We find the defendant guilty of murder in the first degree!" Father Schmidt laughed out loud, breaking the silence in the room. He shook his head from side to side in disgust while his attorneys placed their hands on his shoulder. "I ask that the jury be polled," said McManus. The jury was then asked individually if they agreed with the verdict. Each one answered in the affirmative. Then the clerk asked Father Schmidt for his pedigree information. He said that he was thirty-two years old and born in Aschaffenburg, Germany. When he was asked for his address, he paused for a moment and gave 405 West 125th Street, the location of St. Joseph's Church. He gave his occupation, in a faltering voice, as "priest." The clerk asked if he was married. Father Schmidt did not answer but stood in silence. The clerk asked the question again. In a barely audible voice, he replied, "yes." The spectators began to gather around the defense table. Some people were cursing at the defendant, while police surrounded Schmidt and pushed people away from him.

"The prisoner will be remanded in custody until sentencing on February 11," said Judge Davis. He pounded his gavel for order. "Is that date acceptable, gentlemen?"

"That's fine, Judge," replied Whitman.

"Yes, your honor," said McManus.

The court officers placed handcuffs on Father Schmidt, who turned to talk with Koelble. "I'm satisfied with the verdict," he said. "I would rather die today than tomorrow." Reporters gathered around the jury panel and began to question each one. As more spectators crammed into the small courtroom, police quickly escorted the defendant out the side door and locked it behind them.

Schmidt was taken back into the frightful cellars of the Tombs. When the heavy metal door slammed shut behind him, Father Schmidt fell to his knees. He joined his hands together in prayer, ready to speak to God who asked so much and to whom he gave so little. But no prayers were uttered. He looked instead at the barren walls in front of him, the concrete barrier to the world outside where life flourished and his persistent desires could be satisfied, even under the endless scrutiny that had always caused him grief. He thought of the wonderful days of unrestricted love in the glorious forests of Aschaffenberg, the willing, young chaplains at the seminary, and the procession of cherubic, nameless altar boys with rosy cheeks and delicate smiles. But most of all, he remembered Anna. Sweet, wonderful Anna, whose mystical powers of flesh and yearning delivered him into the dungeons from which there was no escape, and maybe, into the hands of Satan himself.

And he remembered. . . .

19

The Sacrifice

On that fine September night when he last saw Anna, he prayed in the cool, comforting darkness of St. Joseph's Church. He prayed with all his might, all his ability and passion. So intense were his prayers that he imagined even the floor upon which he knelt trembled by the power of his faith. Like when he was a little boy in Aschaffenberg, he witnessed the sacred vision of St. Elizabeth on the day of his communion, that joyous moment when the earth moved under his feet and he experienced the glory of God Himself. He was a blessed boy, known to everyone in the village as "der kleine Pastor [the little chaplain]." Even then, he realized he was a holy child. He felt it. St. Elizabeth was his own and he never forgot her soothing words to him, "Do wirst ein Priester warden! [You shall become a priest!]" It was a revelation that warmed his soul and provided a troubled boy with the guidance for which he craved. Most children were like seaweed, adrift in a vast ocean with no purpose. They never received the type of affirmation he did at such an early age. Yes, he was a fortunate one to be blessed in such a manner, and he always tried to live up to that responsibility in every way. Of course, being human, he could not be perfect. Hans was cursed with an insidious weakness that weighed heavily upon his soul and because of it, he plunged deeply into the quagmire of flesh and hedonism. But despite his many failures, he still considered himself a holy man.

On occasion, he was able to rescue himself from the depths of sin by the power of prayer. When he indulged in his youthful, wicked ways, he recognized he had needs unlike most other boys. But he was weak and could not break the chains of sexual bondage. He could only control his damnable urges to a certain point, until he stumbled into the pit of self-indulgence once again. He prayed for forgiveness and sought reconciliation with God, which absolved his guilt for a time. Then, he fell back again. This cycle repeated itself over and over, throughout his life. In the privacy of the confessional, he frequently relieved his desires while the sinners confessed their many sexual sins. It only seemed natural to him. If God did not want Schmidt to be a priest, he would not have spoken to him. "Se nones vocates fac ut voceres,"[1] the voice had told him. The meaning was clear. God wanted to inspire his soul to prepare for priesthood. Why else would He talk to him in such a personal way? He tried to stay pure, tried with all his strength, but it was not meant to be. There were too many temptations, too many opportunities, and so many young men like him who shared the same forbidden needs.

When he first met Ernest, he realized there was no one quite like him. He was beautiful, desirable, and willing; a soul mate for a troubled and confused spirit. Muret was a gift from God who, in His divine mercy, wanted to alleviate Schmidt's suffering in this world. And Hans was thankful. He never loved a man like he loved Ernest. They shared their desires passionately and for a time, he knew true peace and happiness. But there was also Anna. Sensual, exciting, voluptuous Anna, who taught him the possibilities of carnal pleasures with a woman. He loved her also, loved her as God wanted him to. That was why he married her, to keep their union holy and pure in the eyes of the Almighty. It was not his fault that she was with child. He told her to be careful, to watch her cycle, to cleanse herself after their consecrations. But Anna was frivolous, earthy, and neglectful of her responsibilities. A baby would undoubtedly expose them both to derision and disgrace.

He had known the sting of ridicule many times in his life, especially in Mainz where ignorant people called him "verrueckter Hans [crazy Hans]" and "verrueckter doktor [crazy doctor]." No, the pregnancy could not be allowed to continue. St. Elizabeth would not permit it. Anna must be sacrificed, and a blood sacrifice it must be. For only through the cleansing of the blood can peace be achieved. Like Abraham, who was called upon to slaughter his own son, the sacrifice had to be one who was loved. Only through such an offering could he return to the path of righteousness and the world be made right again.

He got up off his knees and made the sign of the cross in front of the altar. Bitter tears streamed down his face while the knowledge of what he must do descended upon him. He walked out of the church and over to Amsterdam

Avenue, where the activity of the street was still vibrant even at this late hour. Prostitutes gathered near the corner of Broadway while their customers haggled and shouted prices at the snarling women. Speeding trucks, carrying the next day's goods, rumbled northbound, up to Washington Heights and on to the spacious farmlands of Hunts Point. He turned the corner and started up Broadway as his right hand tightly grasped the twelve-inch knife under his coat. The full moon was bright and clear, and glowed fiercely against a darkened sky. He breathed in the crisp air, which made his mind sharp and clear. It was just past midnight when he reached the front steps of 68 Bradhurst Avenue, where Anna, he was sure, was asleep in their bedroom. He looked up as if he expected to see her by the window. Careful not to draw attention to himself, he climbed the steps toward the third-floor apartment. He appealed to St. Elizabeth to stay close to him.

He placed his key in the lock and turned it quickly. Once inside, he gently closed the door behind him. From his waistband, he removed the knife and placed it on the sofa. He draped his coat over the back of the chair, mindful not to crease the garment and later present a shabby appearance in public. He unfastened his collar and placed it on top of his coat. Through the open door of the bedroom, he saw Anna in bed. She lay on her side facing the only window in the room that looked out over 145th Street. Her steady, rhythmic breathing was the assurance that she was in deep sleep. The sheets were down by her waist. Though it was a chilly evening, the apartment was uncomfortably warm. Anna wore a white chemise she had purchased at a sale in a Broadway store not long ago. Her friend, Annie, had taken the time to hem the piece because it was too long and Anna herself was not a good seamstress. He picked up the knife and cautiously entered the bedroom.

Light from the street lamps illuminated the room faintly, an eerie glow that pulsated with the kaleidoscope of bright signs along Broadway. The holy man stood over Anna, knife in hand; his eyes fixated on the woman he made love to so many times, his passion still burning, despite the knowledge of what he was about to do. She stirred briefly and shifted her position until she lay on her back. Her full breasts rose and fell with each breath, her lips parted slightly, lips that once touched his, that ran over his body, whispered her love, her devotion, and spoke the words that still echoed in his ears. It was not his choice, this offering. It was not his doing. A sacrifice can only be ordered by God and it was He who demanded it. Maybe it was better this way. A baby would be too much trouble, too many questions, too much hurtful speculation in the parish. "Dein Wille geschehe! [Thy will be done!]" he said gently.

He bent over and kissed her gently on the lips while he held the knife firmly behind his back. She let out a sigh. Before Anna finished her breath, he cut. He plunged the knife deeply into the side of her neck, just below her left ear and dragged it across her throat, all the way to the base of her right ear lobe. Blood flowed like a river. She shuddered and made a loud gurgling sound. Her hands instinctively went up to her neck. He pushed her arms down and pulled the blade, still embedded in her neck, back in the opposite direction.

She gasped and struggled for air. He could feel the life ebbing out of his beloved Anna. The sorrow, the grief, it was overwhelming to him. He held her hair in one hand and continued to work the knife with the other. Her body went limp and became motionless. The blood poured off the side of the bed and onto the floor. It spilled onto his shoes and the bottom of his trousers. He stepped back and placed the knife down on the sheets. Overcome with a kind of sadness he never knew before, he began to cry. It was not easy to do such a thing in the name of the Lord. But as a holy man, he felt an obligation to complete that which was demanded of him. He stepped back for a moment and fell into a chair. For several minutes, he remained still. Then he suddenly removed his shirt and trousers and folded them neatly on the back of the living-room chair. He sat down and stripped off his underclothes until he was naked.

After several minutes of careful cutting, the head was amputated from the body. He held it high, staring into Anna's lifeless eyes and her beauty, even in death. He carried the head into the bathroom and turned on the light. Holding the skull upside down like a large bowl, he stared at his reflection in the mirror. He lifted the head high like a chalice and offered it up to heaven. "Et sic fiat sacrificum nostrum in conspectus tuo hodie, ut plaeat, Domine Deus,"[2] he prayed. He brought it to his lips and drank some blood from the neck cavity. "Suscipiat Dominus sacrificium de minibus tuis, ad laudem et gloriam nominis sui, ad ultilitatem quoque nostram, totiusque Ecclesiae suae sanctae."[3] He returned to the bloody bed where he placed the head back in its rightful position. As he fervently prayed aloud, "Orate ut meum ac vestrum sacrificium acceptabile fiat apud Deum Patrem omnipotentem,"[4] he removed all of Anna's nightclothes until she was completely naked. He studied her body and quickly became aroused. A large pool of blood had gathered at the top of the bed. The sight of so much blood was too much for him to take. In an act of narcissistic passion, the holy man climbed on top of Anna and completed a sexual union with her body.

When he was finished, he walked over to the bedroom window and looked down into the street. He saw people walking along the sidewalks and traffic moving in the streets as if nothing had happened. Life goes on, he thought. Tragedy only hurts the people who experience it. In his sermons, he often referred to that concept. People tend not to empathize with each other during times such as these, he thought. The proof was right there in front of him. Pedestrians continued to go about their business while Anna lay dead in a pool of her own blood, a mere stone's throw from where people hugged their children, drank their coffee, and cooked their food. He turned away in disgust and returned to the bed. He took a towel and covered the head. Wrapping the bedding completely around the body, he lifted Anna and carried her into the bathroom. He placed the corpse into the bathtub and removed the sheets. Then, with methodical purpose and a sharpened twelve-inch blade, he continued his butchery.

He honed the knife to razor sharpness, while at the same time, dreaded the work to come. Starting with the upper torso, he began to slice away at the bicep part of the arms. It took just a few cuts to reach the ligaments below the shoulder bone. Within minutes, one arm was completely removed from the trunk. He used a saw when it became too difficult with the knife. Working at a steady pace, he managed to dissect both arms and both legs within the hour. He could have finished sooner but was forced to stop every few minutes to clean spots of blood that fell onto the tiled floor or dripped down the bathroom walls. Once the limbs were severed, he placed the four pieces on a blanket spread out over the floor. Then he left the apartment and walked over to 144th Street to a vacant lot. He picked up some heavy rocks and carried them back to the room. Using a brown, heavy-duty paper that he had bought on Eighth Avenue the day before, he wrapped each piece tightly along with the rocks and then secured the bundles with string and white insulated wire. He then turned his attention to the chest cavity and the hips.

The body was much easier to lift without the arms and legs. He laid the body on its back at the bottom of the tub. With both hands, he plunged the knife deep into the abdomen and sliced across the belly. When the incision reached all the way to the right side, he flipped the body over and continued the cut until it returned to the starting point. He did this several times, using more force on each repetition, until the blade finally went through the internal organs and a complete separation was attained. Using the same paper, he wrapped each piece neatly into two large bundles. When he had laid all the pieces onto the living-room floor, he was amazed that a human being could be reduced to such a variety of odd packages.

Taking the head back into the bathroom tub, he held it under the faucet as he washed it clean of blood and debris. He patted it dry and then placed it back on the blanket. Taking the heaviest rock, he placed it next to the skull and looked for more wire. There was none left over and he had used all the string as well. He decided to wrap it anyway. He wrapped the paper around the head and the rock many times, using all he had left. He took all the pieces and placed them on the floor near the front door. It was time to clean up.

He took a scrub brush and a bucket of soapy water to the bathroom. Beginning with the walls, he drenched the tiles and tried to erase all traces of the blood. It had dripped down to the floor and seeped into the joints and along the moldings at the bottom of the wall. He used the brush vigorously on each spot, determined to eliminate all evidence of the slaughter. The bedroom was worse. Blood was all over the floor and the mattress was soggy. He knew it could never be cleaned. Removing all the sheets and blankets, he lifted the mattress from the frame. After checking the hallways to make sure no one was around, he carried the mattress out of the building, dragged it to a nearby lot and set it afire. As the flames consumed the bedding, he began to feel more confident.

By then, it was nearly three in the morning. He was exhausted and yet, in a strange way, exhilarated. But there was still one more task to complete. He had to dispose of the body parts. It would not be a good idea to simply dump the pieces into a garbage can. Someone could find them and the police would surely come. And it seemed to be disrespectful to simply throw Anna into a garbage dump. He decided that it would be best to drop the pieces into the river. He picked up the head, tucked it under his arm and left the apartment.

By then, the full moon had moved behind a layer of deep clouds so he felt secure as he stepped onto the sidewalk. The streets were empty, showing little of the frantic activity that erupted each morning during the rush hour. He held the package containing the head under his left arm and walked quickly over to Amsterdam Avenue where he made a left turn at the corner. He passed row after row of closed shops and vegetable stands that lined the boulevard south up to the junction at 135th Street.

When he reached the intersection at Convent Hill, he heard the faint sounds of music. He saw that an all-night revival meeting, on the southwest corner, had its doors open for services. As he moved closer, he recognized the hymn as "Nearer My God to Thee." Inside, a dozen hagglers, drunks, and hobos, all half asleep, lounged in the wooden pews and chairs while the old black organist played at the front of the room. He entered the tiny chapel and took a seat in the back row. Careful not to draw attention, he placed the package on the seat next to him. The music was soothing and restful, so unlike the stolid Catholic hymns in the old country. America's gospel music was alive, vibrant, and spiritual; it stirred the soul and celebrated a sort of primordial faith that was conspicuously absent from the Catholic Church. Germany had nothing like it. He closed his eyes and let the hymn sweep over him. The power of faith was a wonderful thing. It provided the strength and inspiration he needed to go on. After a few minutes' rest, and with a revived sense of purpose, he picked up the bundle and continued on his way.

At West 129th Street, he boarded the Ft. Lee ferry bound for the Jersey side of the river. At that time of the morning there were only a few other passengers on board. He moved to the stern of the vessel. When the boat reached the halfway point, he placed Anna's head on top of the wooden railing. He turned suddenly. His right elbow made contact with the package, knocking it off the railing and sending it plummeting into the waves below. He studied the package as it disappeared into the churning wake of the ferry's propellers, bobbing up and down quickly in the foam, until it vanished completely into the darkened waters of the Hudson.

He returned to the Manhattan dock and then hurried back to the apartment. He calculated that it would require six additional trips on the Ft. Lee ferry to dispose of all the body parts. Though he was tempted to take both legs at one time, he decided against it because it might be too conspicuous. He realized he would have to finish up on the following day. But he made one more trip that night to dump the bottom section of the torso. Afterward, he was fatigued to the point of dizziness. He never imagined that a sacrifice would be such hard physical labor. When he returned to the flat for the last time, it was nearly six o'clock in the morning and the rush hour in the city was just beginning. But he had to get over to the parish quickly. He tossed the bedding into the bathtub and covered the bundles with a fresh sheet from the closet. As he locked the apartment door, he looked down the stairs to be sure no one was present. He bounded down the steps and onto the sidewalk, where he adjusted his collar and buttoned up his coat. He walked briskly to 125th Street.[5]

Within ten minutes, he was at St. Joseph's rectory. As he entered the hallway to the priest's room, he passed Father Daniel Quinn, an assistant to the parish monsignor. "Good morning, Father," he said softly.

"Good morning, Hans, how are you today?"

"Fine. And you, Dan?"

"We looked for you last night at the evening coffee," Father Quinn said, without answering the question.

"I had a sick parishioner. He needed attention," Father Schmidt replied as he continued on his way. He entered the sacristy and removed his coat and shirt. He glanced at the clock above the door. It was nearly 6:55 A.M. The day's first mass was scheduled to begin in five minutes. He quickly donned the vestments and adjusted his cassock. The morning sun poured in through the six-foot window, flooding the room with a brash light. He closed the curtains together with a quick tug, plunging the room into a tranquil darkness. He kissed the crucifix on the private altar and genuflected before its presence. Outside the door, the congregation began to assemble in preparation for mass. Two altar boys from the St. Joseph's grammar school entered the priest's room.

"Good morning, Father," they said in unison.

"Let's get ready to start," he replied. They stood shoulder to shoulder by the entrance to the altar, waiting for the priest to join them. He made the sign of the cross and hurried to where the boys were. One of the children pointed to the priest's shoes.

"Mud?" the boy whispered. Schmidt glanced down at his feet and saw that his left shoe was covered with specks of dried blood. He grabbed an old cassock from a drawer, wiped the shoe clean, and then tossed the garment into a nearby trash pail.

"Now," said Father Schmidt, as he regained his composure. The taller of the two boys rang a bell, the signal for the flock to stand in unison. Father Schmidt went to the center of the altar, stood before the tabernacle, and bowed his head.

"In nomine Patris, et Filii, et Spiritus Sancti, Amen," he intoned, as the crowd made the sign of the cross. A sudden chill enveloped him. In his entire career, he had never felt so fulfilled, so capable and supremely talented as he did that morning. He could lead the lost, this prince among paupers, this conqueror of evil and loyal messenger of God.

"Intoibo ad altare, Dei. [I will go to the altar of God.]" It was plain to him and certainly would be to everyone else, if they were blessed enough to peer into his soul, that he had become exalted, sanctified to the highest degree, and set on the path of righteousness and glory in the eyes of the Lord. And now, if only for a brief moment, he could walk with the angels once again.

"Ad Deum qui laetificat juventutem meam, [To God, the joy of my youth]" he recited.

The mass was about to begin.

20

Sing Sing

On the morning of February 11, Father Schmidt was brought back to the same first-floor courtroom where he was convicted the week before. District Attorney Whitman joined James Delehanty to hear the sentence from Judge Davis, who had already indicated that he would not show mercy to the defendant. Koelble and McManus were prepared for the worst. They knew there was little sympathy for their client. Newspaper reporters filed into the press section and chatted among themselves while they waited for the judge. When the police escorted Schmidt into the room, his hands chained to his waist, some of the spectators cursed him and yelled obscenities. He quickly took a seat between his two attorneys. His appearance had changed noticeably from the time of the guilty verdict. He had lost weight, and though he was only thirty-two years old, Schmidt's dark hair had begun to turn gray. During the trial, he wore his black cassock and white collar, but at the sentencing, he wore a blue shirt and dark pants.

After Court Clerk Penney called the proceedings to order, Judge Davis entered the room and reviewed the day's calendar. "Mr. Delehanty? Ready to proceed?"

"Yes, your honor, the People are ready."

"Mr. Koelble?"

"Yes, your honor, we're ready."

Delehanty addressed the court first. "Your honor, I move that the judgment of the law be pronounced against the defendant, Hans Schmidt, on his conviction of murder in the first degree."

McManus rose to his feet and made his own motion. "I move for a new trial on the grounds that the verdict was against the law and it was against the weight of the evidence, upon the ground that error was committed on the admission and exclusion of the evidence and upon the ground that the court has misdirected the jury in matters of the law. And finally, your honor, the defendant moves in arrest of the judgment upon the ground that the facts stated in the indictment do not constitute the crime charged."

Judge Davis was visibly annoyed with the defense motions, especially since McManus claimed that Davis had misdirected the jury during his charge. Davis was aware that insanity was a complicated issue, but he felt that he had done his best to explain it to the jury.

"All those motions are denied," Davis declared.

"Exception!" replied McManus.

"Prisoner, please rise!" shouted Court Clerk Penney. Father Schmidt stood with his counsel by his side while Judge Davis read from a prepared statement.

"The judgment of the court is that you, Hans Schmidt, for the murder in the first degree of one Anna Aumuller, whereof you are convicted, be sentenced to the punishment of death, and it is ordered that within ten days after this session, the Sheriff of the County of New York deliver you, together with the warrant of this court, to the Agent and Warden of the State Prison at Sing Sing, where you shall be kept in solitary confinement until the week beginning Monday, the twenty-third day of March 1914, and upon some day within the week so appointed, the said Agent and Warden at Sing Sing is commanded to do execution upon you, Hans Schmidt, in the mode and manner prescribed by the laws of the State of New York."

The defendant bowed his head and turned briefly to his attorneys. He touched their hands in gratitude and said goodbye. As he was taken from the court, he handed a reporter a piece of paper upon which he had written a short verse.

> *Beyond this vale of tears,*
> *There is life above,*
> *Unmeasured by the flight of years*
> *And all that life is love.*[1]

Within the hour, Father Schmidt was on his way to Grand Central Station. Inspector Faurot and Detective Cassassa placed him in the back of their

912 Hudson and drove up Broadway, through its dazzling mixture of horse-drawn carriages, noisy automobiles, and clumsy trucks. They passed Grace Church on Tenth Street and continued into Union Square where lunchtime crowds hurried along on the sidewalks. When they reached West Forty-fourth Street, Faurot drove by the Shubert Theater where *A Thousand Years Ago* was featured. At the Little Theater on Broadway, Bernard Shaw's comedy *The Philanderer* was a popular attraction. One block away at the Astor, there were two showings daily of an eight-reel film titled *Quo Vadis*, one of the very first full-length movies. The price of admission was twenty-five cents for the matinee and fifty cents for the evening show at 8:30 P.M. Stage actress Christie MacDonald was at the New Amsterdam Theater on Forty-second Street in *Sweethearts*, while vaudeville was going strong at the Palace on Broadway and Forty-seventh. But the real excitement in midtown was taking place at Hammerstein's Roof where Evelyn Nesbit Thaw, "The Girl on the Red Swing," the central figure in the Stanford White murder case, was packing a full house twice a day for celebrity-obsessed New Yorkers, who could not get enough of her bawdy show.

Father Schmidt sat quietly in the rear seat, next to Cassassa, as he watched the colorful panorama of the theater district go by. Though it was off the route for the trip, Faurot purposely drove over to the East Side to pass St. Boniface's rectory on Forty-seventh Street. When he cruised by the church, Cassassa could not help but point it out.

"Isn't that the Church of St. Boniface?" he remarked to Faurot.

"Well, I think it is," he replied. "Isn't it, Father?" Schmidt looked up. He removed his hat and placed it on his lap. Then he ran his manacled hands through his black hair.

"It's been a long time since I've been there," he said.

"You know," said Faurot, "I always liked this area of town. Along Second Avenue, I mean. Lots of cafés and restaurants. It has a nice feeling here."

"Yeah," Cassassa said, hoping that the prisoner realized this would be the last time he ever laid eyes on the streets of Manhattan. Schmidt looked over the block of Forty-fifth Street that he had visited many times when he was a priest at the church.

"I don't know if I ever told you this, Frank, but my father never wanted me to be a copper," Faurot said. "He was a cook, the old man. He tried to make me go that way but I fell into police work by accident. But, to tell you the truth, I wish I was a cook."

"I wish you were, too," replied Schmidt as he put his hat back on his head.

They arrived at Grand Central and pulled up to the sidewalk along Vanderbilt Avenue. As they entered the massive main promenade, Faurot checked the schedule, which showed their train to Ossining was on time and waiting on track fifty-one. When they boarded, other passengers avoided them once they saw the chains around the wrists of Father Schmidt. The trio took their seats in the back of a railroad car and settled in for the trip. It was nearly 2:00 P.M. when the train pulled into the station at Ossining, the last stop for Father Schmidt.

"It ought to be burned down," said Arthur Conan Doyle, the famous author of the Sherlock Holmes books, after a visit to Sing Sing in 1914. By then, the prison had achieved a reputation as one of the most repressive penal institutions in America. Built in 1825, by convict labor, using stone that was mined and cut onsite, its original design had not changed much in ninety years. The state simply added more buildings, never updating the existing structures. The original cell-block, which consisted of 800 cells, was still being used in 1914. It was a fearsome place and closely resembled something out of medieval times than twentieth-century American architecture.

Captain Elam Lynds, a strict disciplinarian who believed that penitence was the only path to redemption, supervised the construction of Sing Sing over a period of three years. Each windowless cell was only seven feet long by three feet wide and six-feet-seven inches high. It was little more than cubbyhole of stone for a human being. The design called for a building 876 feet long with cells stacked four levels high. There was no electricity, no running water, and no heat, even during the winter. Sanitary measures consisted of nothing. There was only a wooden bucket placed in each cell, to be emptied when full. The men sat in the frigid darkness each day and night with mostly nothing to do and no one to talk to. Reporter Richard Harding Davis once wrote of Sing Sing, "These cells are so small that if you try to turn or walk in one of them you wipe the damp walls with your body. The cells are unsanitary, filled with vermin, exhaling decay."[2]

As might be expected, diseases of all types were rampant in the prison. Even the warden himself kept his distance form the prison cell-block. "Dysentery, scurvy, Asiatic cholera, smallpox—all took their overwhelming tolls," one warden said later. "Prisoner's diet was barely enough to keep body and soul together. Two eggs a year for each man. Famished prisoners timidly entered the mess kitchen to beg for more food but were driven away probably lashed for their temerity. Sing Sing prison seemed to have been actually a devil's workshop."[3]

Nineteenth-century penologists believed that inmates should be treated harshly in order to keep them under control. When they were not working, prisoners were expected to spend most of their time in their cells reading the Bible. Only after an inmate confronted his criminal past and acknowledged his guilt could he begin to rebuild his shattered past. It was thought to be the only way to right a wronged life. Prisoners were not allowed to talk or to communicate with each other in any fashion. They were expected to eat in silence, work in silence, and live in a silent world where any infraction of the rules was treated with physical torture.

Captain Lynds once told a reporter, "I consider the chastisement by the whip the most efficient and[,] at the same time, the most humane punishment which exists . . . I consider it impossible to govern a large prison without a whip. Those who know human nature from books only may say the contrary."[4] Torture devices, such as the water bath, the iron cap, steel yokes, and dark cells were used routinely at Sing Sing. Each use of these disciplinary measures was faithfully recorded in the keeper's log that documented decades of oppression and terror used to control the inmate population.[5] Prisoners wore striped uniforms, were chained together at the ankles, and marched everywhere in lockstep, like robots, one behind the other.[6]

Many of the inmates succumbed to the unbearable conditions at Sing Sing. "The number of men the prison has killed, has driven mad, has for life crippled with rheumatism or inoculated with unspeakable diseases will never be known."[7] Inmates often fell into an endless cycle of despondency and despair. Suicides were frequent and it was not uncommon for a man to lie dead in his cell for days before someone discovered the body. One physician described his rounds at the facility like this: "I had to knock on the door of each dark cell to discover if the occupant had fallen ill, lost his mind or died in the night."[8]

Record keeping at the prison was sporadic and unreliable. Incoming wardens were shocked to discover an institution whose administrative activities had descended into chaos. One warden found that the prison register called for 795 inmates. An actual head count turned up only 762. "How these missing prisoners had left the prison and when, could not be ascertained," he said later.[9] In reality, methods used at Sing Sing were not much worse than any other prison during that time. But what set the facility apart from other penal institutions were its executions.

During the nineteenth century, legal executions in New York usually took place in the county where the crime occurred, though the procedure remained under the jurisdiction of state officials. The law permitted executions anywhere in the state, a practice that allowed for a level of abuse and brutality that was limited only by the prison warden's imagination. Any location, it seemed, could be used as an execution venue. A tall tree, a village square, or a hastily constructed scaffold were all acceptable to the state. Bedloe's Island, located in New York City's harbor, was one of the most popular sites for execution. For generations, many seafaring criminals and pirates were put to death on that barren island.[10] Ironically, Bedloe's Island later became better known as the site of the Statue of Liberty.

During the late nineteenth century, penal reformers began to make subtle changes in the way the state managed its inmate population. After decades of effort and legislative lobbying, conditions began to improve inside the state's prisons, though penal reform did not begin in earnest until the turn of the century. It was an excruciatingly slow process.[11] The hated lockstep method of walking was curtailed and eventually discarded. Physical tortures were banished. By 1900, all executions were scheduled at either the Auburn prison upstate or Sing Sing, which was destined to become the flagship for capital punishment in the Western world.[12]

On the late afternoon of February 11, the giant steel-plated door of the South Gate swung open. Father Schmidt, Inspector Faurot, and Detective Cassassa entered the prison. Prison guards, led by Principal Keeper Frederick Dorner, met the group just inside the walls. They walked briskly toward the admissions building while behind them, the heavy gate swung closed, a symbolic reception into a new and frightening world. Within minutes, Schmidt stood before the record clerk who loudly demanded the prisoner's name, address, and date of birth. To the standard question, "to what do you attribute your crime?" Schmidt paused for a moment.

"St. Elizabeth," he replied.

The clerk looked up from his log at Faurot, who simply shrugged his shoulders. Most prisoners actually answered this question, "evil companionship." Other causes included alcohol, need of money, revenge, drug abuse, or home conditions.

After paperwork was completed, Schmidt was issued his inmate number. Then, he was taken to another building where his clothes were removed and discarded. The supply clerk issued one prison-made, ill-fitting uniform, which was the only set of garments allowed to an inmate. At the hospital, he was given a complete physical, and a dental exam, and ordered to take a shower. From the hospital, Schmidt was taken to the "bucket rack" where he was issued a slop bucket, his toilet for the time he would be at the prison. Guards then escorted the new inmate to his individual cell in the old stone cell-block. When the metal door slammed shut for the first time, Schmidt felt a sense of loss and dejection he had never known before. "The first turn of the lock in the heavy steel door is one of the greatest tragedies that can come into the life of any man," said one prison warden, "now, if ever, a man, no matter how hardened and stolid he may be, will shed tears."[13] For the next several months, and throughout the sweltering hot summer of 1914, Father Schmidt languished in his concrete cell. Like the other hundreds of prisoners, he read the Bible each day, worked from sunup to sundown, and emptied his slop bucket each evening.

At 9:15 A.M., on October 29, 1914, Alfonse Koelble took the train out of New York City up to the village of Ossining. During the hour-and-a-half trip, which took him past the sleepy Hudson shoreline communities of Tarrytown, Ardsley, and Dobbs Ferry, Koelble studied the wide expanse of the river. Across the choppy waters, he could see tiny villages on the opposite side. The majestic palisades stood hundreds of feet high on the western bank, reminding him immediately of the prison walls at Sing Sing. Along the base of the cliffs, where brightly painted homes dotted the shoreline, dozens of sailboats and pleasure craft bounced lightly with the rhythm of the waves. Koelble dreamed of the day when he could retire from the Manhattan rat race and live in a place where all he had to do was get up in the morning and go fishing. One of the great pleasures of his life was on those rare occasions he and a few friends, none of whom were lawyers, got together and fished the wild waters of Montauk Point off eastern Long Island. In 1910, Koelble discovered tuna fishing, the greatest joy of his life. One day, with a little luck, he would buy a home on the Atlantic side of the island and live in peace, away from city traffic, the chaos of Manhattan life, and the ugliness of things such as murder.

The train pulled into the Ossining depot at 10:50 A.M. Sing Sing was the only prison in the world where a commuter train cut directly through the facility. The station was built in that manner to expedite prisoner processing from New York City. Koelble picked up his bag and walked the short distance to the reception area while the train crawled out of the station. After he entered the double steel doors into a waiting lobby, Koelble nodded to the guard behind the large desk. One of the clerks recognized him and performed the usual routine of personal identification.

"I'm here to see Schmidt, Hans. I'm the attorney of record." The young officer checked the visitation log, which listed all the approved visitors for an inmate. "Alfred Koelble, lawyer," was the first name on the list.

"Approved!" he shouted to another officer on the other side of an iron gate. Koelble entered the secure area and walked through a darkened corridor to another room that contained a wooden table and two chairs. There were no lights and only a tiny window, one foot square, with iron bars, at the far side of the room. A kerosene hurricane lamp sat alone on the table. Its solitary flame provided an unsteady light that flickered slightly every time the door was opened or closed. Koelble sat down, opened the briefcase and removed his papers.

"Schmidt will be right up," the officer said.

"OK, thanks," he replied. He prepared himself for the interview because every meeting with Schmidt was an ordeal. The man changed his moods and demeanor so quickly that Koelble had a difficult time just talking to him. Schmidt was evasive, and whenever he was asked a question he could not answer, he would quote the Bible. It was very annoying. Koelble knew Hans was not telling the truth, but he had no alternative. Anyway, it was not his job to get at the truth. As a lawyer, he had other priorities.

Ten minutes passed before the guard returned. Schmidt walked behind the officer while another guard followed him. He was handcuffed and chained at the ankles. When he walked, he had to shuffle along since the length of the chain was intentionally less than the length of one average stride. Schmidt sat down in a chair opposite Koelble. He turned to make sure the guards had left the room.

"Alphonse!" He smiled. "Greetings, my friend."

"Hello, Hans. How are you?"

"Well, under the circumstances. But I wish I could get some acceptable food. They serve crap here."

Koelble looked up from his papers. He studied the man who now looked so unlike a priest. He had lost more weight and let his beard grow unkempt. His hair had not been cut since the day he was arrested, over a year before. Koelble thought to himself that Schmidt looked like a lot of the other inmates.

"I understand you wanted to give another statement, Hans."

"It's so God damn cold in this place. How can they treat people like this? Yes, Alphonse, I want to tell the truth, you know."

"I thought what you told the court before was the truth?"

"So did I," Schmidt said, "But I think I should add some details that maybe I might have left out."

"Well, I don't know how the court is going to deal with this, Hans. As you know, the matter is still before the appeals court. We should have done this months ago."

"Do you have any tobacco, Alphonse?"

"No. What is it you have to say?"

"Not that I indulge a great deal. But from time to time, a man likes to smoke a little, you know." Schmidt lifted his hands up to show his wrists chained. "Usually I don't wear these in the cell. Only when they move me. I understand on death row, the guards don't take no chances. By the way, I hear Lieutenant Becker is a popular guy there. He keeps the rest of the boys up on police procedures and the like. It's very interesting subject matter. The advancements in the criminology field are many, Alphonse. Fingerprints, psychology, third-degree methods. It's all so scientific. I tell you, criminals don't have a chance."

Koelble stared at the priest whose face was partially obscured by the shadows. Koelble was not confident about his client's mental stability. He never was. Even before the arrest, when he first met Schmidt on the Manhattan lecture circuit, the priest seemed unstable. He frequently tripped over his own words and if he spoke for longer than several minutes, his voice tended to become louder and confrontational. Schmidt always seemed angry about something. But the priest had a certain condescending manner about him that he transmitted to the people around him. Though it was never spoken, one always had the feeling that no priest could be more pious than Father Hans Schmidt.

"Yes. They don't have a chance, Hans. What is it you'd like to say? I have to appear before the judge later this week. We have to be ready." Schmidt shifted in his seat, rattling the chains. He took a deep breath and looked over his shoulder as if to see if any of the guards were loitering about.

"I know I'm going to die, but I really should get some things straight. After all, I have to answer to God for my crimes and I don't want to face Him as a liar, you know."

"Hans," Koelble pleaded, "is there anything that you can say that will help?"

"Listen, Alphonse. Anna requested me to have her examined as to a possible pregnancy. She was examined by Dr. Arnold G. Leo of West 135th Street. I had known Dr. Leo for several months through the person who is known as Dr. Ernest Muret but whose right name is Ernest Arthur Heibing. Anna told me that she was of illegitimate birth, that she often felt the shame of it, as she had often stated, she repeated that a marriage with a priest was illegal and wrong, that if a child was born it would then have to bear the same shame of illegitimacy that she had. At times she said we would marry but usually she kept urging me to have an operation performed. She said two other operations of a similar kind hadn't hurt her and she threatened to try it herself if I procured no one to do it." Schmidt wrapped his arms about himself. "Goddammit!" he shouted over his shoulder, "It's cold in here!"

"Then I hired a flat at Bradhurst Avenue. On Labor Day, I found her in bed complaining of pain. She said that she had tried something on herself and that she was in pain. She urged me to have the operation, as she said, completed. I called on Dr. Muret and Dr. Leo and together we three went to the Bradhurst flat. Anna was lying in bed and was complaining of pain in the abdomen. I cannot fix the exact time at which we reached the apartment but it was in the neighborhood of three o'clock. Anna was in a negligee. She insisted that I not be present at the operation. She said the exposure of a woman's person to her lover would either diminish or destroy his love. I accordingly went into the kitchen which adjoined the bathroom. I could hear Anna's groaning. Some time after we arrived there, Muret passed to the bathroom and in his hand he held a fetus. It was well enough to tell its sex; it was a boy child." With this last statement, Koelble noticed a certain tone of pride in Schmidt's voice, as if the baby boy was something that he could boast about.

"Alphonse, I never saw the fetus again."

"I believe you, Hans, really," he said.

"Anna lay on the bed pale with eyes closed. I knelt down and talked in her ear. She made no reply. Some of her clothes and other things were placed on the bed to prevent the blood from soaking the mattress. When she fainted, I saw Muret place pieces of cotton in the vagina. Anna was bleeding freely and blood was noticeable under her. All three of us were panic stricken..."

"I can imagine," Koelble interjected.

"...and Anna became weaker and weaker and later, Muret said she was dead. We left the flat and later, I appealed to Dr. Leo and begged him to sign a death certificate. He strongly objected because he did not want to get into trouble."

"I see, Hans."

"Muret and I returned to the Bradhurst Avenue flat, arriving there between 11:30 P.M. and midnight. Muret said the thing to do was to cut up the body of the unfortunate girl and get rid of the remains in such a manner as would escape detection. I expected to help him in performing this horrible task but I grew faint after the first effort." Schmidt looked at his hands, clenched into fists and turned them over, palms up, as if he saw them for the first time. "Muret tried at first a small saw but whether he brought it in a bag or not, I do not recall. He said it was impossible to do the work with such a saw so I left the flat and went to the apartment where I had the counterfeit press. I had some knives there."

"Knives? What kind of knives, Hans?"

"Guard! Guard!" Schmidt yelled. "Bring us some hot broth. Have mercy on a poor old priest for once, I say! Bitt! [Please!]" But there was no answer. Schmidt leaned back on the bench until his shoulders rested on the damp wall. Since there was little light in the tiny room, Koelble could barely see in the darkness. "I had bought the knives to be used for counterfeiting. Not for any other purpose. So I returned to the flat and then Muret and I cut up the body. I think it took him about an hour. He performed the work in the bathroom and he handed the various parts to me which I took into the kitchen and wrapped up. I gathered up some stones outside and I took out the parts that very night. But I could not take all of them. It was late already and I had to say mass, you know."

Koelble stopped and looked up from his notes. "Yes, that revelation hurt us at the trial."

"Well, what was I to do? I was assigned by the pastor. I did not want to disappoint him. And after all, people expected to see me." Schmidt shifted his position on the bench and moved back slightly. "Alphonse, there were many who needed my guidance, who needed the help of the Lord. I think it was not too much to ask of me to complete my sacred duties that morning despite the pressures that I was under."

"Why didn't you let one of the other priests perform the mass?"

"I did not see a need to. After all, whose business is it other than mine? And God's. Besides," Schmidt leaned closer to Koelble, "I wouldn't want anyone to get wrong ideas about me. Ich bin nicht gewissenlos. [I am not irresponsible.]"

"Truly."

"So later that day, Bertha Zech arrived. Together we completed the packing of the parts of Anna's body. Most of the wire I used I had purchased in stores in the neighborhood. I think the work was concluded Tuesday afternoon. Bertha took away the smallest parcel having the head. We did talk over the matter, Alphonse, though we avoided the subject as much as possible. Muret suggested to me in the very beginning that I pretend to be insane. He said he would help me out in the insanity defense. It would be the easiest way out for all concerned. He said Thaw was never half as crazy as I was now. He said with the insanity plea, it would not come to trial at all, but I would be sent to an asylum where they would dismiss me after some time when I was cured."

"Hans, you told the police months ago that *you* took the head from the apartment," said Koelble.

"I did?"

"Yes, I'm sure of it."

Schmidt paused for a moment and joined his hands under his chin as if he were praying. His eyes rolled back and he rocked back and forth in his seat. "How could I have made such an error? I was sure she took the head. Or maybe it was the thighs she took. I mean does it make a difference who took what, after all?"

"Not to me," said Koelble, "but your previous statement to the police was different. That's all I'm saying."

"Well, after so much time, it's hard to keep track of all nine pieces. The head? You know, I think Bertha did take the head. It was wrapped up very neatly and not very heavy, after all. I'm sure she could have handled it."

"Hans, the police keep asking me about Louisville," said Koelble. Schmidt sat up suddenly. He ran his hands through his dark hair and down the sides of his unshaven face. Without displaying so much as a blink of an eye, he rubbed his forefingers on his temples.

"Louisville, Louisville!" He shook his head. "God damn it, what is it with these people?"

"I only ask because they asked me."

"Why don't they leave a man alone? Aren't they happy yet? I'm destroyed. My reputation is completely ruined after what that Whitman fellow said about me. I mean who would come to a mass that I performed? Sometimes I really wonder what I've done to deserve this kind of treatment."

Koelble began to assemble his notes and papers into a pile. He set all the files on top of one another and inserted them into his briefcase. "Hans," he said as he rose to his feet, "the appeal is set. I think we might have at least a chance at a new trial."

"Louisville ist in der Vergangenheit! [Louisville is history!]" Schmidt said as he looked off to the side. He ran his left hand through his hair then folded his arms on his chest. Koelble stood up and methodically placed his papers inside the briefcase.

"I haven't been feeling well, Hans. Terry is going to take over for a while," Koelble said as he put on his jacket.

"Why don't they just leave a man alone?" Schmidt repeated.

"I'm going to take a little time off. The appeal is in progress and he will follow the case until I get back."

"What must people think of me? It's always bad news, every day. I guess I should have been more careful. Yes, that's it. I should have been more respectful of other people, more considerate. Like when I was at the St. Boniface Church, the people loved me there. I never wanted to leave, but that damn Father Braun. He always made trouble..."

"I'm tired," Koelble said. "I need a little rest. I'll be back in two weeks or so. In the meantime, Terry McManus will...."

"...for me. I think it was because of Anna. I think he wanted her and he took out his frustrations on me."

"By the way, Hans, the warden informed me you'll be transferred over to another building soon, the Death House. There was no room before. The place was full." Koelble looked over at Schmidt and realized he had not heard a word he said. "I'll see you soon, Hans," he said and left the room.

"Thank you, my friend. Keep up the good work," Schmidt said. "I'm very impressed with your legal skills." He sat in his chair, deep in thought. The chains rattled slightly every time he moved. While Koelble made his way down the narrow path outside the building, Schmidt chewed the ends of his fingernails and spit them out, one by one, onto the floor. He began to recite a prayer from the mass, the Confiteor, except he could not recall the words past the opening sentence, "Confiteor Deo omnipotenti...[I confess to Almighty God]." But he was not upset with that failure of memory. For he always had trouble with that part of the mass.

"Louisville ist in der Vergangenheit," he repeated softly.

21

Death Row

The death house at Sing Sing during the nineteenth century was not much more than a wooden shack containing only eight cells. It was built by convict labor in 1889 specifically to provide a permanent location for the electric chair, the state's new instrument of execution.[1] After twenty-five men were executed during the 1890s, it became obvious that a new facility was needed to handle the increase in death sentences. In 1899, under the direction of Principal Keeper Alfred Conyes, a group of prisoners constructed a new building to replace the dilapidated old structure. It was comprised of a dozen cells, with the electric chair located at its center; concrete walls replaced the wood, while steel bars were installed on all the windows, making an escape more difficult, if not impossible.

The death house was a cold and forbidding place for a man to spend his last hours on earth, even worse than the harsh realities of the main facility. Those who were condemned there were not permitted out of their cells. They had to remain in strict confinement until the day of their execution, because authorities felt that a man who was scheduled to die had nothing to lose and would try anything to escape. Security was intense, and in its seventy-year history, the few escape attempts ended in tragedy for all prisoners involved.[2]

Some men waited for years for their appeals to be heard in Albany's courts. Guards were on duty twenty-four hours a day, seven days a week, especially watchful for the possibility of suicide. On January 13, 1916, prisoner Angelo Leggio, 24, was found hanging from the bars of his cell with a sheet wrapped around his neck. Keepers Frank Kagley and Peter Fitzmaurice said they observed Leggio asleep at about 5 P.M. but less than ten minutes later, they found him dead, suspended from the cell door. "Leggio was depressed when he heard that he could not get a new trial and would follow his accomplice William Flack to the electric chair," said Warden Kirchway. "So far, we have not found the keepers at fault."[3]

Father Schmidt had spoken with Leggio only an hour before his death but the young man had given no indication that he had planned to take his own life. Suicides on death row are not common. "Attempts to commit suicide in the death house are rare," wrote prison physician Dr. Amos Squire. "Hope of commutation endures to the very end. So I doubt if many condemned persons would so far abandon that hope as to try to kill themselves, even if they had the opportunity. Nevertheless, strict precautions are observed to prevent the law from being cheated."[4]

Most of the time, the condemned walked in circles or lay in their beds all day, smoking cigarette after cigarette, cursing and denouncing the injustice of having to die for crimes many of them said they did not commit. Inmates were allowed to have tobacco but not matches. Every time a prisoner needed to smoke, he had to ask a guard for a light. A keeper on death row spent the majority of his shift time running from cell to cell, lighting cigarettes and pipes for the inmates. Inmates were also allowed to play checkers with each other, a privilege denied to the general population at Sing Sing; though they could not see each other when they played because the boards were set up outside in the corridor between the cells. They had to reach between the bars to move the pieces. The game provided soothing therapy to the condemned. "Many men have kept their minds composed during their concluding days of life by defending their reputations for being expert checker players," a prison doctor later remarked.[5] Only a few visitors were allowed to see inmates and those were carefully screened and controlled. Members of the press were sometimes permitted to interview prisoners with the warden's approval, though it was not granted often.

The electric chair, a device that inspired controversy and revulsion since the very day it was installed, had been in continuous operation since 1890. By the winter of 1915, some 127 men and one woman had gone to their deaths by electrocution at Sing Sing. Some of these men had to be taken forcibly from their cells and dragged kicking and screaming to their deaths.[6] A prison doctor described one such execution that took place in the summer of 1912.

"It was a ghastly occasion—I shall never forget it as long as I live. . . . The shrieking and wailing I heard that day is indescribable. The whole thing was like a nightmare, unreal and yet horrible. I am sure all of the witnesses in the room were indeed sorry they were there."[7]

Most inmates went quietly to their deaths. Some, like George Appel, who murdered a police officer in New York City, preferred to have a final caustic word as they sat in the chair. A minute before the current was switched on that ended his life, he turned to the witnesses and said, "Well, folks, pretty soon you're going to see a baked Appel."[8] Others were bitter. Before one inmate was strapped in, he pulled out a handkerchief and wiped the seat. A few minutes before, his partner in crime had been executed in the same chair. "After that rat sat in it," he said to the warden. "I want it clean."[9]

At times, witnesses fainted or ran from the gallery in terror at the awful spectacle of a botched execution. Since the chair was only in use since 1890 and death by electricity was still an inexact science, mistakes were made on occasion. Sometimes, insufficient current was used, or the prisoner was not strapped properly, or the contact points were not secure enough to deliver the lethal jolt. In these cases, it required a strong witness to remain in position as the executioner made adjustments while the prisoner, partially burned and crying in agony, sat in the chair knowing what was to come.

The first official New York State executioner was Edwin F. Davis, who was appointed in 1890 to execute the first man to die by electrocution, William Kemmler.[10] He was later paid $150 per death, a generous figure if he was called upon to kill several of the condemned in one day. The most prisoners executed in one day was on August 12, 1912, when seven men went to their deaths in less than one hour at Sing Sing.[11] The man who pulled the switch that day made $1,050, a very large sum for that time.

Of course, an executioner could make a substantial salary if death sentences increased. That may explain why New York's executioner also served in Connecticut, New Jersey, and Pennsylvania. It was not uncommon for him to kill a prisoner in New York, then get into his car and drive over to Pennsylvania, for example, and kill another one or two in the state prison at Scranton. But not everyone was happy with the new execution device. The electric chair was considered inhumane by many and its survival was tenuous at best. Under the headline, "Far Worse Than Hanging," the *New York Times* loudly denounced the state's first execution in 1890. "Probably no convicted murderer of modern times has been made to suffer as Kemmler suffered. That suffering has culminated in a death so fearful that people throughout the country will read of it with horror and disgust."[12] Other newspapers, such as the *New York World*, the *New York Herald*, the *Sun*, and London's *Standard* and *Times* echoed these sentiments.[13] Technicians, however, made continuous improvements in the procedure and despite its many detractors, the electric chair replaced hanging as the favored method of execution. Slowly, the spectacle of electrocution became accepted and death sentences gradually increased. It was part of a trend that began at the turn of the century and continued for decades to come, reaching a peak in 1936 when twenty-one inmates were executed at Sing Sing.[14] For nearly that entire era, the man who operated Ossining's prolific electric chair was Robert G. Elliot, responsible for an incredible 387 executions during his long tenure as America's most famous executioner.[15]

Surrounded by a steady procession of death and despair, Father Schmidt pondered over his future. Though he had relied on an insanity defense that had served him well in Munich, it failed miserably in New York, thanks to Bertha Zech and Inspector Faurot. He realized that the only escape from the execution chamber was a new trial. In July 1914, Alphonse Koelble put together his brief and filed it with the state court of appeals. Under Koelble's direction, Schmidt gave additional depositions in which he modified his story of Anna's death once again. He said she died from a failed abortion performed by Dr. Muret. Later, he simply assisted in the disposal of her body, his only crime, he said. In October 1914, he wrote a letter to Bertha Zech asking her to tell the truth.

"This is the most important letter that I have written in my life," he began. "It is the letter upon which depends my life. Neither Dr. Leo or of Ernest can I expect that they should make any admissions."[16] Schmidt said that he understood why Muret would not make any admissions. He was already in federal prison on counterfeiting charges and Schmidt had promised Muret he would not involve him in Anna's murder. "No doubt you have read in the papers how I acted during Ernest's trial," he wrote in the letter, "that I took the whole matter upon myself without reserve, that I did anything possible in order to save him."[17] But that was before death row. Schmidt had changed his mind now that the electric chair was a real possibility. He implored Zech to help him. "You know that I am not of a mean and contemptible nature, that my main principle in life was not to hurt anybody. I always wanted to settle everything in peace and harmony. The only person in this world who can save me is you. Be magnanimous."[18] Schmidt knew that he needed to implicate Zech in order to corroborate his own version of Anna's death. "I am exceedingly sorry, dear Bertha, that it was all necessary to drag you into this matter. I can vividly imagine how you feel about it."[19]

Zech responded by going to Assistant District Attorney James Delehanty and submitting a deposition, which denied all of Father Schmidt's allegations. "I did not know Anna Aumuller and I never visited her, either in 68 Bradhurst Avenue, or at any other place," she said, "I was not present at any abortion committed upon her. I did and witnessed none of things described as having occurred in the Bradhurst Avenue flat. I was not present when Anna Aumuller died and I had nothing whatever to do with the disposition of her body."[20] His entire story, she said, was a lie made up to expedite his new appeal and implicate other people for what he did. "I did not directly or indirectly have anything to do with Anna Aumuller at any time and I am wholly innocent of the charges made against me in his affidavit."[21]

Koelble decided to obtain a full statement from Father Schmidt and send it to the state court of appeals. He returned to the prison where he met with Schmidt again. "I am innocent of said crime and my previous statement that I caused her death by cutting her throat is untrue," Schmidt said in the deposition of October 30, 1914, "as she died as the result of a so-called criminal operation on Labor Day, September 1, 1913. I am not now nor was I ever insane."[22] He repeated his claim that Anna had two previous abortions, one performed in the Bronx and the other in Vienna in 1911. On both occasions, she was the one who decided that she did not want the baby because Anna was an illegitimate child herself and felt the shame of it many times. Though Schmidt said that he would marry her, she hesitated because "she had no right to be the cause of my leaving the priesthood and that if I did it was only a matter of time when I would abandon her."[23]

After the operation was completed, according to Schmidt, Anna suffered from internal bleeding. "Anna was bleeding freely and blood was noticeable under her," Schmidt said. "All of us were panic stricken. Bertha Zech said, 'I hope to God she will come out of it!' Anna became weaker and weaker and later Muret said she was dead."[24] Schmidt said when he realized that no one, including his friend Dr. Leo, would sign a death certificate under such circumstances, they decided to dispose of the body themselves.

"I felt then as I feel now that I was morally responsible for Anna's death and I promised Muret, Bertha Zech, and Dr. Leo that I would take all the blame on myself to protect them all."[25] He went on to say that he deceived his attorneys after he was arrested and pretended to be insane when he was interviewed by doctors. He knew that the crazier he behaved, the more likely it would be that he would be sent to a mental hospital and then released sometime in the future.

"I kept faith with Muret, Bertha Zech, and Dr. Leo until I was sentenced to death. I have protected all three of these persons as long as I could. The facts present in this affidavit are the absolute truth and any statements I have made at any time in conflict therewith are untrue. . . . I concealed the truth from my attorneys to save the others though the attorneys wished to save me. . . . I have no desire for life but I feel I have a right to be spared from the ignominy of death as a cold-blooded murderer."[26]

Koelble included Schmidt's latest affidavit along with his request for a new trial based on several points. First, Koelble insisted that the explanation offered by Father Schmidt in his deposition on October 30, 1914, was the truth. The killing of Anna Aumuller was not a murder but an accidental death caused by a failed abortion. He said that his client deserved a new trial so that a jury could have a chance to decide if the defendant was guilty of only manslaughter. If the truth had been available at the original trial, Koelble reasoned, then it was most likely that his client would be found not guilty of murder. He acknowledged that Schmidt could have been found guilty of other offenses, but for those crimes he would not have received the death penalty. Koelble wrote in his application for a new trial, "I respectfully submit on the facts that there is no reasonable doubt but that Hans Schmidt is telling the truth and certainly there would be a reasonable doubt in the mind of any fair-minded juryman upon a new trial that Schmidt had committed a brutal murder."[27]

Second, Koelble stated that Judge Vernon Davis made a reversible error at the close of the trial when he charged the jury. This error centered upon the judge's definition of legal insanity to the jury, including his use of the word "wrong." Koelble complained that Judge Davis gave the jury a false instruction of the meaning of wrong as defined by the law. "It is claimed by the defense that this act of killing was done pursuant to the command of God given to the defendant," Davis told the jury. "That will not excuse the commission of the crime if at the time he committed the act he knew the nature and quality of the act and that it was wrong, contrary to the law."[28] Koelble submitted to the court that Judge Davis's interpretation of insanity was incorrect and because of it, the jury decided the case based on a misunderstanding of the concept of insanity.

In the meantime, Dr. Muret, who was convicted of federal counterfeiting charges, was incarcerated in the federal prison in Atlanta, Georgia. When he learned of Schmidt's October deposition, Muret was not happy. Muret's attorney informed him that he might face murder charges in New York if it could be proven he participated in Anna's death. Muret, whose real name was reported to be Arthur Heibing, submitted a statement of his own to the Manhattan District Attorney's office. "I never met Anna Aumuller in my life," he said. "In reading the affidavit of Hans Schmidt, I saw that he quoted me as to various conversations I had with him concerning the sickness and death of Anna Aumuller, the disposition of her body, and matters that came up after her death. The statements made by him are untrue. I know nothing of, and had absolutely nothing to do with it."[29]

Within a few days, Dr. Arnold Leo, who had offices on West 135th Street, also learned of Father Schmidt's most recent statement. He became furious when he read it because he had tried to help Schmidt when they met in 1912 and considered him a friend. Leo contacted District Attorney Delehanty and provided his own deposition to be submitted to the court. He said that he had read the October 30 affidavit of Father Schmidt "in which he made certain statements about me and my connection with the deceased Anna Au-muller."[30] Dr. Leo stated that he had met Anna only once when she came to his office for a skin ailment in July 1913. "I did not go to . . . Schmidt's flat . . . at any time in my life. I did not accompany him or Muret to the Bradhurst Avenue flat. I did not, as stated in the affidavit, decline to perform an operation for the reason that I was not consulted about it, nor did I see the woman, nor did I do any of the things described."[31]

Dr. Leo denied almost everything Schmidt said he did in his affidavit, except to say that he did know Dr. Muret and Father Schmidt. "I never asked the defendant to take the blame of the death of this girl upon himself and relieve me of the charge, nor did he ever make any promise respecting that matter, as I never was implicated with him in any matter of this sort and never had any occasion to ask or receive any promise whatsoever from him."[32] Delehanty later submitted the affidavit and the Zech deposition as proof that Father Schmidt was concocting false stories for his own benefit.

On December 15, the prosecution team submitted their memorandum to the court in opposition to the defense motion for a new trial. Previous case law was on their side. In *People v. Priori* [163 NY 99] it was determined that only newly discovered evidence could be used as a basis to justify a new trial. In the *Priori* decision, the judge wrote that the evidence "must have been discovered since the trial and it must be such as could not have been dis-covered before the trial by the exercise of due diligence." Delehanty sum-marized his position in this way:

An analysis of the proof offered in support of this motion in the light of the Priori opinion shows that it does not at all conform to the rules laid down by the Court of Appeals for the government of such motions. The Priori opinion has been affirmed time and again in later cases in the Court of Appeals and states the settled law of the case. A mere inspection of the proof offered on this motion shows that if it is not merely concocted, it is clearly evidence that was discovered since the trial and it is clearly evidence which could, with due diligence, have been presented upon the trial. No more extended argument upon the law will be made for the reason that the proposition seems too clear for discussion.[33]

Delehanty said to the court that Father Schmidt's present explanation for the death of Anna Aumuller was nothing more than a series of lies from a man whose entire life was a lie. Affidavits submitted to the court by the prosecution proved how untruthful that explanation was, wrote Delehanty. "The proof against him, coming from so many sources widely separated, shows that he has been concocting stories which were designed eventually to be presented to this court if his sham of insanity failed . . . and his statements will show how utterly unreliable is the story which he has finally chosen to submit to the court."[34] The appeals court announced it would review the record and make a decision the following year.

In the meantime, Schmidt sat in prison as his case crawled through New York's courts. During that period, thirty-two men went to their death in the electric chair at Sing Sing. Most were remorseful for their crimes and ultimately came to accept their fate. Others became withdrawn, despondent, or morose. Lt. Charles Becker, sentenced to die after his retrial in 1915, returned to prison that spring to await his fate. Father Schmidt and Becker later became friends and frequently advised each other on the progress of their cases. By July 1915, Becker had exhausted all his appeals and a Governor's reprieve was the only option left. Ironically, the Governor was none other than Charles Whitman, the former Manhattan district attorney who had put him on death row two years before. It was the first time that a sitting Governor had ever faced such a dilemma. Many people wondered how Whitman could be expected to show mercy to Becker when it was he who put him in the shadow of the electric chair. Despite a tearful, personal appeal from Helen Lynch Becker, the defendant's wife, who showed up at the Governor's hotel room in the upstate city of Poughkeepsie to beg for her husband's life, Whitman denied clemency.

"What did you expect?" said an accented voice from the next cell.

"Oreste? That you?" Becker asked.

"Yeah. They're all the same. They're only out for themselves. Do you think this Whitman was gonna give a you a break? You is a dreamer, Lieutenant," said the inmate. Oreste Shillitoni, age 21, an Italian gang member from Manhattan whose crimes caused a full-scale shutdown of Manhattan's borders, was scheduled to die in June. Though he was a loner and rarely shared his feelings with any of his fellow prisoners, Shillitoni took a liking to Father Schmidt and, oddly enough, Lieutenant Becker. Ironically, most men on death row did not consider themselves murderers. Though all were convicted of murder, the average inmate visualized himself as a victim of circumstance caused by a drunken rage, a hateful wife, or simply down on his luck. Chances were that he would never commit a murder again. Shillitoni was different. He was a real killer.

On the afternoon of May 3, 1913, Shillitoni got into a verbal argument with another small-time hood named John "Kid Morgan" Rizzo near the Mulberry Street bend. Words became fists and soon the men were fighting.

Two cops from the West Thirtieth Street Station, officer Charles Teare, age 36, and officer William Heaney, age 26, happened by and attempted to arrest the two men. Shillitoni pulled out a handgun and shot Rizzo dead in front of the two police officers. Officer Teare then used his nightstick on Shillitoni's head, knocking him to the ground. A gun in each hand, the young thug shot and killed both policemen and took off, running down Mulberry Street toward Hester Street. The double police killing set off one of the largest, most intensive manhunts the city had ever seen. For the next six weeks, police, soldiers, bounty hunters, and others scoured New York in search of the brazen killer. Police detained thousands of citizens on their way to and from work simply because they resembled the gunman. River crossings on both sides of Manhattan were shut down and no one was allowed to leave or enter unless properly identified. Businesses came to a standstill while the ongoing drama played itself to the end. On June 14, Shillitoni, trembling in fear of being murdered by vindictive cops, surrendered to a detective on West 152nd Street.

"You know, Lieutenant," said Shillitoni, "you mighta been better off if you just went on a lam. You can't get justice in this town."

"Yeah, you should know, Oreste," replied Becker. "Look where it got you!" With that remark the prisoners erupted in laughter. Most of the men liked Becker, even though he was a cop. He was a part of the Manhattan streets, a cop who tried to make some money and got death row instead.

"At least your cell is closer to the door, my boy!" added Becker. Even Shillitoni laughed at that remark. Becker tolerated the young Italian but he hated him like all police hated cop killers. One of the last regrets Becker had was that he might not live to see Shillitoni die. But Shillitoni had his own ideas. He was already planning an escape. With a little luck, he thought, he could be out in a month or two.[35]

On the morning of July 30, 1915, death came calling for Lt. Charles Becker. It was 5:15 A.M. when five large uniformed men appeared in front of his cell door. The commotion awakened Father Schmidt, whose cell was directly next to Becker's. Accompanied by the prison chaplain, Father William Cashin, they prepared Becker for the execution. Cashin was the Catholic chaplain for Sing Sing since 1912. He was a slender man with a long, cheerless face and never seen without his black cassock and white collar. During his tenure, he had comforted thousands of unfortunate men and women inside the prison walls. To the men on death row, Father Cashin always seemed ready for a funeral. He had a kindly, if not unrealistic, demeanor that was both desired and reviled by the condemned. Some saw his presence as a symbol of death while others the faithful, welcomed his prayers and blessings.

"No word was spoken," reported the *New York Times*, "but Becker got up promptly, followed by the priest and started for the door. He had to be reminded by Father Cashin that he had not donned his coat. As they slowly walked down the corridor, between walls of white curtain that had been stretched in front of the other cells, mumbled 'good-byes' were heard from some of the cells as they passed."[36]

"So long, boys!" Becker called out. "I'll be seeing you again!" He began the walk to the end of the hallway where the only door led to the execution chamber. "To those who had known him in his days of prosperity, the sight of Becker was a shock," said the *New York Times*. "Instead of the powerfully big man he had been, he appeared to have shrunken. His shoulders sagged and there were deep creases in his face, while his eyes peered out almost furtively over deep black circles."[37] He turned to take one last look at the place where he had spent the last months of his life. Then, from inside the darkened cells, other inmates began to yell out their own farewells. Hans Schmidt whispered prayers to his friend as Becker passed by.

The refurbished death chamber had its walls and ceiling painted bright white. As he walked through the door, Becker recited the litany along with Father Cashin. When he first laid his eyes on the chair, Becker's voice cracked. The priest spoke louder and more quickly in order to distract his attention. When Becker sat in the chair, he faced three small glass windows at the end of the room while his back nearly touched the partition to the autopsy area. This made for some painful moments for the doomed prisoner at those times when other inmates preceded him to the electric chair. Autopsies were conducted immediately after an execution. It would not be unusual for an inmate when he entered the death chamber to see the body of his friend, still warm, being wheeled into the autopsy area behind the flimsy partition. As Becker was hastily strapped into the chair at 5:42 A.M., his last words were, "Into thy hands, O Lord, I commit my spirit." Because Lieutenant Becker was a large man and physically strong, it required three sustained jolts of current to kill him. He was pronounced dead at 5:53 A.M.

After the pronouncement, Becker was wheeled into the autopsy room while attendants cleaned up the death chamber. Though no other executions were scheduled for that night, the room was maintained in a neat and orderly manner. Nothing was allowed to be out of place. "The physicians who performed the autopsy reported that Becker had been in perfect health," one news report stated. "Pinned to the undershirt on the left side over his heart, physicians found the small photograph of Becker's wife which had been in his cell. The face was turned toward the body. On the back was a penciled request that the photograph be buried with him."[38]

For Becker, the wait was over. For Schmidt, the march to death continued.

22

Appeal

One of the busiest nights ever on death row was September 3, 1915. On that date, five men were scheduled to die in the electric chair. Multiple executions were not rare at Sing Sing, but this was the first occasion that five men were executed and the most since 1912, when seven prisoners went to their deaths in the space of one hour. One of the five condemned was a man named Antonio Salemne, age 26, a Sicilian immigrant who killed his young wife in a jealous rage in upstate New York.

Unlike many of his contemporaries, Salemne was a well-educated man who could read and write. Though he came from a poor family, his parents were able to send him to school and teach him how to behave like a gentleman. He met an eighteen-year-old girl, Francesca Francioso, in Rochester and soon fell in love. Her parents were thrilled to have such a refined young suitor for their daughter.

On the wedding night, Salemne discovered that his new wife was not a virgin. According to the Sicilian code of honor, this was a great insult to a husband who would become subject to ridicule in the community. Anger and resentment seethed inside the young man until he could not take it anymore. On the morning of June 12, 1914, after he finished shaving, Salemne cut the throat of his sleeping wife with the straight razor. He surrendered to the police explaining that the insult to his manhood could only be rectified by the blood of his wife.[1] When Salemne arrived at Sing Sing, he met Schmidt and they became friends, perhaps because of the similarities in their cases. Salemne was also a devout Catholic.

At dawn on September 3, the execution of the five began. First, guards took William Perry, age 27, from his cell and escorted him down the hallway to the death chamber. Perry murdered his girlfriend after a dispute in Harlem in 1914. Then Louis Roach, age 40, a farmhand who killed his boss in upstate Montgomery County, was executed. Pasquale Venditti, age 47, a Brooklyn laborer who shot his landlord, and Thomas Tarpey, age 42, a British war hero who killed a co-worker in Brooklyn, were next. When guards came for Salemne, he thanked the priest for his comfort and said goodbye to the other inmates. He walked to his death unassisted while guards waited by the chair, which was still warm from the previous executions.

"Be strong, Antonio!" Shillitoni called out as Salemne passed by on his way to death. "God will provide for you! Say your prayers!"

"Arriverderci, Oreste. Buona fortuna! [Good bye, Oreste. Good luck!]" Salemne answered.

When the parade of deaths was over, the inmates could hear the dreadful noise of the autopsies being performed on the other side of the cell-block wall. Within minutes, they were overcome by a mass hysteria of fear and disgust. Locked in their cages like helpless animals awaiting slaughter, the men began to scream and wail. They cursed and swore at the guards, the jail, and the chair. They cried for salvation and begged for their lives. Principal Keeper Dorner summoned Chaplain Cashin to the cell-block. The frantic priest tried to comfort the inmates but it was to no avail. Walter Watson banged his skull on the metal bars until his forehead bled. Another prisoner chewed his own wrists almost to the bone. In the background, the men heard the shrill sound of saw cutting human bone barely twenty feet away.

"God help us!" one man screamed.

"Bastards!" another yelled.

"Shut up, you God damn cowards!" shouted Shillitoni, who was in the last cell, closest to the death-chamber door. The men raged on until they were too exhausted to continue. One by one, they retreated into the farthest area of their cells, in realization that there was little they could do to help themselves. Keeper Dorn sent in a gallon of ice cream and distributed oversized portions to each inmate. It soothed the men into silence and contentment, at least for the rest of the day.

Though Father Schmidt and his crimes were well known on Death Row, most inmates still considered him a priest and they frequently asked him for spiritual guidance. Some of the condemned rejected him because they saw his crimes as a violation of priesthood, which was held in high esteem at that time even by criminals. One of the few who befriended Schmidt was Walter Watson, a Brooklyn painter who murdered his wife in a jealous rage the previous year.[2] He was scheduled to die in March, one month after Schmidt.

On November 23, 1915, the court of appeals announced its decision in *People v. Schmidt.* The judiciary panel, led by Judge Benjamin N. Cardozo, was not impressed with the history of the case and especially with the defendant's behavior toward his attorneys. Judge Cardozo said, "In his affidavit, he tells a most extraordinary tale. He now says that he did not murder Anna Aumuller and that his confession of guilt was false. . . . He believed that he could feign insanity successfully and that after a brief term in an asylum he would again be set to large."[3] The court pointed out that Schmidt said he had made a deal with his colleagues not to implicate them but all the parties involved deny such an agreement was ever made. "Whether they were parties or not to the fraud upon the court is of little importance now," Cardozo added. "The defendant now says he was sane; that the tale of monstrous perversions and delusions were false; that he did not hear the divine voice calling him to sacrifice. He asks that he be given another opportunity to put before a jury the true narrative of the crime."[4]

The judges pointed out that New York statutes allow a new trial only when the defendant can produce new evidence that would have changed the verdict if it had been known before the first trial. The defense offered by Schmidt on appeal was well known to him and easily available to him months ago. All he had to do was to tell the truth to his attorneys, which he did not do. "He chose to withhold it because he had faith in his ability to deceive the courts of justice. . . . Even if the entire tale were true, the courts are powerless to help him."[5] The court of appeals, by law, could not order a new trial under those circumstances. "A criminal may not experiment with one defense," Cardozo said, "and then when it fails him, invoke the aid of the law which he has flouted, to experiment with another defense, held in reserve for that emergency."[6]

In response to Koelble's assertion that Judge Vernon Davis made an error in his charge to the jury on February 4, 1914, the court was more responsive. When Davis gave his explanation of the legal term of insanity, he used the word "wrong" in an incorrect manner and may have confused the jury. To this, the judicial panel agreed but decided that the error did not rise to the level necessitating a new trial. In a sharply worded opinion, Judge Cardozo analyzed the situation in which the defendant found himself.

We have considered the charge of the trial judge upon the subject of insanity, because the question is in the case, and the true rule on a subject so important ought not to be left in doubt. But even though we hold that there was error in the charge, we think the error does not require us to disturb the judgment of conviction. It is of no importance now whether the trial judge charged the jury correctly upon the question of insanity, because in the record before us the defendant himself concedes that he is sane, and that everything which he said to the contrary was a fraud upon the court. It is of no importance now whether the defendant would be relieved of guilt if his diseased mind had revealed the divine presence to his eyes and the divine command to his ears, because he tells us that he never saw the vision and never heard the command. He concedes, therefore, that the issue of his insanity was correctly determined by the jury; he concedes that even if there was an error in the definition of insanity no injustice resulted; and his position is that having fabricated a defense of insanity in order to deceive the trial court, it is now the duty of another court to give him a new trial because his fabricated defense was imperfectly expounded.[7]

In other words, Schmidt was asking for another trial because his deception on the court had failed. The court was not sympathetic. "The principle is fundamental that no man shall be permitted to profit by his own wrong . . . and we will not aid the defendant in his effort to gain the benefit of a fraudulent defense. The judgment of conviction should be affirmed."[8] Cardozo's opinions were highly regarded in the legal community.[9] His rejection of the appeal was a tremendous blow to the defense. Schmidt, it was said, was resigned to his fate. But for Koelble, the struggle continued.

When asked by reporters what his plans were, Koelble said " he could not tell what his next step would be until he read the text of the decision. His possible courses, he said, are motion for rearguement [sic] of the case before the court of appeals, an appeal to the Supreme Court of the United States, an application for a new trial on the ground of newly discovered evidence and an appeal to the governor for clemency."[10]

Though Schmidt had high hopes that his conviction would be overturned, his time was running out. Alphonse Koelble made a motion on January 2, 1916, that the court should revisit the issues because when the original appeal was denied, his client was deprived of his constitutional right to due process. Koelble also said that since Schmidt's federal charges were still outstanding, it would be legally incorrect to execute him before that case could be resolved. Koelble's motion was unusual in that the defense counsel was required to notify the district attorney of any motions put to the court, which he failed to do. However, due to the urgency of the matter, the appeals court went forward with the motion anyway. On January 7, the court issued its decision.

"This motion is irregular," the judge wrote in his decision, "since such an application requires notice to the District Attorney and we have no evidence that the prescribed notice had been given. Notwithstanding this irregularity, in view of the fact that the execution of the judgment is fixed for the week beginning next Monday, we have looked carefully into the merits and find nothing which would justify us in granting a reargument."[11] Though Koelble admitted that Schmidt had deceived him and his co-counsel, Terence McManus, his client, he said, should not have to suffer for it. To that point, the court disagreed. "In affirming the judgment this court held the defendant was unharmed by an error relating to a defense which he alleged and admitted under oath to be fraudulent and a sham. His counsel now insists that by so holding we deprived him of rights guaranteed by the Constitution of the United States. We can perceive no basis for this assertion. The request of counsel for a certificate that a Federal question was involved in the appeal cannot be complied with for it is not the fact. The motion for a reargument must be denied."[12]

As far as the courts were concerned, it was a closed case. There was only one option left for Koelble and Father Schmidt: an appeal to the governor. Immediately after his motion for another review was denied, Koelble appealed to Governor Charles Whitman, the same man who had commandeered the prosecution of his client when he was Manhattan's district attorney. This situation challenged the notions of fairness but it was not the first time that Whitman found himself in such a difficult position. Barely six months before, Lt. Charles Becker's lawyers found themselves in the same predicament. But this time, Whitman was responsive. Perhaps he was affected by the avalanche of criticism over the Becker case in which he refused clemency; or maybe he saw legal issues in the Schmidt case that deserved additional scrutiny. But on January 12, Governor Whitman granted a one-month reprieve for Father Schmidt up to February 14.

"In July last, Schmidt's attorneys made a motion for a new trial on the ground of newly discovered evidence asserting that he had been guilty of manslaughter and not murder. The court however expressed the opinion that if Schmidt had been caught in a trap of his own making, his only remedy was in an appeal to the Governor. 'In the light of the opinion of the court of appeals,' said Governor Whitman, 'It seems but fair that counsel for Schmidt should be able to present the matter for determination.' "[13]

Koelble tried hard. He previously hired Dr. Henry Cattell, a specialist from Philadelphia, and had him perform a new autopsy on the remains of Anna Aumuller. Koelble hoped to show that she had undergone an abortion before she died. If it could be shown that Anna died from a failed operation, it would strengthen his case and might force the court to order a new trial. When Dr. Cattell examined Anna, he came to the conclusion that the original postmortem was incorrect and Anna had died from a poorly performed abortion by incompetent doctors. "I find nothing in the postmortem examinations to warrant the statement that the said Anna Aumuller came to her death from bleeding occasioned by the severance of her throat," he wrote in his affidavit. "I do find, however, every evidence from the parts examined and from the knowledge derived from similar cases of abortion, that the said Anna Aumuller came to her death from bleeding and shock due to an abortion."[14]

But District Attorney Delehanty was emphatic. "As shown in the various papers submitted in behalf of the state in opposition to this application, the story now told by his defendant, when examined in the light of the almost successful sham of insanity which he perpetrated throughout his trial, is nothing more than a further attempt by sham to escape the penalty for his crimes."[15] New autopsy reports meant little, said Delehanty, because the examining doctors were paid by the defense and therefore their conclusions were biased. However, it still did not matter because any of that information was still available prior to the earlier trial and should have been brought out then. It was the defendant, by his deceitful sham of insanity, who prevented his attorneys from presenting a truthful defense. It was undeniable, Delehanty told the governor, Father Schmidt had convicted himself.

On the frigid morning of February 12, death row guard Patrick O'Toole came to see the prisoner. "Father, are you awake?"

"Yes, I'm here. Where can I go?" He sat up in his bunk, covered by blankets and brushed his hair back.

"I've got some bad news. The Governor denied clemency. We just got the word."

Father Schmidt stared at O'Toole for a moment. Then he fell backward on his cot. He brought his hands up to his face and covered his eyes. "I thought God was on my side. I don't know what happened."

"Sorry, Father," said the young guard, "the warden said the day will be February 18."

"The eighteenth? Why, that's not much time at all! What do they expect from me?"

"I don't know," said the guard as he walked away. "I was just told to bring you the news."

Father Schmidt buried his face into the pillow. He began to cry. "Why has this happened to me?" he wailed. "Should I have been an atheist?"

He rolled off the bed and fell to his knees on the cold, hard floor. "Warum, Herr Gott? Ich war doch ein gutter priester! [Why God? I was a good priest!]" he shouted. The words echoed off the stone walls and shattered the silence along the row of the condemned. His sobbing was loud and uninhibited. He begged. He cried. He lifted his hands and heart to the heavens. He stared at the holy crucifix in the corner of his cell and tried to understand.

But he could not.

23

Execution

Warden George Kirchwey announced that, contrary to rumors, he would not prohibit reporters from witnessing Schmidt's execution. "I have not barred reporters," he told the *New York Times*. "What I ordered was that only twelve persons be allowed to witness executions; reporters can be among them. The law limits the number of witnesses to twelve."[1] When it was pointed out to the warden that forty witnesses attended Becker's execution the previous year, Kirchwey had no comment. The Becker execution was special in many ways. There were pressures from powerful, diverse sources to bend the rules in that case. However, for the Schmidt execution scheduled for Thursday, February 18, Kirchwey decided not to send invitations to newspapers as was the custom. Reporters had to contact the warden personally if they wanted to view the event.

After all the appeals were exhausted, including the possibility of a reprieve from Governor Whitman, Father Schmidt accepted the inevitable. Koelble visited his client on Tuesday to ask if there was anything he could do. Schmidt handed him a written statement that he requested to be given to the press. "I charge bad faith on the part of nobody," he said. "This is only a weakness of the judicial system, as there is a weakness of human nature. But I happen to be the victim this time and I hope and pray that time will prove every one of my contentions and that my judicial murder will help to abolish executions for not one third of the men who have been in the death chamber with me, including Becker, were guilty of murder."[2]

At 5:00 P.M. on Wednesday night, the prison chaplain, Father William Cashin, visited Schmidt in his cell. Schmidt gave his only set of rosary beads to Cashin with instructions to deliver it to his mother upon his death. The two priests then prayed together on their knees. Schmidt asked that a mass be said in the morning before he entered the execution chamber. Cashin told him they would need permission from Warden Kirchwey for that.

"I just can't say a mass on my own, Hans. We'll need to get the okay from the warden," Father Cashin explained.

"Well, I don't see what the problem is; after all, we are holy men. I once saw the face of God on the Wertheim cloth, you know. You would think that the warden would want to bring religion into this horrible place."

"I understand, Hans," replied Father Cashin. "I'll work on it." He picked up the prayer book and placed it inside his leather pouch. The tired priest smoothed his cassock and sat down on the cot next to Schmidt. "Hans, there's one more thing. And I want you to know that the only reason I mention this is that the monsignor at the church asked me." The frail priest placed his arm around the prisoner's shoulder in a fatherly manner. "Hans, what of the little girl in Louisville?"

"What girl?" he replied.

"The girl that went missing in Louisville in 1909, Hans. Alma Kellner."

Schmidt jumped up. "God damn it! I never heard of her! Why are they trying to blame her death on me? It was that damned Frenchman, that horrid maintenance man. I met him once, an awful man. They convicted him, you know. He killed that girl. Always trying to put things on me. Of all people, all the good I've done, Father. It's just not fair!"

"I understand, Hans, but the monsignor was concerned. . . ."

"Concerned? Is he kidding? Does he know where I am?" Schmidt shook his head in a condescending manner that made Father Cashin see the futility of the conversation.

"I know, Hans, but there are. . . ."

"And the air in this place is sickening. I think it is killing me, Father, I don't know how guards can work in this dungeon. How can they breathe?" He spread the lapels of his shirt apart. Taking deep, exaggerated breaths, he tilted his head upward and stood on his toes.

"Keep calm, Hans. We'll pray for you." Father Cashin made the sign of the cross.

"Before you leave, let's say a prayer together then," Schmidt whispered, "a prayer for Alma's killer."

The two men knelt on the floor and prayed for the salvation of the man who took the little girl's life. After a few minutes, Father Cashin rose to his feet and placed the rosary in his pocket. In a moment, a guard appeared at the door. Father Cashin put on his coat and patted the young priest on his shoulder but Schmidt did not acknowledge him. The chaplain exited the cell and made a vow to himself to say the last mass for his friend.

In a few moments, Schmidt stood and began to pace. The size of the cell permitted only eight steps from front to rear. While the guard watched carefully from the opposite side of the bars, Schmidt fell on the bunk bed like a burlap sack and lay motionless for thirty minutes. Then he jumped up suddenly.

"I'm an innocent man!" he yelled. "Innocent as the day is long! I never hurt that poor girl, as God is my witness! I never hurt her!"

"You disgraced the church, you bastard!" said another prisoner. "Why don't you shut up?"

"I never disgraced the church!" he yelled. Schmidt turned to the guard who sat quietly in his chair, across from the cell. "Can you do something about the air in here, God damn it! I can't breathe, I tell you!"

"Calm down, Father, the air is fine," said Watson from the cell immediately adjacent.

"No it's not, Walter. The warden did something to the air on purpose. It is so hard to breathe in this damn place!" It was frigid in the cell-block. The winter breeze came in through windows, doors, and cracks and crevices that were everywhere in the old building. "And it's cold as ice," he shouted. "A man could get pneumonia in here. Are they trying to kill us?"

A few minutes past 7:00 P.M., Principal Keeper Fred Dorner appeared at Schmidt's cell to inform the prisoner that it was time for his bath. Every condemned inmate was required to wash on the night before the execution. After the bath, Father Schmidt was outfitted with a new set of prison-issued clothes. If an inmate could afford it, he was allowed to wear the clothes of his choice. It could be a suit and tie, a robe, or anything of his choosing, with the permission of the warden. The traditional apparel was black or dark pants, a white shirt, and slippers. After Schmidt dressed, a barber was sent to his cell. He received a shave and a neat haircut. Though a common understanding was that the top of the head needed to be shaved clean, it was not so. Human hair, so long as it was neatly trimmed, did not interfere with the efficiency of the electrocution process.

According to tradition, the condemned man was allowed to order anything he wanted for his last meal. At times, prisoners would demand the most outlandish meals simply to make preparation more difficult for the kitchen staff. Out-of-season fruits, hard-to-get items such as lobsters or crabs, flavored ice creams, and freshly rolled cigars were only a sampling of what some of the inmates ordered. Prison cooks went along with the requests and did the best they could. Ironically, most of the condemned gave away their meals at the last minute because they were too nervous to eat. "Occasionally a man will eat heartily and with relish on the eve of his execution," wrote Dr. Squire in *Sing Sing Doctor*, "but not often. During the concluding days his digestion is seldom upset, but his desire for food usually diminishes. Nevertheless an elaborate meal is almost always ordered—sometimes merely as a forlorn effort to reassert individuality and recapture a semblance of personal integrity through the exercise of this privilege, even though it is impossible for the man to swallow a bite."[3] For his last meal, Schmidt ordered sauerbraten, string beans, mashed potatoes, cheesecake, and coffee.

Throughout the evening, Schmidt shouted out vows of innocence one minute and then lay on his bunk in silence the next. "Schmidt's conduct was a surprise to prison officials," one report said. "His last night on earth he spent alternately raving and protesting his innocence and declaring that he had made his peace with God."[4] One of his final acts that night was to give his pillow to Watson, who had less than a month to live himself.

"Thanks, Father," Watson said through the bars. "I guess I can use it for the time I have left." Watson took the pillow, placed it on the metal bars and rested his head. "When it's my time, I'll give it to Roy. Where I'm going, I won't need it."[5]

"Well, for the present time, you'll be comfortable," replied Schmidt.

"Hey, Father? Thanks for the roast beef, too."

"Sauerbraten, it was," said Schmidt.

At 3:00 A.M., while death row slept, a dark automobile pulled up to the front gates of Sing Sing. The driver was a short, pudgy man who mostly kept to himself and rarely socialized. He lived in a modest home outside the small upstate village of Auburn, New York, where neighbors thought he was some sort of salesman. His name was John Hilbert, an electrician who once labored under Edwin Davis, New York's first official executioner.

Davis was a secretive man who always imagined that the state wanted to steal his electrocution techniques and put him out of a job. He jealously guarded his procedures and refused to share his knowledge with anyone. Davis held on to his position for twenty-four years and eventually executed 240 prisoners under the authority of the state. But officials worried about what would happen if Davis became sick or passed away, leaving New York without an official executioner. After much effort, Davis was persuaded to train a successor. He chose Hilbert, a man very much like himself, withdrawn, sullen, and unresponsive to those around him. Before he retired, Davis managed to sell his execution methods to the state for $10,000. He abruptly resigned in 1914, and Hilbert, who was paid fifty dollars per execution, stepped up to the job. Because the pay was low, he was forced to obtain additional work and later became the executioner for Massachusetts, New Jersey, and Kansas as well.

"Morning, Mr. Hilbert," said the guard at the gate.

"Yup, morning," the driver replied. The gate swung open and the noisy roadster cruised onto the prison grounds. Hilbert parked on the south side of the death house to ensure easy access to his car after his work was done. He never lingered once the execution was completed. As soon as the inmate was declared dead, Hilbert removed his electrodes, which he carried with him to each electrocution, picked up his fee from the warden's office, and quickly drove away. Hilbert, like Davis before him, received many threats against his life and family. For that reason, he took pains to hide his identity from the public. He would not allow any photographs to be taken of himself and frequently gave a false name when he was in town. His address was kept a secret and when it was time to leave the prison after an execution, he would never go straight home. He would drive in the opposite direction for miles, through twisting country roads and deep into the northern Westchester hills, until he was sure he was not followed. Hilbert was particularly mindful about reporters. The print media, especially in New York City, had an ongoing obsession to reveal the identity of the executioner. Despite many years of trying, the press was never able to obtain a photograph of the elusive John Hilbert.[6]

At 4:00 A.M., Father Cashin arrived at Schmidt's cell with the good news that Warden Kirchwey had granted permission for the mass. He quickly set up a temporary altar in the cell, replete with a chalice, a crucifix, and a small quantity of wine, which he had smuggled into the prison. He donned the church vestments and lit candles. Together, the two priests said mass while the other inmates prayed in unison for clemency and redemption, in that order. "For the first time in the history of Sing Sing, a full mass was said for a prisoner about to die in the electric chair," reported one newspaper. "A temporary altar was erected in Schmidt's cell in the death house with everything necessary for the purpose."[7]

By 4:30 A.M., eighteen witnesses had assembled in the office of Warden Kirchwey. He had allowed an additional five reporters after some of the press made a complaint to Governor Whitman's office that newspapers were being shut out of the execution. The warden informed the witnesses what was expected of them and how to behave during the execution process, but Kirchwey himself would not be present at the execution process. He was a staunch opponent of capital punishment and during his tenure at Sing Sing, he never attended a single execution.

All witnesses were to remain absolutely silent in the execution chamber. Before they left the office, each witness was searched by guards for cameras and other contraband. No photographs were allowed and every man had to sign a paper indicating that he understood the rules. Principal Keeper Dorner led the group across the yard to the death house where they entered through a private doorway at the rear. The witnesses first passed through a small vestibule that was used as a coat room and then they entered the death chamber itself where several rows of chairs had been set up for the event. The nervous men took their seats in silence while they examined the room around them.

It had a gray cement floor and pallid walls. Above them, bright, garish lights illuminated the space. On their left were two doors. One led to the cubicle where executioner Hilbert stood ready to turn the switch upon the physician's command. The other led to the autopsy room, only yards away from the electric chair. On the right side of the room, in the corner, another door, painted dark green, led to the cell-block. Above the entrance was a large sign that read, "Silence."

In the center of the room was the electric chair, resting upon a rubber mat and secured to the floor with one-inch metal bolts. Constructed entirely of wood, stained a brownish color, its thick arms held a pair of restraining straps on each of its sides. The chair had a large back that was tilted slightly to the rear. There were a total of eight black leather straps with heavy buckles that were designed to run across the chest, abdomen, and each arm and leg. A slim headrest, which could be adjusted according to a man's size, protruded from the high back. The chair was twenty-four inches wide, viewed from the front and twenty-six inches deep, viewed from the side. Its height from floor to the top of the tilted back was fifty-five inches. It looked like an ordinary chair that should have been in the waiting room of a train station or an old library. Witnesses stared at the device with both fascination and revulsion. Five minutes of ominous silence passed.

On the other side of the wall, guards in the cell-block had made slits at the bottom of Schmidt's trousers. Like almost all inmates, he chain-smoked incessantly. He took one final puff from his cigarette and discarded the butt onto the cell-block floor. Father Cashin recited prayers from his book and was the first one out of the cell. Schmidt fell in behind him while two guards positioned themselves on either side of the prisoner.

"It's time," one of the men said.

"Don't worry," replied Schmidt. "I'm a punctual man."

Suddenly, the green door swung open and witnesses heard a loud voice, "Auf wiedersehen Ire alle! [Goodbye everybody!] Especially Walter. See you soon, my friends."[8] A few seconds later, Schmidt stepped into the death chamber. It was 5:50 A.M.

His beard had been shaved off and his hair was cut very short, almost to the scalp. He looked very different from how he looked at his trial and for a few moments, those who knew him were not sure it was the same man. Keeper Dorner and Father Cashin escorted Schmidt to the chair, located eight feet away from the first row of witnesses. "He walked with a firm step, repeating in clear tones, the litany of the dying," said one newspaper report. "Firmly, he paced the few steps to the death-dealing chair."[9] Pausing in front of the chair, Schmidt reached inside his shirt and removed a crucifix. He held it high above his head with two hands. Four guards suddenly rushed forward to restrain him. They had mistaken his movement for an attempt to resist. "One minute! One minute!" he pleaded. "I want to say one word before I go. I beg forgiveness of all I have offended or scandalized and I forgive all who have offended against me!"

The guards forced Schmidt to sit into the chair. He prayed loudly while the keepers applied the leather straps tightly around his chest, arms, and legs. They quickly attached the electrodes to his ankles and his biceps while Father Cashin recited his litany for all to hear. A brown metal cap containing a black mask sewn into its brim was fitted over his head. In a muffled voice, he called out his last words in life. "My last word is to say goodbye to my dear old mother!" His hands curled around the edge of the chair's arms. "Scarcely had he repeated these last words when Dorner, who was in charge of the execution, gave the signal to the executioner."[10] The guards stepped back.

Hilbert studied the prisoner for a moment to be sure he was securely fastened. Then he quickly turned the dial. Over 1,700 volts of current slammed into the prisoner. Hans Schmidt's body stiffened violently and strained forward against the straps that held him to the chair. There was a loud crackling sound, then hissing, and, finally, a deep steady hum. The first current was initiated at 5:52 A.M. and lasted for one minute twelve seconds. A noticeable puff of smoke appeared at the top of his head and witnesses perceived a definite odor of burning. Schmidt's hands and neck turned a bright crimson color. When the current was turned off, Prison Physician Dr. Mereness performed a brief examination with his stethoscope and announced the prisoner was still alive. A second jolt was administered for ten seconds, and a third quickly followed. Dr. Mereness then pronounced the prisoner dead at 5:58 A.M.

Two guards returned to the chair and quickly unbuckled the heavy belts. The witnesses lingered about, not really sure the procedure was over. Newspaper reporters feverishly wrote in their paper pads, eager to record every second of the experience. The entire event, from beginning to end, lasted just six minutes. "He was one of the bravest men ever executed in the electric chair," said one news report.[11] Schmidt's body was lifted out of the chair and placed on the gurney. The uniformed men then rolled the cart a few feet away to behind the partition, where the autopsy began immediately. The witnesses filed out and headed toward the exit. As they reached the door, the buzzing sound of the autopsy saw broke the silence and made the men walk faster. They could not help wondering that justice sometimes works in a mysterious way. Like that of his victim, Schmidt's body would endure the cut of a blade.

"His last night on earth he spent protesting his innocence," said the *Albany Times*, "and declaring that he had made peace with God. The guards had expected a scene when the slayer was to be executed. But his actions surprised them. He was the coolest man in the death chamber. He almost domineered those who assisted in putting him to death."[12] The *Evening Telegram* told its readers that "Hans Schmidt, the first Catholic priest ever to be executed in the United States, went to his death in the electric chair at Sing Sing Prison today for the murder of Anna Aumuller."[13]

Father Cashin later claimed the body of Hans Schmidt on behalf of his mother, Gertrude, who was still living in Schweinblein. However, the family was unable to ship the remains back to Germany. Eventually, Father Cashin made arrangements to bury Schmidt in New York. According to the family's wishes, the burial location was kept secret.

Freedom

Clad in a blue suit, black topcoat, and gray hat, the frail, slightly built man walked a little slower than he did when he first arrived in 1910. He was a lot thinner then and a lot happier. As he approached the front gate of the prison, he turned to get a last look at his friends who were not as lucky as him. The man yelled back, "Goodbye! Au revoir! See you soon!" Joseph Wendling, age sixty-two, had received the parole that he had sought for sixteen years.

Beginning his life sentence at the Frankfort Reformatory, he had spent twenty-four years in various Kentucky prisons for the murder of Alma Kellner in 1909. Though he was thought to be a model prisoner at first, Wendling proved to be the opposite. Less than a year after he arrived, he escaped from prison by hiding in a delivery truck. He remained at large for nearly a week while frantic authorities searched everywhere for the convicted murderer. He was found roaming the streets of downtown Frankfort masquerading as a woman and living in the seamier part of town. Despite additional security measures, Wendling escaped again in 1921. This time, he was caught when he tried to get back into the prison using a rope to climb over the walls. He wanted to attend a disciplinary hearing the following day, and because of his record, the panel refused to consider a release for many years. Eventually, Wendling settled into prison life and never tried to escape again.

When Joseph Wendling became eligible for parole in 1919, Alma Kellner's uncle, Frank Fehr, appeared at the hearing and voiced his opinion against the release of the man he believed had killed his niece. He appeared at every parole hearing since then and was vociferous in his opposition. But after he received an eighteen-page letter from Wendling in 1933, Fehr abruptly reversed his position. He wrote to Governor Ruby Laffoon and said he would accept full responsibility for the parole. By late 1934, the prison board had become sympathetic and began to look at his parole favorably.

The parole notice was received by Warden Thomas Logan of the Eddyville Penitentiary and became official on January 25, 1935, seventeen years after Father Schmidt's execution. Wendling's release was conditional on two points. The first was that he had to agree to return to France immediately. The second condition was never made public. Governor Laffoon signed the parole, which was recommended by the State Welfare Board the previous autumn.

"I'm not at liberty to say what the condition, besides deportation, was," Fehr told reporters.[1] Fehr's role in the process was essential to the board's review on the case. Though he always insisted that Wendling confess before he would drop his opposition to parole, the prisoner refused. For the entire twenty-four years that he was in prison, Wendling denied killing Alma Kellner.

Accompanied by two Kentucky State police officers and Warden Logan, Wendling was taken from the Eddyville facility by car and into the city of Louisville for completion of formalities. Later that day, Warden Logan and Wendling began their train trip to New York City. According to the parole agreement, he was scheduled to board a ship back to France. Wendling's passport was obtained several weeks before and his fare paid by funds he accumulated during his incarceration. The Welfare Board insisted that the costs of his release should not be paid by the state's taxpayers. That was also part of the agreement. Kentucky authorities wanted the money for Wendling's deportation to come from his own pocket. Outside of Louisville, his parole received very little attention. Twenty-four years was a long time, and the world had moved on.

On the cold morning of February 2, while Warden Thomas Logan followed closely behind, Wendling boarded the French liner *Champlain* at the West Forty-third Street docks. "He came to New York last Thursday, accompanied by Warden Thomas Logan, who stayed with him until the ship sailed, going with the passenger to his cabin in the tourist class. In the interim they had seen New York together, visiting picture houses and viewing the places popular with visitors to the city."[2] Wendling's destination was Dijon, France, where his parents once lived on a farm. "Although I have not heard from them," he told reporters, "I hope they are still living. If they are not, then the farm will become my property and I will probably live on it."[3] He carried only one bag, which was packed by his loyal wife Madelena, then seventy-five years old and still living in Louisville. If things worked out in France, Wendling planned to send for her. But it never happened. She died the following year.

The ship drifted out from the dock until four colorful tug boats bumped alongside and gently nudged the vessel out into the harbor. Logan and his men stood on the wharf and watched as huge billows of smoke poured from the *Champlain*'s double stacks. She turned her bow slowly to the south and crawled down the river. The powerful tugs veered away one by one, moving on to their other assignments. On board, Wendling grasped the smooth wooden railing and watched the mighty canyons of Manhattan drift by. He took deep breaths of fresh air and realized it was the first time in over twenty-five years that he was not under the yoke of prison life. It was freedom he felt; that precious commodity more valuable than gold once it's gone.

The *Champlain* picked up speed, cutting through the water easily as she steamed for the open Atlantic, due east toward the coast of France. On the dock, Warden Logan studied the vessel until all that remained was the tiny image of her stern and a twisting column of smoke as the ship methodically sank below the horizon. After a few minutes, the colossal ship was gone; only a dim memory, an intangible vision, and for a moment, it was as if it never existed at all.

Notes

INTRODUCTION

1. Carson, Butcher, and Mineka, 336–338.

1. THE CHAPEL

1. "Dispose our days in Thy peace; command that we be saved from eternal damnation and numbered among the flock of Thy elect. Amen."

2. "And do Thou, O God, vouchsafe in all respects to bless, consecrate and approve, this is our oblation, to perfect it and to render it well pleasing to Thyself, so that it may become for us the Body and the Blood of Thy most beloved Son, Jesus Christ, our Lord."

2. THE SIXTH

1. Heinrich Schmidt, 416.

2. Ibid., 414.

3. Jeliffe, 719.

4. This analysis of Hans Schmidt was first introduced by Dr. Jeliffe in his testimony to the court in January 1914. His conclusions were based on interviews with Father Schmidt during the time he was in custody in the Tombs in New York

City. In his notes, Dr. Jeliffe uses direct quotes from Father Schmidt, who described his childhood experiences in Aschaffenburg, including his first sexual encounter with a male friend who lived in the same village.

5. Schadler, 440.

6. Ibid., 441.

7. Jeliffe, 718.

8. Schadler, 445.

9. Karl Schmidt, November 8, 1913, 474–475.

10. Jeliffe, 800.

11. Heinrich Schmidt, 411.

12. Jeliffe, 799.

13. Ibid., 802.

14. Boxheimer, 1–3.

15. Karl Schmidt, November 8, 1913, 476.

16. Karl Schmidt, October 3, 1913.

17. Karl Schmidt, November 8, 1913, 475.

18. Kraus, 489.

19. Jeliffe, 748.

20. Karl Schmidt, October 3, 1913.

21. Jeliffe, 722.

22. Lichenstein, 675.

23. Jeliffe, 723.

24. Ibid.

25. Lichenstein, 676.

26. Bendix, 502.

27. Boxheimer, 2.

28. Ibid., 4.

29. Katerina Schmidt, 478.

30. According to the testimony of the American vice deputy consul at Frankfurt, William Dawson Jr., who visited Jordanbad and submitted the record of Hans Schmidt's stay to the court.

31. Boxheimer, 5.

32. Karl Schmidt, November 8, 1913, 476.

33. Jeliffe, 725.

34. Ibid., 726.

35. Sieben, 485.

36. Jeliffe, 727.

37. Ibid., 721.

38. Sieben, 486.

39. Kraus, 490.

40. Boxheimer, 5.

41. Quinn, 594.

42. Ibid.

43. Sieben, 485.

44. Harry Thaw, accused of the shooting murder of world-renowned architect, Stanford White, in 1906, was a millionaire playboy. He killed White in a jealous rage over Evelyn Nesbit, Thaw's nineteen-year-old wife. The ongoing scandal, involving Manhattan's high society and blatant influence-peddling by Thaw's family, created the century's first high-profile murder case. The sensational tale was reported around the world. A great deal of attention was focused on Thaw's bizarre sexual practices, which were described in detail by New York's tabloids. Thaw was found not guilty of murder by reason of insanity in his second trial and died in Miami in 1947 (Wolf and Mader, 152–163).

45. Quinn, 604.

46. Sieben, 487.

3. ALMA

1. *Courier-Journal* (Louisville), December 9, 1909.

2. Wilson, 323.

3. Fass, 56.

4. They were later identified as William Mosher, whose handwriting matched the ransom note, and Joey Douglas, a notorious burglar who was well known to the police.

5. Fass, 37.

6. An ex-cop named William Westervelt was convicted on questionable evidence and sentenced to seven years in prison. But he denied any part in the Charley Ross abduction and was released in 1882. Westervelt fell into obscurity, and little is known about his life after prison.

7. *Courier-Journal* (Louisville), December 9, 1909.

8. Ibid., 1.

9. Ibid., 2.

10. *Courier-Journal* (Louisville), December 20, 1909, 2.

11. Ibid., 1.

12. Ibid.

13. Ibid.

14. Ibid.

15. Ibid.

16. Ibid.

17. *Courier-Journal* (Louisville), December 9, 1909, 1.

4. INTO THE CELLAR

1. *Courier-Journal* (Louisville), July 31, 1910, 1.

2. *Courier-Journal* (Louisville), May 31, 1910, 1.

3. Ibid.

4. Ibid.

5. Ibid.

6. Ibid.

7. *Courier-Journal* (Louisville), May 31, 1910, 1.

8. *Courier-Journal* (Louisville), May 31, 1910, 2.

9. Ibid.

10. Ibid.

11. This interview was published in its entirety in the Louisville *Courier-Journal* on May 31, 1910.

5. THE PURSUIT

1. *Courier-Journal* (Louisville), May 31, 1910, 3.

2. Ibid., July 31, 1910, 3.

3. Ibid.

4. *Louisville Times*, August 1, 1910, 1.

5. *New York Times*, July 31, 1910, 14.

6. *Courier-Journal* (Louisville), August 6, 1910, 1.

7. *Courier-Journal* (Louisville), August 11, 1910, 1.

8. Ibid.

9. *New York Times*, August 13, 1910, 12.

10. *Courier-Journal* (Louisville), August 16, 1910, 10.

11. *Courier-Journal* (Louisville), August 17, 1910, 2.

12. *Louisville Times*, November 28, 1910, 1.

13. *Courier-Journal* (Louisville), December 1, 1910, 2.

14. *Louisville Times*, December 2, 1910, 1.

15. *Courier-Journal* (Louisville), December 2, 1910, 1.

16. *Louisville Times*, December 3, 1910, 20.

17. *Louisville Times*, December 3, 1910, 1.

18. Ibid.

19. Ibid.

20. *Louisville Times*, December 24, 1910, 1.

6. AT DAWN

1. Kouwenhoven, 394.

2. Ibid., 396.

3. Willard, 375.

4. The Burr mansion was actually built at another location. In 1820, the Astor family had the building rolled on logs to its new location on Varick Street. In 1822, it was reopened as a public house with a music room and refreshments. The family then "sold or leased lots to carpenters and masons, who erected row after row of houses on speculation. By the mid-twenties, this once remote neighborhood was full of people" (Burrows and Wallace, 447).

5. Russell, 322

6. For a contemporary description of the real-estate empire held by Trinity Church during this era, see Charles Edward Russell's detailed article (originally published in 1909), "The Tenements of Trinity Church" in *Tales of Gaslight New York* (2000), Castle Books. He estimated their holdings to be worth $100 million in 1908, making the church the largest landholder in New York and probably the richest in America. Trinity derived an enormous amount of income from these investments. How the church spent this money and where, Russell said, remained a mystery because Trinity's finances were kept secret from the public.

7. The *Lusitania* was one of the most extravagant ocean vessels ever built and one of the fastest. Used as a passenger and cargo vessel since 1906, she became the most popular ship afloat. During the tension-filled years before World War I, an increasing number of ships were sunk by German submarines, who claimed the vessels were being used to transport war material to Germany's enemies. Despite many warnings from German authorities, the *Lusitania* decided to sail to England on May 1, 1915. A few days later, she was hit by a single torpedo off the coast of Ireland and sunk in just eighteen minutes. Over 1,200 lives were lost.

7. CLIFFSIDE PARK

1. *New York Press*, September 6, 1913, 1.
2. Ibid., September 7, 1913, 1.
3. Ibid., September 6, 1913, 1.
4. Ibid.
5. Ibid.
6. *New York Press*, September 7, 1913, 1.

8. WEEHAWKEN

1. *New York Press*, September 8, 1913, 1.
2. Ibid.
3. Ibid.
4. *Sun*, September 8, 1913, 1.
5. Ibid.
6. *New York Press*, September 6, 1913, 1.
7. Ibid., September 7, 1913, 1.
8. *Sun*, September 8, 1913, 1.
9. *Sun*, September 11, 1913, 2.
10. Ibid.
11. *New York Press*, September 8, 1913, 1.
12. Ibid.
13. The trochanter is a bony structure that sticks out at the end of the thigh and serves as an attachment for various muscles of the leg.

14. *New York Press*, September 8, 1913, 1.

15. *Sun*, September 11, 1913, 3.

16. *Sun*, September 11, 1913, 2.

9. FAUROT

1. The largest street sign in the world was erected on the west side of Broadway between Forty-third and Forty-fourth streets. Wrigley's Company paid one million dollars to lease this space and put up a sign that was 200 feet long and 100 feet high, which drew massive crowds and needed squads of police to maintain order (Traub, 51).

2. Ibid., 41–42.

3. *New York Herald*, September 15, 1913, 1.

4. Sachs, 151.

5. Brooker, 141.

6. Ibid.

7. Ibid.

8. Ibid.

9. *Evening Telegram*, September 14, 1913, 3.

10. *New York Times*, September 15, 1913, 3.

11. *Sun*, September 15, 1913, 2.

12. *New York Herald*, September 15, 1913, 1.

13. Faurot, 303.

14. *New York Press*, September 15, 1913, 2.

15. *New York Times*, September 15, 1913, 3.

16. By 1905, there were over three million outdoor electric lights on the streets of New York City. Broadway was lit up like no other street in the world, thanks to the visionary ideas displayed at both the Chicago World's Fair in 1893 and the fantastic Pan American Expo held at Buffalo in 1901. Both expositions showed what could be possible using electricity in a modern metropolis. Pioneered by the Croatian genius, Nikola Tesla, street lighting brought American cities out of medieval darkness and into a new and exciting era. But New York City would not be the first to receive lighting. That distinction belonged to Buffalo in 1896 when Niagara Falls provided the power to generate 15,000 horsepower of Westinghouse electricity. But it was Tesla's ideas that made it possible. An introspective man who shunned the public spotlight, Tesla was one of the greatest inventors the world has ever seen. He was almost supernaturally gifted. Eccentric, flamboyant, and deeply envied by Thomas Edison and George Westinghouse, his theories were often beyond the understanding of his contemporary scientists. Because of those professional jealousies, Tesla was not readily accepted by his colleagues. "If there ever was a man who created so much and whose praises were sung so little, it was Nikola Tesla" (Cheney, 89).

17. *Sun*, September 15, 1913, 2.

10. THE RECTORY

1. *New York Times,* September 15, 1913, 2.
2. *New York Herald*, September 14, 1913, 1.
3. *Sun*, September 15, 1913, 2.
4. *New York Herald*, September 15, 1913, 2.
5. Ibid.
6. *New York Times*, September 15, 1913, 2.
7. *New York Herald*, September 15, 1913, 2.
8. *Sun*, September 15, 1913, 2.
9. *Evening Telegram*, September 14, 1913, 3. A crude diagram of a human form was drawn on a piece of paper by Faurot. It was given to Father Schmidt, who then drew slash marks on the body to indicate exactly where he had severed Anna's body. The paper was signed by Detective O'Connell, Detective O'Neill, Detective Cassassa, Inspector Faurot, and Father Schmidt.
10. *New York Times*, September 15, 1913, 2.
11. *Sun*, September 15, 1913, 2.
12. *Evening Telegram*, September 14, 1913, 3
13. *New York Times,* September 15, 1913, 2.
14. Ibid., 1.
15. *New York Times*, September 18, 1913, 2.

11. MURET

1. *Evening Telegram*, September 15, 1913, 2.
2. *New York Herald*, September 15, 1913, 1.
3. *Sun*, September 15, 1913, 1.
4. *New York Herald*, September 16, 1913, 1.
5. *New York Times*, September 15, 1913, 1.
6. *New York Herald*, September 16, 1913, 1.
7. Ibid.
8. Ibid.
9. Ibid.
10. Hirt, 287–289.
11. September 16, 1913, 1.

12. STIGMATA

1. *New York Herald*, September 16, 1913, 1.
2. Ibid.
3. *New York Herald,* September 16, 1913, 2.
4. *New York Herald*, September 15, 1913, 2.
5. *New York Press*, September 24, 1913, 1.

6. *New York Herald,* September 16, 1913, 2.

7. Ibid.

8. Marshall, *New York Times*, December 3, 1911, 8.

9. Ibid.

10. *New York Times*, October 11, 1913, 1.

11. During the years 1912 and 1913, thirty-four persons were executed at Sing Sing while dozens more sat on death row. Since the electric chair was introduced to New York State in 1890, thanks to the efforts of an eccentric dentist named Dr. Alfred Southwick, executions increased dramatically. On August 12, 1912, seven men were executed in a single night, the most in the history of the state (Hearn, 122).

12. Ellis, 431.

13. Marshall, *New York Times*, November 27, 1910, 1.

14. Steffens, 447.

15. Marshall, *New York Times*, November 27, 1910, 2.

16. Ellis, 433.

17. Logan, 9.

18. Ibid.

19. Knappman, 265.

20. Ironically, after Whitman was elected governor in 1914, Lieutenant Becker made an appeal for clemency to the governor's office. It was the first time in the state's history that a governor was asked to commute a death sentence that he himself had obtained as a prosecutor. Many observers felt there was an obvious injustice in this situation. How could Whitman decide the case when it was he who convicted Becker in the first place? In the end, Whitman denied clemency and Becker was executed on July 30, 1915. His wife engraved these words on her husband's tombstone: "Charles Becker, murdered by Governor Whitman." The stone was replaced when Whitman's office threatened Mrs. Becker with a defamation lawsuit.

21. Steinberg, 257.

22. *New York Times*, September 25, 1913, 7.

23. Ibid., 1.

24. Ibid., 7.

25. *New York Times*, December 24, 1913, 18.

26. *Evening Telegram*, September 15, 1913, 3.

27. *Sun*, September 15, 1913, 2.

28. *New York Times*, September 24, 1913, 1.

29. *New York Times*, September 25, 1913, 7.

13. BELLEVUE

1. *Sun,* September 17, 1913, 2.

2. *Sun,* September 16, 1913, 3.

3. Ibid.

4. *New York Times*, September 21, 1913, 1.

5. The M'Naghten Rule is a landmark in British and American criminal justice. This case, decided in 1843, established the accepted criteria for legal insanity, an area of the law that was ambiguous, poorly defined, and vastly abused in criminal courts. Simply stated, the M'Naghten Rule says that a defendant can only be considered insane if, at the time of the commission of the crime, he did not know what he was doing or did not know that the act was wrong. Contrary to public perception, an insanity defense is rarely used in America's courts and rarely successful.

6. Jeliffe, 716.

7. Gregory, 846.

8. Ibid.

9. Ibid.

10. Ibid.

11. This meeting between Schmidt and doctors Jeliffe, Karpas, and Gregory was described in detail by each of the psychiatrists in their court testimony during the Schmidt trial in January 1914. When Dr. Gregory intentionally cut his finger to draw blood, he suspected that he would get a strong reaction from Father Schmidt. He already knew from the depositions taken in Germany that Schmidt had a morbid fascination with blood.

14. IN THE TOMBS

1. *Evening Telegram*, September 15, 1913, 3.

2. A coroner's inquest had the power to order a defendant imprisoned and held for the Grand Jury, which happened in this case. Once the determination was made that a defendant was responsible for the death in question, he could be, and usually was, sent to jail to await further court action. A coroner could pass on bail recommendations to the district attorney's office as well.

3. *New York Press*, September 29, 1913, 1.

4. *New York Press*, September 22, 1913, 12.

5. Ibid.

6. *Evening Telegram,* September 25, 1913, 5.

7. *New York Times*, September 23, 1913, 5.

8. *New York Press*, October 4, 1913, 3.

9. Ibid.

10. Ibid.

11. Coroner's Inquest, 1.

12. Ibid.

13. Ibid.

14. *New York Press,* October 3, 1913, 1.

15. Ibid.

16. Coroner's Inquest, 1.

17. *New York Times*, September 15, 1913, 8.

18. Sutton, 181–182.

19. Anbinder, 231.

20. The location was also an execution site in pre–Revolutionary War days. One of the most famous executions of the era took place in 1741, when seven black slaves were executed for their role in an arson conspiracy earlier that year (King, 453).

21. Anbinder, 231.

22. *New York Times,* September 15, 1913, 8.

23. Ibid.

24. For a detailed description of the shocking conditions at New York City's jail during the nineteenth century, see Charles Sutton's *The New York Tombs: Its Secrets and Mysteries* (1973).

25. *New York Tribune,* December 29, 1913, 5.

26. *New York Herald,* September 18, 1913, 2.

15. TRIAL

1. Logan, 188.

2. Slocum had a promising career in baseball that was curtailed by a serious drinking problem. On New Year's Eve in 1890, he killed his girlfriend, Ella Perkins, by bludgeoning her with a baseball bat in their apartment on Roosevelt Street. He was executed at Sing Sing prison on July 7, 1891.

3. When it was discovered that Feigenbaum was in London in 1888 during a series of mutilation murders, speculation increased that he was "Jack the Ripper," but no proof was ever established that he was responsible for the killings. Feigenbaum never offered a motive for the Hoffman murder and the attempted murder of her sixteen-year-old son. He went to his death in the electric chair at Sing Sing on April 27, 1896.

4. Ironically, Schmidt's trial was scheduled to be held in the same room where Lt. Charles Becker was tried in 1912.

5. Logan, 243.

6. It was a strategy that would be affirmed in 1914 when Charles Whitman was elected governor of New York.

7. *New York Times,* January 22, 1914, 2.

8. King, 45.

9. Ibid.

10. King, 53.

16. CLOSE UNION

1. Schadler, 438.

2. Ibid.

3. Ibid., 440.

4. Ibid., 448.

5. Heinrich Schmidt, 410.

6. Ibid., 411.

7. Cesare Lombroso, an Italian physician heavily influenced by Darwinian theory, was convinced that criminals were a sort of biological throwback on the evolutionary scale. He believed that deviant behavior manifested itself by physical characteristics such as wide noses, low foreheads, and undersized skulls. He coined the phrase, "born criminal," a term used to describe the inevitability of poor genetics. Lombroso's work was later disproved, mostly by the work of another researcher, Charles Goring, who published *The English Convict: A Statistical Study* in 1910. Goring showed that there was no physical differences between a group of 3,000 convicted criminals and another group of British soldiers. Lombroso's conclusions were based not on his own misconceptions, but on faulty research methods, a condition that later became known as the Lombrosian Fallacy (Vito and Holmes, 96).

Richard Dugdale's *The Jukes: A Study in Crime, Pauperism, Disease, and Heredity* (1875) described an upstate New York family whose propensity for crime extended from one generation to the next beginning in the early eighteenth century. "Dugdale found that, over the next 75 years, heirs included 1,200 persons, most of whom were 'social degenerates'" (Schmalleger, 94). Using complicated charts and far-reaching assumptions that were later discredited, Dugdale concluded that criminal behavior was genetic in nature.

8. Karl Schmidt, November 8, 1913, 475.

9. Ibid., 476.

10. Katrina Schmidt, 478.

11. Boxheimer, 481.

12. Sieben, 485.

13. Ibid., 486.

14. Seebacher, 492.

15. McGuire, 638–639.

16. Poe, 23.

17. JELIFFE

1. Jeliffe, 714.

2. Ibid., 715.

3. Ibid., 716.

4. Ibid., 719.

5. *New York Times,* January 23, 1914, 1.

6. Jeliffe, 720.

7. Ibid., 749.

8. Ibid., 746.

9. Ibid., 747.

10. Ibid., 760.

11. Ibid., 827.

12. Ibid., 792–793.

13. Ibid., 756.

14. Ibid., 754.

18. ZECH

1. According to the list of evidence in the trial transcript, exhibits 20 and 21 were two photographs of Anna Aumuller. Exhibit 20 was a portrait-type image that was reproduced in New York City newspapers. Exhibit 21 was an image of Miss Aumuller in a festive costume and reproduced in the *New York Herald* on September 15, 1913.

2. Hays, 389.

3. *New York Times*, February 4, 1914, 4.

4. Vernon Davis, 1370.

5. Ibid., 1371.

6. Ibid., 1375.

7. Ibid., 1376.

8. Ibid., 1380.

9. Ibid., 1391.

19. THE SACRIFICE

1. "If you do not have a vocation, make yourself one."

2. "And may our sacrifice so be offered in Thy sight this day as to please Thee, who art our Lord and God."

3. "May the Lord receive this sacrifice from your hands to the praise and glory of His name, for our good, and that of all His holy church."

4. "Pray that my sacrifice and yours may be acceptable to God the Father Almighty."

5. This narrative of the murder of Anna Aumuller conforms to the sworn statement of Father Schmidt on the night of September 13, 1913, and the court testimony of Dr. Smith Ely Jeliffe, Dr. Perry Lichenstein, and Dr. Menas Gregory who interviewed the prisoner and discussed with him the details of what he did inside the Bradhurst Avenue apartment on the night of the murder.

20. SING SING

1. *Tribune*, February 12, 1914, 6.

2. Richard Harding Davis, 2.

3. Lawes, *Years*, 87.

4. Christianson, 128.

5. In one year, 1,213 punishments were given out to 890 prisoners (Lawes, *Years*, 86). In another year, 613 men out of a population of 796 received punishments of every sort; most of those received disciplinary measures more than once. One man was punished twenty-times that same year (86).

6. The striped uniform was worn well into the twentieth century. One stripe signified a first-time offender; two stripes for the second-timer and three stripes for a

three-time loser. Four stripes were career criminals who were considered lost causes and treated the harshest by guards (Cheli, 20).

7. Richard Harding Davis, 2.

8. Squire, 11.

9. Lawes, *Years*, 83.

10. One of the most famous executions on Bedloe's Island took place in 1860. Albert Hicks, who had hijacked a sloop off the coast of Long Island and murdered its four-man crew, was taken to the island and hung in front of 10,000 spectators who had gathered offshore in small vessels and excursion boats hired especially for the occasion.

11. It was not until Warden Lewis E. Lawes took command of Sing Sing in 1920 that things really began to change. His visionary leadership brought a new understanding of the state's responsibility toward its prison inmates. A strong opponent of the death penalty and a shameless self-promoter as well, Lawes brought the aged facility into the light of the twentieth century. Lawes lectured across the country on the evils of capital punishment and wrote several books, including *Twenty Thousand Years in Sing Sing*, which were well received by the public. Several of his writing projects were made into successful films during the 1930s, and he became a sought-after celebrity in Hollywood.

12. New York executed more inmates than any other state in America up until 1972 when the U.S. Supreme Court put a temporary hold on executions in its decision in *Furman v. Georgia*.

13. Lawes, *Death*, 57.

21. DEATH ROW

1. One of the men who worked on the construction project, Thomas Pallister, was later convicted of murder and, ironically, sentenced to death. While waiting to be executed, he and a fellow prisoner broke out of Sing Sing. The next day, their bodies were found floating in the Hudson River. Each had a bullet in his head. The incident remained a mystery, and no one was ever charged in their murders (Blumenthal, 13).

2. Although three death row inmates escaped from the prison, one was quickly recaptured in nearby Ossining. The others were later found dead.

3. *New York Times*, January 14, 1916, 4.

4. Squire, 179.

5. Ibid., 178.

6. There are documented cases of prisoners who fought all the way to their executions. Most, however, were resigned to their fate and went peacefully to their deaths. Two brothers, known as the "Mad Dog Espositos" had to be carried to the chair in 1942 in a semiconscious state as the result of a self-initiated starvation to protest their own executions. In 1936, Mary Frances Creighton, convicted of the murder of her boyfriend's mother, became the only person in Sing Sing history to

be executed while unconscious. Hours before she was scheduled to die, she apparently collapsed from the pressure and had to be lifted into the electric chair.

7. Squire, 147.

8. Drimmer, 347.

9. Ibid., 352.

10. The state's first execution was a disaster when the chair did not function as planned. Kemmler may have suffered terribly in the apparatus while technicians tried desperately to correct the problem. The *New York Times* said Kemmler "died this morning under the most revolting circumstances. An execution that was a disgrace to civilization. It was so terrible that words fail to convey the idea" (August 7, 1890, 1). Author Craig Brandon, in his book on the history of the electric chair, points out that many newspapers expanded on the details of the execution. "The details of the botched execution were ghastly enough, but many of the newspapers, because their reporters were not able to be present, invented even more terrible accounts—that Kemmler's body caught fire, that flames erupted from his mouth, that he cried out in pain when the current was turned on" (Brandon, 181).

11. Lorenzo Cali, Vincenzo Cona, Filepo DeMarco, Salavatore DeMarco, and Angelo Guista were executed on August 12, 1912, for the murder of a Westchester County woman. A sixth man, Santo Zanza, had already gone to his death in the chair on July 8, 1912. Though four of the men were unaware that a killing had taken place during a burglary they committed together, all seven were convicted and sentenced to death. The sentence was proper under the felony murder rule that states if a nonparticipant in a crime dies, all the suspects involved can be charged with murder, even if they were not present during the actual killing.

12. *New York Times,* August 7, 1890, 1.

13. Drimmer, 31.

14. Twenty inmates were executed at Sing Sing in both 1932 and 1944.

15. A quiet, unassuming grandfather who shunned publicity and lived a normal life with his family in Queens, New York, Elliot was originally an assistant to Edwin Davis, the state's first executioner. Unlike other men who fell into their jobs by chance, Elliot always wanted to be an executioner, even as a child. As an adult, he was frequently described as a morose, isolated individual who suffered psychological problems from his dreadful position. "Friendless, lonely, a social outcast. That according to common supposition, is the miserable existence that is mine," Elliot once wrote. "It has been said that I am a recluse, living in an atmosphere of funeral gloom" (Elliot, 9). Nothing could be farther from the truth. In reality, Elliot was comfortable with his work and saw it as a necessary occupation in service to the public. Some of his most famous executions were Nicola Sacco and Bartolomeo Vanzetti in July 1927, Ruth Snyder in 1928, and Bruno Hauptmann, the kidnapper of the Charles Lindbergh baby, in 1936. Elliot kept a written diary of every execution he performed which was published in 1940 under the title, *Agent of Death.* During his career, Elliot earned $57,600 from the state of New York for his services (Drimmer, 53).

16. Hans Schmidt, October 2, 1914, 1.

17. Ibid., 2.

18. Ibid.

19. Ibid.

20. Zech, November 17, 1914, 1.

21. Ibid., 2.

22. Hans Schmidt, October 30, 1914, 6.

23. Ibid., 7.

24. Ibid., 11.

25. Ibid., 11.

26. Ibid., 18.

27. Koelble, 3.

28. Vernon Davis, 1386.

29. Heibing, 2.

30. Leo, 1.

31. Ibid., 2.

32. Ibid., 3.

33. Delehanty, 3.

34. Ibid., 4.

35. Armed with a handgun that was smuggled in by persons unknown, Shillitoni escaped from death row on June 21, 1916. He shot two guards, killing one, and managed to climb the outer wall of Sing Sing despite a barrage of fire from machine guns, rifles, and shotguns of the prison guards. Shillitoni made it to Ossining Hospital where he was befriended by a nurse. He was later captured after the nurse told the police where he was hiding. Shillitoni was executed on June 30, 1916 (Hearn, 140).

36. *New York Times*, July 31, 1915, 3.

37. Ibid., 1.

38. Ibid., 1.

22. APPEAL

1. Hearn, 135–136.

2. Walter Watson, age 42, had separated from his wife, Elizabeth, that year. He became enraged over the breakup and threatened to kill her if she did not return. On March 22, 1915, Watson went to visit her in her new apartment. When she refused him entry, he broke down the door and stabbed her to death in front of their six children. Watson was executed on March 3, 1916.

3. Cardozo, 1.

4. Ibid.

5. Ibid., 2.

6. Ibid.

7. Ibid., 7.

8. Ibid., 8.

9. Benjamin Nathan Cardozo was later appointed by President Herbert Hoover to the U.S. Supreme Court where he served with distinction from 1932 to 1938.

10. *New York Times*, November 24, 1915, 6.

11. *New York Times*, January 8, 1916, 5.

12. Ibid.

13. Ibid., January 13, 1916, 8.

14. Cattell, 2.

15. Delehanty, 2.

23. EXECUTION

1. *New York Times*, February 9, 1916, 12.

2. Ibid., February 18, 1916, 12.

3. Squire, 206.

4. *Syracuse Herald*, February 18, 1916, 3.

5. Roy Champlain, age 30, was on death row for the 1915 murder of his uncle in upstate Wellsville. Champlain was executed on June 2, 1916.

6. In 1926, Hilbert was scheduled to execute two men at Sing Sing. Just before the executions took place, he had a mental breakdown and later resigned. Rumors spread that his dreadful work had weighed heavily on Hilbert's mind and it caused him a great deal of emotional grief. "With the passage of time, he began to be depressed," commented Dr. Squire. "On each occasion when he came to Sing Sing to officiate in an execution, I noticed that he was not as he had been when I first knew him. I could see too well that he was slipping" (Squire, 202). Other sources said that he was despondent over family issues. The truth would never be known. In 1929, Hilbert was found dead with a gunshot wound to the head, an apparent suicide, in the basement of his home.

7. *Syracuse Herald*, February 18, 1916, 2.

8. On the morning of February 17, 1916, there were nineteen men on Sing Sing's death row waiting to die.

9. *Syracuse Herald*, February 18, 1916, 3.

10. Ibid.

11. Ibid.

12. *Albany Times,* February 18, 1916, 1.

13. *Evening Telegram*, February 18, 1916, 1.

24. FREEDOM

1. *Courier-Journal* (Louisville), January 25, 1935, 1.

2. *New York Times*, February 3, 1935, 31.

3. Ibid.

Bibliography

Anbinder, Tyler. *Five Points*. New York: Penguin Putnam, 2004.

Ashbury, Herbert. *The Gangs of New York*. New York: Avalon Publishing Group, 2004.

Bann, Mary. Transcript of Testimony, Manhattan Criminal Court [216 NY 324], January 21, 1914.

Bendix, Ludwig. Transcript of Testimony, Manhattan Criminal Court [216 NY 324], January 21, 1914.

Blumenthal, Ralph. *Miracle at Sing Sing: How One Man Transformed the Lives of America's Most Dangerous Prisoners*. New York: St. Martin's Press, 2004.

Boxheimer, Johann G. Deposition for Trial at Munich, Germany [216 NY 324], January 19, 1909.

Brandon, Craig. *The Electric Chair: An Unnatural American History*. Jefferson, NC: McFarland & Company, 1999.

Braun, John S. Transcript of Testimony, Manhattan Criminal Court [216 NY 324], January 22, 1914.

Brooker, Carlton. Transcript of Testimony, Manhattan Criminal Court [216 NY 324], January 21, 1914.

Burrows, Edwin G., and Mike Wallace. *Gotham*. New York: Oxford University Press, 1999.

Cardozo, J. The People of the State of New York. Appellant. Court of Appeals of New York. *Respondent v. Hans Schmidt*, 216 N.Y. 324 (1915).

Carson, Robert C., James N. Butcher, and Susan Mineka. *Abnormal Psychology and Modern Life*. New York: Longman, 1998.

Cattell, Henry. Affidavit filed at Philadelphia, PA, November 20, 1914.

Cheli, Guy. *Sing Sing Prison*. Portsmouth, NH: Arcadia Publishing, 2003.

Cheney, Margaret. *Tesla*. New York: Barnes and Noble Books, 1993.

Christianson, Scott. *With Liberty for Some: 500 Years of Imprisonment in America*. Boston: Northeastern University Press, 1998.

Coroner's Inquest. Criminal Courts Building, held by Coroner Israel F. Feinberg, October 2, 1913.

Davis, Richard Harding. "The New Idea at Sing Sing." *New York Times,* July 18, 1915.

Davis, Vernon. Charge to the Court. Court of appeals, State of New York [216 NY 324], February 5, 1915.

Delehanty, James A. Memorandum in Opposition to Motion for a New Trial. December 21, 1914.

Drimmer, Frederick. *Until You Are Dead*. New York: Windsor Publishing, 1990.

Dugdale, R. L. *The Jukes: A Study in Crime, Pauperism, Disease and Heredity*. New York: Putnam, 1877.

Elliot, Robert G. *Agent of Death*. New York: E. P. Dutton & Co., 1940.

Ellis, Edward Robb. *The Epic of New York City*. New York: Carroll & Graf Publishers, 2005.

Fass, Paula S. *Kidnapped: Child Abduction in America*. Cambridge, MA: Harvard University Press, 1997.

Faurot, Joseph. Transcript of Testimony, Manhattan Criminal Court [216 NY 324], January 23, 1914.

Goring, Charles. *The English Convict: A Statistical Study*. Montclair, NJ: Patterson-Smith, 1913

Gray, Christopher. *New York Streetscapes: Tales of Manhattan's Significant Buildings and Landmarks*. New York: Harry N. Abrams, 2003.

Gregory, Menas, M.D. Transcript of Testimony, Manhattan Criminal Court [216 NY 324], January 29, 1914.

Hays, Harold M. Transcript of Testimony, Manhattan Criminal Court [216 NY 324], February 3, 1914.

Hearn, Daniel Allen. *Legal Executions in New York State, 1639–1963*. Jefferson, NC: McFarland & Company, 1997.

Heibing, Arthur. Deposition at Federal Prison, Atlanta, GA, November 12, 1914.

Hirt, Anna. Transcript of Testimony, Manhattan Criminal Court [216 NY 324], January 22, 1914.

Jackson, Kenneth, ed. *The Encyclopedia of New York City*. New Haven, CT: Yale University Press, 1995.

Jeliffe, Smith Ely. Transcript of Testimony, Manhattan Criminal Court [216 NY 324], January 28–29, 1914.

King, Moses. *King's Handbook of New York City 1892: An Outline History and Description of the American Metropolis*. New York: Barnes and Noble Books, 2001.

Knappman, Edward W. *Great American Trials*. Detroit: Visible Ink Press, 1995.

Koelble, Alphonse. Deposition at State Court of Appeals [216 NY 324], December 21, 1914.

Kouwenhoven, John A. *The Columbia Historical Portrait of New York*. New York: Icon Editions, Harper and Row, 1953.

Kraus, Peter. Transcript of Testimony, Manhattan Criminal Court [216 NY 324], November 8, 1913.

Lawes, Lewis E. *Life and Death in Sing Sing*. New York: Garden City Publishing Company, 1928.

———. *Twenty Thousand Years in Sing Sing*. New York: Ray Long & Richard Smith, 1932.

Lichenstein, Perry. Transcript of Testimony, Manhattan Criminal Court [216 NY 324], January 28, 1914.

Logan, Andy. *Against the Evidence*. New York: Avon Books, 1970.

Marshall, Edward. "American Police Are Regarded With Suspicion." *New York Times*, November 27, 1910.

———. "Newspapers Are Great Detectives, Whitman Says." *New York Times*, December 3, 1911.

McGuire, Frank, M.D. Transcript of Testimony, Manhattan Criminal Court [216 NY 324], January 28, 1914.

Morris, Lloyd. *Incredible New York: High Life and Low Life of the Past Hundred Years*. New York: Random House, 1951.

Poe, Edgar Allan. *The Complete Tales and Poems of Edgar Allan Poe with Selections From His Critical Writings*. Text established, with bibliographical notes, by Edward H. O'Neill. New York: Barnes and Noble Books, 1992.

Quinn, Daniel. Transcript of Testimony, Manhattan Criminal Court [216 NY 324], January 22, 1914.

Sachs, George. Transcript of Testimony, Manhattan Criminal Court [216 NY 324], January 22, 1914.

Schadler, Elizabeth. Transcript of Testimony, Manhattan Criminal Court [216 NY 324], January 26, 1914.

Schmalleger, Frank. *Criminal Justice Today: An Introductory Text for the Twenty-First Century*. Upper Saddle River, NJ: Prentice Hall, 1999.

Schmidt, Hans. Deposition at Sing Sing Prison, Ossining, NY, witnessed by Alphonse Koelble and George Jenkins, Notary Public [216 NY 324], February 15, 1914.

———. Deposition at Sing Sing [216 NY 324], March 13, 1914.

———. Deposition at Sing Sing [216 NY 324], October 30, 1914.

———. Letter to Bertha Zech, translated by Edward J. Rosenthal, Official Interpreter, Court of General Sessions, New York, NY, October 2, 1914.

Schmidt, Heinrich. Deposition for trial [216 NY 324] at Frankfurt, Germany, November 8, 1913.

Schmidt, Karl. Deposition for trial [216 NY 324] at Frankfurt, Germany, November 8, 1913.

———. Letter to Hans Schmidt, defendant's exhibit "Q" [216 NY 324], dated October 3, 1913.

Schmidt, Katerina. Transcript of Testimony, Manhattan Criminal Court [216 NY 324], November 8, 1913.

Seebacher, Johannes. Deposition for trial [216 NY 324] Frankfurt, Germany, November 8, 1913.

Sieben, Jacob. Transcript of Testimony, Manhattan Criminal Court [216 NY 324], November 8, 1913.

Squire, Amos O. *Sing Sing Doctor*. Garden City, NY: Doubleday, Doran and Company, 1938.

Steffens, Lincoln. "New York: Good Government in Danger." In *Empire City*, edited by Kenneth T. Jackson and David S. Dunbar. New York: Columbia University Press, 2002.

Steinberg, Allen. "The Becker-Rosenthal Murder Case: The Cop and the Gambler." In *Famous American Crimes and Trials, Volume 2: 1860–1912*, edited by Frankie Y. Bailey and Steven Chermak. Westport, CT: Praeger, 2004.

Sutton, Charles. *The New York Tombs: Its Secrets and Its Mysteries*. Montclair, NJ: Patterson Smith, 1973.

Traub, James. *The Devil's Playground*. New York: Random House, 2004.

Vito, Gennaro F., and Ronald M. Holmes. *Criminology, Theory, Research and Policy*. Belmont, CA: Wadsworth Publishing Company, 1994.

Willard, Eugene Sands. "The Most Valuable Ten-Acre Lot in the World." In *Tales of Gaslight New York*, compiled by Frank Oppel. Edison, NJ: Castle Books, 1909.

Wilson, Colin. *The Mammoth Book of True Crime*. New York: Carroll & Graf Publishers, 1998.

Wolf, Marvin J., and Katherine Mader. *Rotten Apples: True Stories of New York Crime and Mystery, 1689 to the Present*. New York: Ballantine Books, 1991.

Zech, Bertha. Deposition taken by Assistant District Attorney James Delehanty [216 NY 324], November 17, 1914.

———. Transcript of Testimony, Manhattan Criminal Court [216 NY 324], February 3, 1914.

NEWSPAPERS

Albany Times (later became the *Albany Times-Union*): February 12–16, 1916.

Courier-Journal (Louisville): August 8, 1909, through June 1, 1910. January 25, 1935.

The Evening Telegram (New York): September 1, 1913, through February 28, 1914.

Louisville Times: August 8, 1909, through June 4, 1910.

New York Herald: September 1, 1913, through February 28, 1914.
New York Post: September 1 to December 1, 1913.
New York Press: September 1, 1913 to February 18, 1916.
New York Times: September 1, 1913, through February 28, 1916.
New York Tribune: September 1, 1913, through February 16, 1914.
Sun (New York): September 1, 1913, through February 28, 1914.
The Syracuse Herald: February 18, 1916.

Index

About the Author

MARK GADO is a police detective in New York where he has received dozens of awards and commendations during his 29-year career. He is a Vietnam combat veteran (1967–68) and was part of the Ground Zero rescue effort in September and October 2001. Gado writes on criminal justice issues and historical crime for Court TV's Crime Library. *Killer Priest* is his first book.